AutoCAD®

Professional Tips and Techniques

Lynn Allen
Scott Onstott

BICENTENNIAL
1807
WILEY
2007
BICENTENNIAL

WILEY PUBLISHING, INC.

ACQUISITIONS EDITOR: Willem Knibbe
DEVELOPMENT EDITOR: Heather O'Connor
TECHNICAL EDITOR: Jon McFarland
PRODUCTION EDITOR: Martine Dardignac
COPY EDITOR: Tiffany Taylor
PRODUCTION MANAGER: Tim Tate
VICE PRESIDENT AND EXECUTIVE GROUP PUBLISHER: Richard Swadley
VICE PRESIDENT AND EXECUTIVE PUBLISHER: Joseph B. Wikert
VICE PRESIDENT AND PUBLISHER: Dan Brodnitz
BOOK DESIGNER AND COMPOSITOR: Chris Gillespie, Happenstance Type-O-Rama
PROOFREADER: Nancy Riddiough
INDEXER: Ted Laux
ANNIVERSARY LOGO DESIGN: Richard Pacifico
COVER DESIGNER: Ryan Sneed
COVER IMAGE: ©Ashley Cooper/Corbis

Dear Reader

Thank you for choosing *AutoCAD: Professional Tips and Techniques*. This book is part of a family of premium-quality Sybex books, all written by outstanding authors who combine practical experience with a gift for teaching.

Sybex was founded in 1976. Thirty years later, we're still committed to producing consistently exceptional books. With each of our titles we're working hard to set a new standard for the industry. From the paper we print on, to the writers and professionals we work with, our goal is to bring you the best books available.

I hope you see all that reflected in these pages. I'd be very interested to hear your comments and get your feedback on how we're doing. To let us know what you think about this or any other Sybex book, please send me an email at: sybex_publisher@wiley.com. Please also visit us at www.sybex.com to learn more about the rest of our growing AutoCAD line.

Best regards,

Neil Edde
Vice President and Publisher
Sybex, an Imprint of Wiley

Acknowledgments

I'd like to send out a great big thank you to all of you AutoCAD users out there who make my job worthwhile each and every day and have taught me more than I could ever learn on my own. Thanks to Autodesk for giving me the time and space to work on this book where needed (especially you, Kelly). Thanks to the ever-patient Willem Knibbe, who worked overtime convincing me to write another book and turned my No's into a Yes. Above all, thanks to the amazingly talented Scott Onstott, who was the real reason we were able to pull these great tips together into one action packed book. And to Tiffany, my Maltese puppy, who sat next to me for the many hours I worked on this book... I see many dog biscuits in your future.

—Lynn Allen

I'd like to thank Lynn Allen for co-writing this book with a person she's met only "virtually." Willem Knibbe deserves extra credit for getting this book off the ground while coordinating the efforts of two authors. Thanks to Heather O'Connor for her work in developing the book. Jon McFarland has my appreciation for his fine technical editorial work and his excellent suggestions. Thanks also to Tiffany Taylor for her work as copy editor and Martine Dardignac for keeping everyone on schedule.

—Scott Onstott

Contents at a Glance

Contents

Introduction

You've been working with AutoCAD for quite some time now, and you feel you've got the program under control. You can get your job done, on time, with minimal stress, thank you very much! But you can't help asking yourself if there's a better way:

- Could there be a better way to set up the user interface so I can reach my favorite tools more quickly?

- How can I eliminate some of the AutoCAD tedium that causes me to focus more on drafting than my design?

- What are the top-secret tips and techniques that the AutoCAD pros of the world arc using to get their jobs done faster?

If any of this rings true to you, then you're in the right place, with the right book.

Who Can Benefit from This Book

If you're new to AutoCAD and still trying to figure out the basics, then put down this book and find a nice AutoCAD primer. You won't be happy here. To truly benefit from this book, you need a sound understanding of AutoCAD, and you need to have mastered the basics. *AutoCAD: Professional Tips and Techniques* is intended to take you to the next level—to help you reach AutoCAD productivity heights you never imagined were possible! Anyone using an AutoCAD-based product such as AutoCAD LT, Architectural Desktop, AutoCAD Mechanical, AutoCAD Electrical, or AutoCAD Map 3D can benefit from reading this book.

About This Book

Surveys show that the majority of AutoCAD users utilize, at most, 40 percent of what AutoCAD has to offer. What about that other 60 percent? Where can you find out about the other 60 percent? We've gathered the tricks of the trade from around the world and put them all in one convenient location. No more trolling through blogs and websites, scrounging for tips; you'll find a treasure chest of proven tips and techniques right here. And we don't expect you to digest all this information in one sitting—do yourself a huge favor, and read a little each day, whenever you find some time to add another cool technique to your AutoCAD repertoire. *AutoCAD: Professional Tips and Techniques* digs deeper than most AutoCAD books on the market. Rather than covering all things AutoCAD (which would require a book so long you'd never want to tackle it), we focus on those features we feel will give you the most bang for your buck. You probably don't have lots of time to focus on improving your AutoCAD skills; you need to get right to the good stuff. You want to spend your valuable time reading about techniques that give you the largest productivity jolt possible. And because finding time to improve your skills is difficult at best, we suggest you put aside 15 minutes a day, crack open the book, and read one or two tips. Follow your reading with some hands-on practice, and you'll be in better AutoCAD shape in no time (just like exercise, but without that pesky sweating). Although we did structure the book in logical order, there's no need to go through it from start to finish. Feel free to begin with the chapters that seem the most valuable or interesting to you. We won't tell your teacher you skipped around….

The following is a basic overview of each chapter to help you decide where to begin. Select the chapter that triggers the most pain for you, and you'll be well on your way to more productive and effective design skills. Just a little time each day is all you'll need, to maximize your potential on AutoCAD software. Enjoy!

Chapter 1—Arranging the AutoCAD User Interface It's important to be comfortable with your AutoCAD environment. Knowing how to set up the user interface for optimal productivity is a great way to start down the path of higher AutoCAD satisfaction. Here you'll learn tips that will help you live in harmony with Windows as well as the Auto-CAD UI. If speed is an issue (and you don't get paid by the hour!), you'll find several techniques that will speed up your computer and AutoCAD. Why sit around staring, waiting for your computer to catch up, when you could be designing? This chapter will also help you personalize your AutoCAD world to your liking. If you aren't happy with your current work environment, and you want AutoCAD to feel more like your favorite easy chair, than definitely begin with this chapter.

Chapter 2—Drawing and Editing This is one of our favorite chapters because it deals with commands you use all day, every day. If you can shave one step off a command you use constantly, that's a big deal, right? We also review some valuable commands that few users take advantage of or understand fully. This chapter also contains great tips on selecting objects more quickly (something we're constantly doing) and working more efficiently with the layers in your drawing. Drawing and editing make up the bulk of all things AutoCAD, so you're sure to find some gems here.

Chapter 3—Annotation One of the least rewarding parts of our design jobs comes into play with annotating drawings. Text, dimensions, and cross-hatching can boggle the mind with all the system variables and scale factors. Chapter 3 straightens out these notions and puts everything in the proper perspective. Here you'll learn some cool tips to get exactly the results you're looking for (so you no longer have to settle for what you're been dealt by AutoCAD). We also delve into the powerful world of attributes and tables to kick your skills up a notch.

Chapter 4—Layouts and Sheets Projects can get out of control without proper planned organization. The Sheet Set Manager is a great master organizer. This chapter sorts out the infrequently used (but powerful) Sheet Set Manager and tackles the oft-confusing topic of paperspace. You can even venture into conquering fields if you feel inclined to truly unleash the power of AutoCAD.

Chapter 5—Dynamic Blocks Among the greatest features added to AutoCAD are the powerful dynamic blocks. You can set up intelligent blocks that make insertions, modifications, and calculations a breeze. One block—many possibilities. If you want to hone your dynamic block skills, you'll appreciate the insight this chapter brings to the process.

Chapter 6—3D Modeling We don't live in a 2D world, but we continue to draw like we do. If you've wanted to make the leap into the exciting world of 3D, this chapter provides a great kick-start. Even those of you who are 3D aficionados will find tips and techniques that will lead you to greater 3D success. Take a step out of your flat 2D world, and discover the possibilities that 3D design can bring into your AutoCAD life.

Chapter 7—Visualization Let's face it, if your client can't visualize your design properly, you aren't going to win the contract. With all the new visualization capabilities housed in AutoCAD, you can get your design intent across with maximum clarity. This chapter covers the skills needed to get the desired effects, including working with materials and textures. You'll even learn some nifty tips for maximizing your standard zooming, panning, and 3D orbiting skills.

Chapter 8—Sharing Data Even if you live on an island, you need to share your data with others. There are many techniques for sharing data, but this chapter focuses on those that are the most effective and efficient. External references can be a source of headaches, but with a clear understanding of them, you can eliminate 95 percent of the pain. Here you'll discover system variables that make for easy work with Xrefs and DWF files. If you're working on Architectural Desktop, and you've been frustrated by the inability to edit the AEC objects in AutoCAD, you'll learn a workaround that may do the trick. You'll also find some powerful tips for going between AutoCAD and PhotoShop and Office.

Chapter 9—Plotting and Publishing Despite all your hard work online, you still need to output to a piece of paper. With all the nuances of publishing, it's frustrating when you can't get the exact results you're after. Chapter 9 takes the guesswork out of plotting and publishing and helps you fine-tune your results. You'll also learn how to publish your AutoCAD files to the Web and easily transmit them to others. This is a great chapter for you if you've been rolling your eyes over making hard copies!

Chapter 10—Customization Ahhhhhhhh—the real meat always lies in the depths of customizing your system. Here you'll learn how to seize the reins from AutoCAD and take control of your design life! This chapter delves deep into the mystic CUI command, helps you customize your palettes for maximum productivity, and discusses deployment strategies. This is a great way to top off all your other newfound AutoCAD knowledge.

About the Authors

You'll find that *AutoCAD: Professional Tips and Techniques* comes with a bit of attitude. Scott and I (this is Lynn speaking) have seen it all (OK—it feels like we've seen it all), and with that come our distinct viewpoints on the proper way to use the software. We don't expect you to always agree with us (heck, Scott and I didn't always see eye to eye), but we hope you'll open your mind and try a few of our suggestions. You may find yourself a little further down the path to true AutoCAD gurudom!

In my travels throughout the world, I speak to nearly 30,000 users each year—and they're generous enough to share their favorite tips or workarounds, many of which are included in this book. I've also had the distinct privilege to work with many industry experts who have shared their AutoCAD insights with me. As a veteran user of AutoCAD since Release 1.4 (over 20 years ago), I realize that it's nearly impossible to know absolutely everything about AutoCAD no matter how long you've been using it. I spend most of my time traveling from event to event hoping to share my insight to as many AutoCAD users as possible. I'm hoping this book will make its way to those who can't see me in person. If you have some spare time on your hands feel free to visit my blog at www.autodesk.com/lynnallen where you can read about my various adventures and the latest AutoCAD Hip Tips.

Scott is an expert in his own right, with the ability to translate even the most complicated processes and concepts to paper with amazing clarity. Scott independently writes, records, and publishes a series of video tutorials on a wide array of AEC software. Keep up with what he's doing at ScottOnstott.com.

Between the two of us, we have more than 35 years of experience with AutoCAD. We enjoyed putting together this assortment of tips and techniques to help you maximize your use of AutoCAD. We think you'll find that the concepts in this book are as easy to understand as they are powerful. Dig in!

Arranging the AutoCAD User Interface

UI—THE USER INTERFACE—is an acronym that is thrown around a lot. Just for a moment, don't think of it as just those two letters. The UI is what comes between you (the user) and it (the essentially incomprehensible computer). The UI lets you interact with the inner workings of the machine, ideally in an intuitive fashion.

Unlike an automobile with a manual transmission, whose stick-shift and clutch are parts of its permanent UI, your computer's UI is highly customizable. You don't like a stick-shift? Click here, and you have an automatic.

The AutoCAD UI is important. Many people gloss over it, thinking the real meat is in using tools and getting the job done. That may be so, but if you're ever going to enjoy the dining experience, you need to pay attention to how you access and work with the tools.

Tweaking Windows

Although using Windows out of the box works, you'll get more out of your operating system—and AutoCAD—if you make a few alterations. This section offers you tips and tricks for tweaking the ubiquitous Windows.

These aren't exactly AutoCAD tips proper, but knowing a few things about maintaining the health of your operating system can make you a much happier CAD user and human being. In addition, it's a little-known fact that a few parts of AutoCAD's UI aren't controlled by AutoCAD at all. Shhh…in these cases, AutoCAD must defer control to Almighty Windows.

Maintain a Healthy Disk Drive

How can you use AutoCAD successfully if you don't install it on a healthy disk drive? The following basic tips are essential reading for all Windows users.

Defragment and Check the File System

The two most important things you can do to maintain a healthy disk drive are to defragment and error-check the file system periodically. We know it sounds like a hassle, but it isn't:

- These things are easy to do, once you know where to find the tools.

- Defragmenting the file system will speed up your hard drive. If you've never done it before, you'll be pleased because you'll probably feel like you have a brand new computer. Maybe you can justify putting off that hardware upgrade for another year once you see what an amazing tip this is.

In this section, we'll reveal how to defragment on a schedule so you can literally set it and forget it, We'll also explain how to troubleshoot through error checking.

Defragmenting

Files aren't the smallest unit of storage on a hard drive. The information in one file may be stored in multiple clusters across several sectors, all over your hard drive (which is probably more than you wanted to know).

Your data gets scattered in the course of doing your digital business, and over time your hard-drive head (one of the moving parts) has to work harder to put all those tiny clusters back together. If you've ever heard your hard drive grinding away without just cause (that's the head moving frantically), it's time to defragment.

Defragmenting is like rearranging your closet. Everything gets tidied up so you save time searching for what you want. Bonus: You'll prolong the life of a hard drive by defragmenting.

To defragment, click the Start menu, and choose Run. Type `dfrg.msc`, and click OK. Alternatively, right-click your hard drive in Windows Explorer, and choose Properties. Select the Tools tab, and click Defragment Now.

Select the (C): drive under Volume, and click the Analyze button to see a graphical representation of how fragmented your drive is. Red is bad, blue is good, green is neutral, and white is free. If you see a lot of red, then it's definitely time to clean things up. Select Defragment, and let Windows do the rest (if only organizing my closet were so easy!). If you've never done this, or it's been a long time, defragmenting could take hours; consequently, you'll want to defragment at night when you're finished with work. You may also need to do it multiple times to get rid of all the red.

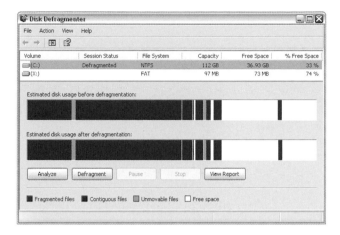

You must have at least 15 percent free space on a volume to defragment it. If you don't have this much free space, make some by archiving old files onto DVD or tape backup.

Error Checking

If your system locks up or dies due to power failure (pay attention, California), there is a good chance your hard drive scrambled a few files in its death throes when the head jerked erratically across the platters as they spun down (sounds horrific, doesn't it?). Checking (and fixing) your hard drive is a good idea if you see the Windows blue screen of death after experiencing a serious crash.

Although it may not solve every problem, a Windows utility called CHKDSK (check disk, in English) may be able to repair the damage.

You have to be logged on with Administrator rights to run CHKDSK.

Click the Start menu, and choose Run. Type **CHKDSK C: /f**, and click OK. The /f switch is necessary because it fixes problems rather than just telling you about them (like your coworkers). If you do this on your C: drive, you'll see a message like this:

```
Chkdsk cannot run because the volume is in use by another process.

Would you like to schedule this volume to be checked the next time the system restarts?
(Y/N)
```

Type **Y**, and the drive will be checked the next time you start the computer. It may take 20 minutes, so plan ahead.

Put Defragmentation on a Schedule

Manually defragmenting your hard drive can get old. Are you really going to remember to defragment on a regular basis, or are you likely to forget about it until your hard drive slows to a crawl again? Fortunately, there is help for the terminally busy (or lazy). If you schedule defragmentation, then you can potentially forget about it forever (and why isn't this part of Windows already?).

Scheduling defragmentation is a simple two-step process. First, make a batch file that runs the command-line version of DEFRAG. Then, schedule the batch file to run as often as you like. Begin by creating your batch file:

1. Open Notepad (found by selecting Start ➔ Programs ➔ Accessories ➔ Notepad), and type the following:

   `DEFRAG C: /v`

   The /v option shows verbose output in the command window while defragmentation is happening. If you don't care to read this information (or don't need help sleeping), leave off the /v switch.

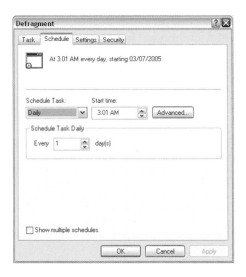

2. Save the file (under C:\Windows, for example) as DefragmentC.bat—the .bat extension indicates a batch file.

3. Click Start menu ➔ Settings ➔ Control Panel ➔ Scheduled Tasks ➔ Add Scheduled Task. The wizard guides you through the steps. Browse for DefragmentC.bat, which you created in the previous step. This is the task you want to schedule.

4. Select a time when you're likely to be away from your computer, but plan to leave it on. We suggest running DEFRAG daily in early morning hours (if you leave your computer on all the time). Open the task after completing the wizard if you want to make any changes.

> Diskeeper is commercial automatic defragmentation software that does a more thorough job than DEFRAG. (www.diskeeper.com).

Take Control of the Swap File

Have you ever opened a number of big drawings, maybe with loads of Xrefs or 3D geometry, only to discover that AutoCAD is taking an inordinate amount of time to do anything? Maybe you also have many different programs running: AutoCAD, Autodesk VIZ, Autodesk Inventor, Microsoft Word, and/or Microsoft Outlook. If you've already defragmented, then there must be another reason for the slowdown. Chances are, you've run out of memory.

When your system is overtaxed with too much information to process, rather than immediately crashing, Windows stores what should be going into the now-full random access memory (RAM) in virtual memory. *Virtual memory* is another way of saying your computer is paging to disk, or recording data to the swap file. Every time your system pages out to disk, you get to sit and wait. Although virtual memory is a poor substitute for physical (real) RAM, it's better than nothing (certainly better than crashing), and we all use it from time to time.

If this is news to you, then you're letting Windows manage the swap file automatically. You can get better virtual-memory performance by setting the swap file two to three times the size of your physical memory (RAM):

1. Choose Start menu → Settings → Control Panel → System. Click the Advanced tab (we're making an expert out of you already!).

2. Click the Settings button in the Performance area, which controls virtual memory (among other things).

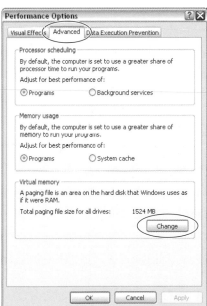

3. In the Performance Options dialog box, click the Advanced tab. Click the Change button in the Virtual Memory area.

4. Click the Custom Size radio button, and set Initial Size at twice the size of your RAM. For example, if you have 1 GB of RAM, set Initial Size at 2048 (RAM is in powers of 2) MB.

5. Set Maximum Size at three times your RAM, and then click Set. Click OK in each of the open dialog boxes, and you're done.

6. After a restart, you should see an improvement in your AutoCAD performance.

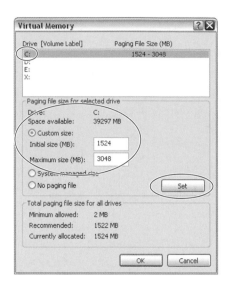

Clean Out Temporary Crud

When I (Scott) went to college umpteen years ago, I remember discovering what were labeled "temporary buildings" on the campus map (they looked surprisingly identical to Army barracks); I learned that these buildings had been there for some 50 years. They were ramshackle, rusting Quonset hut–type structures that didn't fit into the architectural context. I had the aesthetic pleasure of seeing these surprisingly long-lived structures end their "temporary" status when they were demolished to make room for a library renovation.

The moral of the story is that things (and files) labeled "temporary" often hang around long after they stop being useful and start becoming a nuisance. Windows needs help in deciding just how temporary your temporary files are meant to be. You can avoid all manner of strange crashes, hung systems, frozen mice, and other maladies that mystify technical support personnel by periodically cleaning out your temp files:

1. Close all your programs.

2. Open Windows Explorer. A nice shortcut to do this, by the way, is Windows key+E—if your keyboard has a Windows key. Otherwise, right-click the Start menu, and choose Explore (which is also a nice tip!).

3. Highlight the text in the address bar, type **%TEMP%**, and press Enter. This is an environment variable (surrounded by percent symbols) that resolves to the Windows Temp folder, which in my case is

   `C:\Documents and Settings\Admin\Local Settings\Temp`

   This is much easier than trying to scout around for your temp directory yourself; trust me. My user name is Admin, so that's why you see it in this path. Using %TEMP% is the easy way for sure.

4. Delete all the files in the Temp folder (just do it).

5. Did you know that AutoCAD is tied to Internet Explorer? Yes, AutoCAD has many Internet features like hyperlink, Communication Center, and even Help that borrow from IE. So, you should clean out these temporary files as well. Click Start menu → Settings → Control Panel → Internet Options.

6. Click Delete Files in the Temporary Internet Files area to clean out the browser cache. Click OK in the confirmation dialog, and that's it.

Perform Basic Maintenance

It's surprising how many self-identified "power users" neglect basic computer maintenance. If it sounds like you may be one of these folks, it's time you start taking these things more seriously—because it's no joke.

Clean Up Your Hard Drive

We hate to say it, but clean up your hard drive, will you? Uninstall unused applications, and archive ancient data. This task can become a nightmare if you've put it off for years. Spend a few days, if that's what it takes; and while you're at it, organize your file system. Pick an organizational scheme, and stick to it. A great portion of human productivity is wasted trying to find the right files. It doesn't have to be that way!

Back Up Religiously

Blessed are those who back up regularly, for their files will not be scattered to the winds. Be proactive and perhaps a bit cynical: Expect corruption—of the digital sort. Perhaps it's a bit harsh to say this, but if you don't have a backup, then ultimately you're wasting your time. Never before in history has so much human effort been stored in so ephemeral a medium as magnetism on spinning metallic disks.

If you're concerned about a single machine, then a portable hard drive that matches the size of your system disk is a great backup solution. If you need to back up a local area network (LAN), then consider a tape solution or redundant array of inexpensive disks (RAID). Backup systems pay for themselves many times over; it's a false economy to think that backup systems are too expensive.

Windows XP has a built-in backup program: Click Start menu → Run, and type **ntbackup.exe** to launch the Backup or Restore Wizard. Backups should also be scheduled regularly, but that should go without saying.

Practice Safe Computing

Gone are the days when the Internet was a safe network for a few academics and geeks. Now you need protection from malicious adversaries who are into stirring up trouble.

Please tell me that you're using a firewall. In the age of always-on Internet, algorithms are constantly pounding on your digital door. The firewall is the only thing keeping them out.

Let's face it: Windows is chock full of security holes. Microsoft finds more every week, as evidenced by the numerous security patches the company offers via the Automatic Updates feature. Do keep up to date with these, by all means! Usually, people who get hacked could have avoided it by installing readily available security patches. Control how updates are delivered to you in the Automatic Updates control panel.

Windows doesn't come with antivirus software. Clearly, Microsoft has some work to do. Antivirus software is a must. If you're not about to buy a commercial antivirus package, then try one of the free ones like AVG (www.free.grisoft.com). Make sure you set whatever program you're using to update the virus definitions regularly (notice a theme here?).

> If you're into privacy, then try Spybot or Ad-Aware.

Don't open attachments from untrusted senders. Don't even open attachments from those you do trust, unless you know what to expect. Many viruses are spread by joke attachments that carry a humorous message and also a dangerous secret payload. Sorry to get into all this fear-based thinking, but you have nothing to fear when you practice safe computing.

Know Your Display Control Panel

Most folks are aware that the Display Properties dialog box is the place to go to change the resolution of the screen. Fewer know that the Display Properties dialog box also controls how many UI features appear, both in Windows and in AutoCAD. This section will introduce you to the more interesting parts of the Display control panel.

Are Your Graphics Drivers Up to Date?

Before you begin making changes in the Display control panel, update your graphics card drivers to the latest version. Graphics card companies often release new versions that contain bug fixes and/or support for additional features. Follow these steps:

1. You need to find out exactly what graphics driver you have. To do so, minimize all your applications by pressing Windows key+M, or minimize each application manually if you don't have a Windows key (we'd never buy a computer without a Windows key!). Right-click the desktop, and choose Properties from the shortcut menu to open the Display Properties dialog box.

2. Select the Settings tab, and click the Advanced button.

3. A dialog box with your particular graphics adapter appears. Choose the Adapter tab of this dialog, and click Properties.

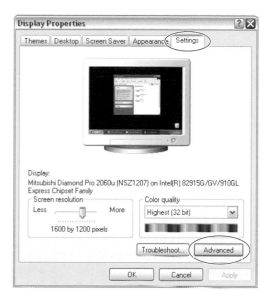

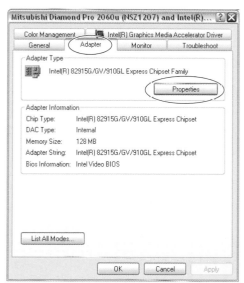

4. The Properties dialog displays the name of your particular adapter or chipset in the title bar. Note that the driver version is shown on the Driver tab—this is what you're looking for, so make a note of it.

5. Now you need to check for driver updates. Use your browser to surf to the manufacturer's website, and locate the driver download part of the site. Search for your adapter or chipset name and/or driver version. If a new version is available, download and install it. Click OK in all the open dialogs; you'll probably have to restart the computer for the new driver settings to take effect.

Update Autodesk's Hardware Certification Database

AutoCAD 2007 has a new feature that monitors your graphics card driver and compares it with Autodesk's Hardware Certification Database. If a new driver is available, a bubble notifies you when you launch AutoCAD. Unfortunately, you need to manually download the Hardware Certification Database to keep this system up to date. This is worth doing to get the best 3D performance out of the installed graphics card:

1. In AutoCAD, use the Options command, and choose the System tab. Click the Performance Settings button to open the Adaptive Degradation and Performance Tuning dialog.

2. Click the Check for Updates button. Internet Explorer launches and takes you to a page on the Autodesk website.

3. The page that appears has instructions for downloading and installing the latest Hardware Certification Database. Close AutoCAD, follow the instructions, and restart AutoCAD. You'll be notified if a new graphics driver is available and whether it's fully compatible with AutoCAD's new 3D features.

Set Screen Resolution and Color Quality

You should set the screen resolution to the maximum you can see (without squinting—squinting causes wrinkles). As you increase resolution, everything gets smaller while screen real estate effectively grows. Use the screen-resolution slider on the Settings tab of the Display Properties dialog box to adjust the resolution.

Everybody wants more screen real estate (it's a valuable commodity); but don't exceed what your tired eyes can comfortably see, or you'll have to boost that eyeglass prescription before you know it (even though Lynn's husband, an optometrist, appreciates the business). Boosting resolution is a poor substitute for a larger monitor after all.

I (Scott) have a 22″ monitor, which is great, and my graphics card supports resolutions up to 2048 × 1536 pixels, but that's way more than I can see—and yes, I'm wearing glasses. I have to compromise and set resolution at a more modest 1600 × 1200 pixels, which is plenty in my humble opinion.

Make certain that color quality is set to Highest (32 bit). Some older graphics cards support higher resolutions only at a lower color depth. It may have been acceptable in the old days to run AutoCAD in 256 colors; but doing so would be a major faux pas today, now that AutoCAD has true color (32-bit) support.

If you perceive a flicker at higher resolutions, there is something you can do that may correct this annoying problem. Click the Advanced button on the Settings tab of the Display Properties dialog box. A dialog box appears that is specific to your monitor. Click the Monitor tab, and change the screen refresh rate from the drop-down list. Try the highest rate, and work your way down the list if necessary until you eliminate that pesky flicker.

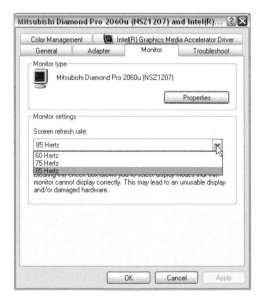

Keeping Up Appearances

If your aesthetic sense has long been offended by the saturated blues and greens of the default Windows XP interface, then rejoice, for relief is on its way. The Appearance tab of the Display Properties dialog box makes it possible to alter many of the UI components under Windows' control. In turn, these affect how AutoCAD appears—because, after all, AutoCAD runs on Windows.

The first drop-down list allows you to toggle between the classic look of Windows 2000 and the updated look of XP. We'd go with XP, but only on the provision that you choose the silver color scheme rather than the default blues or olive green (yuck). The advantage of this color scheme lies in its neutrality—it's not likely to influence your perception of color as much as the other options.

The Font Size drop-down lets you boost size to Large or Extra Large, which is useful if you're doing client demonstrations with an LCD projector and you want text to be readable in a presentation. Because I (Lynn) spend most of my time doing presentations, I use the extra-large font so the audience can easily read the words. I also change the text color to black on yellow because that is the easiest color combination to see (think of construction signs).

If you want to get into the nitty-gritty, then click the Advanced button. In the resulting dialog box, you can control individual interface components. One pet peeve I have is with the extra-large title bar in the XP style. Why must it take up so much room? Whoever designed the default XP style clearly wasn't using AutoCAD, because they don't value screen real estate as much we typically do.

Select Active Title Bar from the Item drop-down, and change Size to 21. Doing so brings the title bar down to a reasonable scale while matching the size of the application and drawing caption buttons in AutoCAD.

The size and font of text on the tool palettes in AutoCAD are controlled by the ToolTip item in the Advanced Appearance dialog box (it's in the

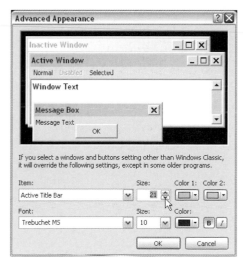

Item drop-down list). Could this be more obscure? I (Lynn) personally find this frustrating because I like the font of the tooltips to be larger than that on my tool palettes.

After you're finished tweaking the appearance of the Windows UI, select the Themes tab of the Display Properties dialog box (if you have one), and save a theme. Should anything change, this will make it easy to recall all your customizations with one click at a later date.

Prepare for AutoCAD Launch

5, 4, 3, 2, 1… Startup switches are options you can add to the shortcut(s) that launch AutoCAD. They allow you to boot up AutoCAD with some preexisting conditions in place. Startup shortcuts are usually placed on the desktop. In the old days (pre–AutoCAD 2000), startup switches were more commonly used, because they set the default folder—something that's handled with a system variable now.

See "Folders: To Remember or Forget?" in Chapter 8.

Startup switches are still useful, giving you the ability to select a particular script, template, configuration folder, view name, support folder, user profile, workspace, and more—to start with AutoCAD. Look up "startup switches" in AutoCAD Help for all the options.

Using Startup Switches

To see how startup switches are used, let's disable the splash screen that appears when Auto-CAD launches (in AutoCAD 2007, it's a transparent green box). That splash screen not only slows you down, but it can be downright annoying after a while:

1. Create a shortcut for launching AutoCAD, if you don't already have one on your desktop. Use Windows Explorer to locate C:\Program Files\AutoCAD 2007\acad.exe (the file that launches AutoCAD), right-click, and choose Send To → Desktop (create shortcut).

2. Get back to your desktop by minimizing everything (press Windows key+M, or tediously minimize the windows one at a time). Right-click the shortcut to acad.exe on the desktop, and choose Properties.

3. Place the cursor at the end of the text in the Target text box, and type **/nologo**. All startup switches are added to the end of the target line and immediately follow a forward

slash. These options are passed to the executable when it starts up. Switch to the General tab, and rename the shortcut AutoCAD 2007. Click Apply, and close the dialog box.

4. Launch AutoCAD with the shortcut, and observe that the splash screen no longer appears.

Other Switches in the Startup

Before we tell you about Lynn's favorite switch, let's look at some of the more popular startup switches. Follow each switch with a space and then what it's asking for (script file, template, layout, and so on):

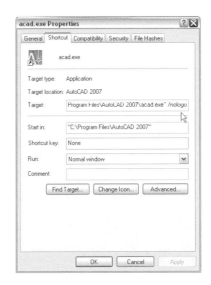

/b Runs a script file upon launching AutoCAD.

/t Creates a new drawing based on the indicated template file. AutoCAD assumes a DWT file type, so complete path information isn't needed. You may decide to have two different startup icons for 2D and 3D. The latter will use the new ACAD3D template file.

/layout Opens a specific layout in the indicated drawing file. The syntax requires you to specify the drawing file and the layout, separated with a vertical bar. For example, if you have a drawing file called Engine and a layout called Assembly: use `"C:\Program Files\ AutoCAD 2007\acad.exe" /layout "C:\ACAD 2007 Project\Engine|Assembly"`.

/v Opens the indicated drawing file, and zooms to a specific view (views are much more popular in AutoCAD 2007).

/p Launches AutoCAD, and loads a specific profile. This profile is in effect only for the current AutoCAD session

/nossm Suppresses the existence of the new Sheet Set Manager upon entering AutoCAD (for those of you who haven't embraced it).

/ld Loads a specified ARX or DBX application. You have to include the complete path information.

/c Specifies the path for the hardware configuration file you want to use during your Auto-CAD session.

When using these switches, be sure to give each icon a new name so you can easily distinguish them. You can also change the tooltip in the Shortcut tab by modifying the contents in the Comment section. The Shortcut tab also allows you to tell AutoCAD you always want it to launch maximized (which is a must if you find yourself maximizing it manually each time).

Loading Sheet Sets Automatically

Before I (Lynn) got into using sheet sets, I used to load the sheet set manually nearly every day (because AutoCAD didn't remember that I had it loaded when I left the drawing). I'm not a fan of tedium, so I decided to do something about it. My favorite switch gives me the ability to automatically load a specific sheet set so I don't have to load it myself after AutoCAD launches. Here's how you do it.

Let's say the name of the sheet set you want to load automatically is `BigClient.dst`. The startup looks like the following (and yes, in case you're wondering, most of the switches follow this syntax: `/switch "name"`

```
"C:\Program Files\AutoCAD 2007\acad.exe" /set "C:\ACAD 2007 Project\BigClient.dst"
```

```
/set is the switch
```

```
C:\ACAD 2007 Project is my directory path
```

Notice the directory is in quotes, and you have to use the complete path statement. Switches are a little wishy-washy on the path statements; some require the complete path information (such as sheet sets), but others don't (such as script files). For those that don't, make sure they fall within the AutoCAD search path.

If you plan to work on the same drawing file for a while, you can set up a startup that launches AutoCAD and goes straight to that specific drawing file. To load the drawing file called `Engine` from your ACAD 2007 project directory, you use the following syntax:

```
"C:\Program Files\AutoCAD 2007\acad.exe" "C:\ACAD 2007 Project\Engine"
```

Cycle through Tasks and Documents

If your resume identifies you as a multitasker, then we're sure you have many programs running and multiple drawing files open in AutoCAD at any given moment, while you're also talking on the phone and drinking coffee. Obviously you can use the Windows taskbar at the bottom of the screen to switch between tasks (which means making a running program active, in geekspeak).

Most true multitaskers already know about the Alt+Tab key combination. Holding down the Alt key while pressing the Tab key displays an icon menu in the center of the screen that you can step through by pressing Tab repeatedly to select a specific task. But did you know that Alt+Shift+Tab steps backward through this list of tasks? This factoid should please those who like to keep as many apples in the air as possible.

AutoCAD also has multitasking hotkeys that allow switching between open drawings, which are AutoCAD's version of tasks. Holding down the Ctrl key while pressing Tab cycles to the next open drawing (although no icon menu appears). Keep holding that Ctrl key down and tapping Tab, and you'll continue cycling through open drawings. If you go too far, press

Ctrl+Shift+Tab to cycle backward through the list of open drawings. The Shift key is used to reverse the cycling direction in all multitasking key combinations.

If you're comfortable switching tasks with Alt+Tab but don't think you'll be able to remember Ctrl+Tab, then the TASKBAR system variable is for you. Set TASKBAR to 1, and all open drawings will immediately appear as separate buttons (a.k.a. tasks) at the bottom of the screen.

If you tend to run AutoCAD without any other programs at the same time, having individual drawings visible as tasks on the taskbar may be the way to go. Then, you can toggle between them using Alt+Tab because each drawing is, well, a task.

Finding Help

Perhaps the phenomenon is confined to roughly half of the species, but rumor has it that it's a rare event indeed when a man will ask for help (and yes, Scott is writing this). All the women out there probably don't need to read this section (but please do anyway, because I'm sure you'll learn new ways to find support).

Read this section, and seek help in secret if you need to, or do it overtly with the full confidence that you'll find the answers you seek. The truth is, much help is at your fingertips, if you know where to look. Of course, this book is the ultimate resource for AutoCAD tips and techniques (even if we do say so ourselves), but you may not always have it handy (say it isn't so!). In such an emergency, you'll want to know how to find help in other forms.

Search Tips

The AutoCAD Help system runs in its own window and can be opened by pressing the F1 key, choosing Help → Help from the menu, or using ? on the command line.

> How many times have you accidentally hit F1 when you meant to press the adjacent Esc key? If you don't want help at your fingertips, see Chapter 10 to learn how to reassign F1 to Cancel (or something else more user friendly).

Click the Search tab, enter a search query, and press Enter. In AutoCAD 2007, you can ask questions in plain language, thanks to the new AnswerWorks engine. AnswerWorks ranks search results with percentages and functions, much like an Internet search engine.

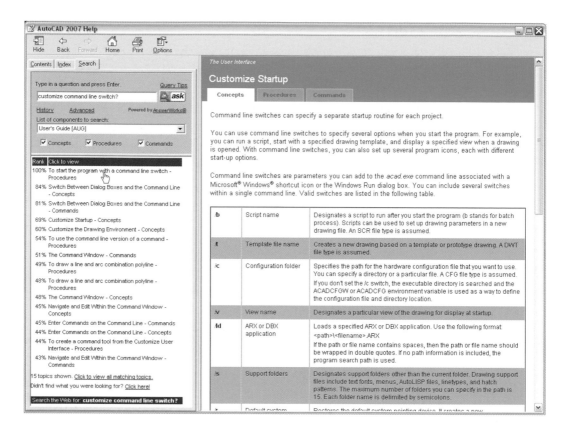

Click Advanced to access a list to search only within a specific component (think book) in the user documentation set, instead of everything together. For example, if you're looking for a customization issue, you can choose the Customization Guide (ACG) from the list; the search results are then updated. Choose a component to search before (or conveniently after) you've performed the search, and the results are updated.

Click a search result, and you see its associated help in the right-hand pane. Now, click the Contents tab—the table of contents tree should expand to the page you just accessed. If the tree doesn't expand, try clicking the Back and Forward arrows (sometimes this does the trick).

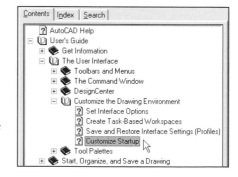

The Contents tab reveals the context in which the sought-for page exists. Browsing through the table of contents in the context of a focused search is the fastest way to find what you're looking for.

Disable Antivirus Checking of Help File

If the AutoCAD Help window takes forever to open, there is a good chance your antivirus software is checking it to make sure it's clean (trust us, it is). This can become annoying if it happens every time you open Help.

AutoCAD Help is a separate but linked task on the taskbar (it disappears when AutoCAD closes). Many antivirus programs think this is highly suspicious, so they get triggered. You'll have to figure out how to reassure your particular antivirus program that everything is OK. This information is usually buried somewhere in the program options. Try excluding the AutoCAD Help file, specifically C:\Program Files\AutoCAD 2007\Help\acad170.chm. You can even exclude .chm files in general, but this is the less secure option.

Use Cursor Help in Dialog Boxes

This underused feature is quite helpful. Most dialog boxes in AutoCAD have a question-mark button on their title bars, next to the close box X. Click the ? button, and the cursor will display a question-mark icon next to the pointer.

Now, click any part of the dialog box you're interested in querying. A tooltip appears that displays information about the control you selected. This is a great way to learn which system variables the Graphical User Interface (GUI) elements control. It's also much faster than going through standard Help.

For example, open the Options dialog (right-clicking the command line is a quick way to get to Options). Select the 3D Modeling tab, and click the question-mark button. Then, click the Visual Style While Creating 3D Objects drop-down list. The tooltip describes this drop-down's function in more verbose prose, and it also reveals the name of the associated system variable—DRAGVS, in this example.

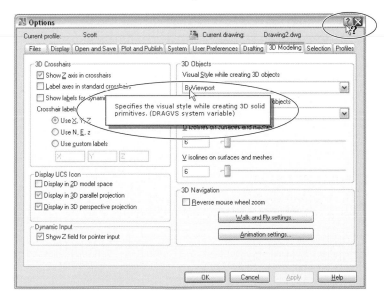

Quick Help Offers Contextual Information

New users of AutoCAD will benefit most from the Quick Help feature. It displays contextual help information in the Info Palette as you work. Every time you enter a command, information appears about the active command. Obviously, this gets old after you fully understand the commands you're using. However, more experienced users can still benefit by opening the Info Palette just prior to using an unfamiliar command.

Press Ctrl+5, or choose Help → Info Palette. Leave the Info Palette floating and visible or put it in a dock, as you prefer. Any command you enter will automatically open its corresponding documentation page in the Info Palette.

For example, let's say you want help using the new Thicken command in AutoCAD 2007. Type **Thicken**, and press Enter, and documentation is instantly available. The Info Palette displays the brief description "Creates a 3D solid by thickening a surface." (You probably could have guessed as much.) A hyperlinked procedure is also shown.

Click To Convert One Or More Surfaces To Solids, and observe that a step-by-step procedure is listed that you can follow. But wait! As soon as you try to follow the steps, the procedure list disappears, because the Info Palette must follow whatever is happening at the moment.

To keep what is currently displayed in the Info Palette, right-click inside the palette, and choose Lock from the context menu. Now you can go ahead and follow the steps as you work. After you've completed the task, you'll have to unlock the palette to keep it responding to input.

Submit Comments about AutoCAD Help

Let the fine folks at Autodesk Technical Publications group who are responsible for the AutoCAD Help documentation know your mind. Now there is an easy way to report errors, omissions, deficiencies, deliberate obfuscation, and/or praise to the technical writers.

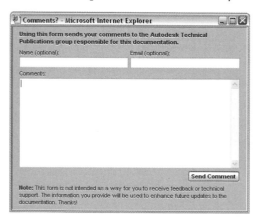

Every page in the Help window has a miniscule link in the lower-right corner that says, "Please send us your comment about this page." (Maybe they're hoping you won't be able to read text that small! No, we're sure that's not it.) Click the link, and a dialog box appears, giving you the power to vent or praise as the case may be. You can optionally enter your name and e-mail address.

Don't use the comment mechanism in the Help system if you want technical support. Instead, submit comments to make AutoCAD Help better in the future.

Online Help

You can access tons of AutoCAD help online. The AutoCAD Help menu has links to many excellent resources, including these:

- e-Learning training is available to subscription customers (a wonderful utility worth trying).

- The Support Knowledge Base is a good place to go when you have a specific technical problem.

- Autodesk User Group International (AUGI) has many interesting resources (www.augi.com). You can also sign up for this organization free of charge (and we all love free).

In addition, point your browser to http://discussion.autodesk.com to access the Auto-CAD discussion groups that are available on the Web and via the news: protocol. Did you know the Thunderbird e-mail client has built-in newsreader support? You can read news and blogs (anything with syndication) while you peruse your e-mail. This is a great way to keep up to date with the latest issues.

Plus, the AutoCAD blogosphere has exploded in the last few months! What's up in blogistan, you say? Quite a lot! Check it out:

Web log Title	Host	http://
Lynn Allen's Blog	Lynn Allen	blogs.autodesk.com/lynn
Between the Lines	Shaan Hurley	autodesk.blogs.com/between_the_lines
The AutoCAD Insider	Heidi Hewett	heidihewett.blogs.com
Beyond the UI	Lee Ambrosius	hyperpics.blogs.com/beyond_the_ui
Beside the Cursor	Richard Binning	integr-8.com/besidethecursor
Will Render for Food	Beau Turner	rndr4food.blogspot.com
Beth's CAD Blog	Beth Powell	bethscadblog.blogspot.com
In the Dynamic Interface	Mark Douglas	mdouglas.blogs.com/in_the_dynamic_interface
The Mad Cadder	Michael Rotolo	themadcadder.blogs.com

continues on next page

Web log Title	Host	http://
Mistress of the Dorkness	Melanie Stone	mistressofthedorkness.blogspot.com
The Autodesk Informer	Ryan Small	autodeskinformer.blogs.com
CAD Managment Topics	Scott Durkee	scottdurkee.blogspot.com
Raster Design with AutoCAD	Jane Smith	rasterdesign.blogspot.com
The Digital Architect	Scott Onstott	scottonstott.com/vodcast

Our apologies to any AutoCAD bloggers who aren't listed here. This is an incomplete list, even at the time of this book's publication. Who knows how many more industry-related weblogs will appear in the coming months and years? Keep them coming!

Using Workspaces

Do you find it impossible to come up with the perfect arrangement of menus, toolbars, and palettes? There are just too many toolbars and palettes and never enough screen real estate to make this wish come true.

Enter *workspaces*. This feature was designed to fulfill this seemingly impossible dream. Workspaces save any arrangement of menus, toolbars, and palettes that you care to create. The idea is that you can save a workspace for every set of tasks that you want to perform. Doing 3D modeling? Save the relevant toolbars and palettes as a workspace. Back to construction documentation? You'll need different palettes, toolbars, …you get the picture—save it all as a workspace.

If you don't want to be bothered to manually save changes to your ever-evolving workspaces, you can elect to automatically save workspace changes. Use the WSSETTINGS command, or click the first button on the Workspaces toolbar. Click the second radio button to make this change.

However, there is some danger with this approach. Everything you change is saved automatically, so there's no room for massive experimentation if you're basically happy with the UI. Perhaps your best bet is to set workspaces to automatically save during a period of experimentation. Then, revert back to Do Not Save Changes To Workspace once you're satisfied that your workspaces are more or less carved in stone.

A hybrid approach is to lock down certain workspaces that *are* carved in stone (read-only) via an Enterprise CUI file. This is an excellent approach to offering standardized drawing environments to everyone on your team. Don't worry about not being able to edit these files, because every user also has their own customizable workspaces that may diverge from the official standards.

See Chapter 10's "CUI for the Enterprise" section for more information.

If you want a particular workspace to appear on startup, use the /w command-line startup switch in the shortcut that launches AutoCAD (see "Prepare for AutoCAD Launch," earlier in this chapter).

Organizing the Interface

AutoCAD 2007 includes several new features that ought to drastically change the way your user interface looks. Working without a command line in favor of dynamic input is a huge step. Cleaning up the UI and anchoring dockable windows provides for a streamlined interface, the likes of which we've never seen before in AutoCAD.

Hide the Command Line

Some veteran AutoCAD users will think this is pure blasphemy, but now is the time to kill (we mean, hide) the command line. Yes, this anachronism from the days of teletypes has finally become—dare we say it?—obsolete. Maybe we won't go that far, because it's a good idea to have our old friend waiting to come out of hiding at a moment's notice in case something goes wrong. But with screen real-estate values going through the roof, it's easier to make the decision.

Dynamic input effectively replaces the command line. Make sure the DYN toggle is on in the status bar if you're planning to hide the command line. The F12 key toggles dynamic input on and off. In addition, right-click the DYN toggle, and choose Settings from the tiny shortcut menu.

Three check boxes appear on the Dynamic Input tab of the Drafting Settings dialog. Select Show Command Prompting

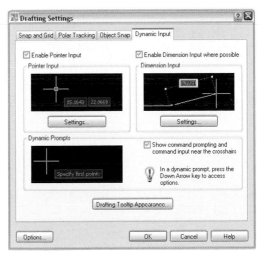

And Command Input Near The Crosshairs. You'll need this option if you plan to hide the command line. Press the Down Arrow key to access command options on screen instead of on the command line.

> See "Input Dynamically" in Chapter 2.

Drag the command-line window out from its dock to palettize it. Turn on auto-hide to save screen real estate. Better yet, anchor the command line—it's a dockable window (see the section "Anchor Dockable Windows").

> Certain commands, such as FILLET and OFFSET, don't display the current settings when using dynamic input. Consequently, you can easily display the command line when this additional information is needed.

Clean Up the UI

You can do a few things to clean up the UI. The first is to hide the layout tabs. Why? Haven't you noticed that the layout tabs occupy an entire row above the status bar, taking up far more space than they're worth?

Right-click a layout tab, and choose Hide Layout And Model Tabs from the shortcut menu. The entire bar housing the layout navigation buttons and tabs disappears, making more space available to the drawing window.

Two new buttons (Model and Layout) appear on the status bar, plus a couple of tiny arrows that give you access to additional layouts that appear in a shortcut menu. So, they provide the same functionality as the buttons and tabs they replace. The only thing we miss is the shortcut menu that appeared on the old layout tabs. Right-click the Model or Layout button on the status bar to display the old UI, if you ever want it back.

Another UI tidbit is to hide unwanted individual buttons on the status bar. When is the last time you used snap? We don't mean object snap, which everybody uses every day. Few use the old-school snap that is tied to absolute space. Why not get rid of its status-bar button? While you're at it, get rid of the Ortho button, too; Polar is much better. Unless you're really into 3D, you may also find it useful to remove the Grid button. The fewer buttons you have on your status bar, the less likely you'll be to select the wrong one.

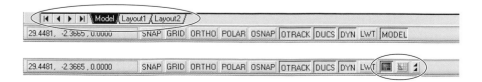

Click the downward-facing arrow in the lower-right corner of the status bar to open the status-bar menu. Turn off any buttons you can live without. These buttons will disappear from the status bar.

Finally, the button adjacent to the status-bar menu is the clean-screen toggle. Click it or press Ctrl+0 (if you aren't on AutoCAD 2007) to experience minimum clutter. AutoCAD is maximized, and all palettes and toolbars disappear. Anchored dockable windows are still usable in this mode. Clean-screen mode gives the drawing window center stage and is most useful in presentations. Many people find it difficult to work for any length of time without palettes and toolbars, so toggle out by pressing Ctrl+0 again.

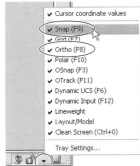

Anchor Dockable Windows

The ability to anchor dockable windows (also known at times as *floating palettes*) is one of the best new features in AutoCAD 2007. In case you haven't noticed, there has been a proliferation of dockable windows in recent AutoCAD releases. These include the following:

- Advanced Settings Dialog
- Command Line
- Dashboard
- dbConnect Manager
- Design Center
- External References
- Info Palette
- Lights In Model
- Materials
- Markup Set Manager
- Properties
- Quick Calculator
- Sheet Set Manager
- Sun Properties
- Tool Palettes
- Visual Style Manager

With all these dockable windows competing for space on screen, there is now officially no room left for drawing. Autodesk probably figured that it couldn't just tell everyone to go out and buy three more monitors, so it invented the *anchor* feature.

Right-click the vertical title bar of any palette (or, more correctly, *dockable window*), and toggle on Allow Docking, if it's not already on. Repeat, and choose Anchor Left or Anchor Right.

The best thing about anchoring is that you can anchor multiple dockable windows on each side of the screen without sacrificing any more pixels. Hover the mouse over any labeled anchored dock, and the associated palettes expand, filling all the available space.

Anchoring is the most efficient way to work with dockable windows. Try anchoring as many palettes on the edges of the screen as your display resolution allows. You'll have instant access to most of the UI without having to hunt for palettes in the menu or, worse yet, try to remember shortcut keys.

> If you want to decrease the amount of time it takes to unhide palettes, check out the cool program at http://jtbworld.blogspot.com/2006/02/autocad-palette-auto-hide-speed.html

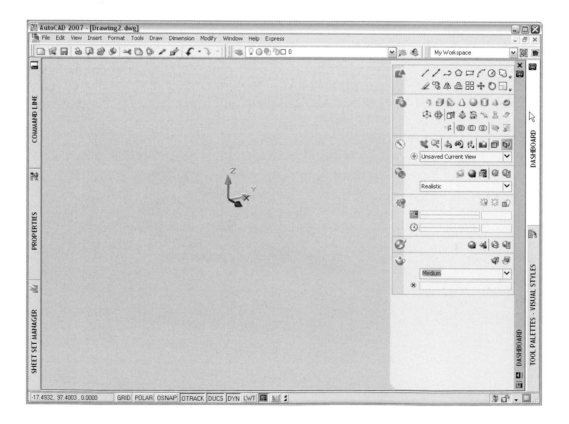

Setup the Dashboard/Tool Palette Connection

The Dashboard is definitely an interesting new feature in AutoCAD 2007. Did you know that there is a mysterious connection between the Dashboard and the Tool Palettes?

The Dashboard is filled with *control panels* (ahem; didn't Autodesk think about the obvious name collision with this well-known Windows feature?). One of these control panels, 2D Draw, isn't visible out of the box—so let's turn it on. Right-click anywhere inside the Dashboard palette. Choose Control Panels → 2D Draw Control Panel from the shortcut menu. The missing control panel appears at the top of the palette; its icon is a 2D triangle and square. Consider using this control panel for basic drafting tools instead of using the bulkier Draw and Modify toolbars.

Each control panel can be activated by clicking its icon. When a control panel is active, it's highlighted in orange, revealing more hidden controls. There is more to the control panels than meets the eye.

Bear with us, and activate each control panel one at a time. After you activate one, hover the mouse over the Tool Palettes to unhide them if anchored (no need to hover if they're floating and staring you in the face). Many of the control panels automatically trigger different tool palette groups to activate. This is the mysterious connection alluded to earlier.

For example, when you activate the 3D Navigate control panel, the Cameras tool palette group is likewise triggered, bringing its one and only Cameras palette to the fore. When you activate the Materials control panel, the Materials tool palette group brings numerous palettes to the fore in the Tool Palettes. Get it?

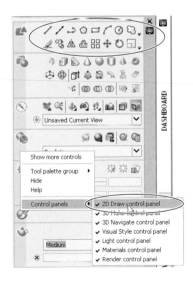

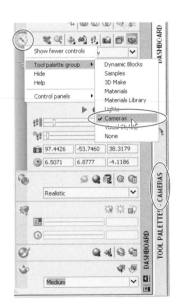

You can customize which tool palette group is connected with each control panel. Activate a particular control panel, and then right-click its icon. From the shortcut menu, choose which tool palette group you want to associate with the active control panel. Now you have the ultimate in customizable interconnected UI convenience!

Lock Down the UI

By now, you've probably spent numerous hours researching the UI, only to realize you haven't gotten any productive work done. Remember that research is an investment in your future productivity. (Tell that to your boss!) When you're finally satisfied with all aspects of your highly customized interface, or you need to get back to work, it's time to lock down the UI.

You lock it down so that some nefarious individual (most likely yourself) doesn't accidentally mess up all the organizing that's been done to make your interface the streamlined masterpiece it has become. Of course, doing this is more critical if you've set the workspace to automatically save changes (see "Using Workspaces," earlier in the chapter).

Click the padlock icon in the lower-right corner of the screen, and choose All ➜ Locked if you're going for a total lockdown. If you're not so sure, lock only toolbars and/or windows, floating and/or docked. Better safe than sorry.

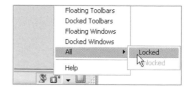

Recover "Lost" Dockable Windows

Have you ever "lost" one of your dockable windows—for example, the Command Line? It isn't visible anywhere on the screen when you toggle it on. Almost immediately, panic sets in. Why did you ever undock it? How will you live without your command line? You toggle the window on and off frantically with shortcut keys, and then you try the menu, before dreading that you might have to reinstall AutoCAD. Wait, don't do that—the fix is easy:

1. Use the CUI command to open the Customize User Interface window.

2. Expand your current workspace in the Customizations In All CUI Files pane.

3. Expand Dockable Windows in the Workspace Contents pane.

4. Select the lost item in the list.

5. Change Orientation to anything other than Do Not Change (Left, for example). Click OK, and the case is closed.

6. Move the recovered dockable window back to your preferred location.

How is it possible to misplace dockable windows? This can happen when you've been using dual monitors in extended desktop mode. You experience the loss when you're away from your second monitor, say with a notebook computer on the road. AutoCAD remembers the position of your floating window but isn't smart enough to know that you can't see it because it's off the screen. You may also lose your dockable windows when you change the resolution of the screen (which once happened to Lynn in front of about 150 people in Denmark!) If neither one of these situations applies to you, dockable windows have also been reported to disappear for no good reason at all.

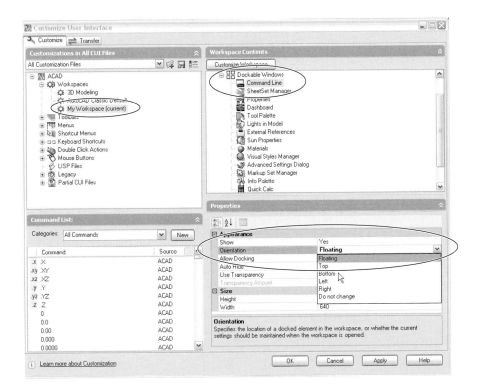

Inputting with the Keyboard and Mouse

Long gone are the days when tablets were popular input devices in the AutoCAD community. Although they had some advantages, they made portability impractical. Today, the keyboard and mouse are the only input devices you'll need to get the most out of AutoCAD. The tips in this section—some new and some old—will help you work more efficiently with AutoCAD.

Input Optimizations

The first big optimization is to enter commands using dynamic input on screen rather than on the command line. Old habits are hard to break, but please give dynamic input a chance. To get the most from dynamic input, turn dynamic prompts on in the Drafting Settings dialog box. Use the Down Arrow key when you want to see options.

Autocomplete is another nifty feature that should be popular among the lazy, forgetful, and/or dyslexic (which should include just about everyone). This tool comes in handy when you can't remember how to spell a specific system variable or command. Autocomplete works both in dynamic input prompts and on the command line. To use this practically invisible feature, key in a few letters of a command or system variable you kind-of remember, and then press the Tab key for a suggested command completion. AutoCAD pages through all the commands and system variables that start with those characters.

For example, type **SP**, and then press Tab. Keep pressing Tab, and complete commands will cycle at the prompt. You'll see these commands:

- SPACETRANS
- SPELL
- SPHERE
- SPLANE
- SPLINE
- SPLFRAME

…on and on alphabetically ad nauseum. If you're too hasty in pressing Tab, and you go past the command you want, press Shift+Tab to go backward. Press Enter to execute the selected command, and you're back in business.

Command cycling is another input optimization of note. Press the Up Arrow key to see the previous command that you used appear at the prompt. This list isn't alphabetical, like Autocomplete—these are the commands you really used, not just thought about using.

Press the same key again to see the command before that, and so on. Use the Down Arrow key to go forward through the cycle. Press Enter to execute, as always.

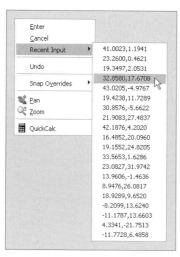

Where is this feature useful? Let's say you observe that you're going through the same repetitive motions while drawing. You're using OFFSET and then FILLET and maybe TRIM repeatedly. Instead of hunting for the correct tool button, just press the Up Arrow key for quicker command access. Anything to save a few microseconds.

The final input optimization to mention is Recent Input. This is similar to command cycling but is used for input instead of commands (thus the well-chosen name). When you're at an input prompt (for example, when you're drawing a line), right-click to access the Recent Input shortcut submenu; here you'll find recently used coordinates and commands with quick reuse potential.

Board the Command Alias Express

Command aliases are abbreviated command names. L is the alias for LINE, A is for ARC, and so on. Surprisingly, command aliases aren't part of the CUI editor; they're still controlled by the ancient ACAD.PGP file. Ever since Autodesk went with the Microsoft standard for AutoCAD, the support folder that contains the program parameters file is buried deep in the file system. Way deep—look how far you have to go to manually reach this hidden folder:

```
C:\Documents and Settings\<username>\Application Data
```

```
\Autodesk\AutoCAD 2007\R17.0\enu\Support\acad.pgp
```

Theoretically, you could edit this text file by hand, but why bother? Instead, use the ALIASEDIT Express Tool to edit the file without leaving the comfort of AutoCAD.

For example, many people prefer to use the alias C for the COPY command rather than CIRCLE. To make this change, use ALIASEDIT. Scroll down the command list, and select the alias C. Click Edit, and change the association to COPY. Click OK in all the dialogs and confirmation dialogs that appear, and AutoCAD will reinitialize so the change is live.

INSTALL THE EXPRESS TOOLS

If you haven't installed all the Express Tools, then drop everything and install them immediately (do a custom install, and select Express Tools). The Express Tools are extremely useful. Some have already found their way into core AutoCAD—they have come of age and are now considered to be grown-up AutoCAD features.

Other Express Tools haven't been so lucky; they still suffer from lack of worldwide acceptance. Some Express Tools are waiting to be *localized*—translated into every language in which AutoCAD is offered. Because the Express Tools don't run on AutoCAD LT, only tools that make their way into the core product are available to LT users.

Function Key Master List

Many of the function keys have been the same since time immemorial (since 1982). But recently a few of them have changed, and it behooves you to make some additional changes on your own. Instead of trying to piece together all this information on your own, you can memorize the following chart, or photocopy it and pin it up (or tattoo it on yourself, if you're into that):

F1	Help
F2	Text Window
F3	Object Snap
F4	Tablet
F5	Cycle Isoplane
F6	Dynamic User Coordinate System
F7	Grid
F8	Orthogonal
F9	Snap
F10	Polar Tracking
F11	Object Snap Tracking
F12	Dynamic Input

All the function keys except F1 are toggles that turn modes on and off. Some of the keys have corresponding buttons on the status bar.

We suggest that you change F1 to Cancel to avoid accidentally hitting the Help function when you miss the Escape key. We also recommend that you change the F4 key from the archaic Tablet to something more valuable. Lynn's is set to 3DOrbit to sync up with the settings in Autodesk Inventor.

> See Chapter 10 to learn how to customize the function keys.

Temporary Overrides Are Here to Stay

Temporary overrides were introduced in AutoCAD 2006 and are worth getting to know only if you can walk and chew gum at the same time. They work when you hold down a key combination (usually involving the Shift key) while doing something with the mouse. A tiny icon appears near the cursor to visually clue you in that something is being overridden at the moment.

This feature comes in handy when you can't be bothered to toggle a mode off because you know you're going to need to turn it right back on in a second (that would mean two clicks or button presses; think of the time waste). Press the correct keys, and the mode in question is overridden—but just temporarily, while you're holding down the keys.

There are two sets of temporary overrides, one for each hand (depending on whether you're right or left handed). One of your hands is on the mouse, right? We certainly wouldn't want you to let go of the mouse. The other hand can hold down a key combo to temporarily override while you continue to use the mouse. (Then, if you really practice, you can answer the phone with your foot.)

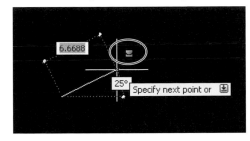

This is the default list of temporary overrides, all of which can be customized with the CUI command (see Chapter 10):

Left Hand	Function
Shift+A	Toggles object snap
Shift+S	Enables object snap enforcement
Shift+E	Object snap override: endpoint
Shift+V	Object snap override: midpoint
Shift+C	Object snap override: center
Shift+Q	Toggles object snap tracking
Shift+D	Disables all snapping and tracking
Shift+X	Toggles polar tracking
Shift+Z	Toggles dynamic UCS
Shift	Toggles orthogonal mode

Right Hand	Function
Shift+'	Toggles object snap
Shift+;	Enables object snap enforcement
Shift+P	Object snap override: endpoint
Shift+M	Object snap override: midpoint
Shift+,	Object snap override: center
Shift+]	Toggles object snap tracking
Shift+L	Disables all snapping and tracking
Shift+.	Toggles polar tracking
Shift+/	Toggles dynamic UCS
Shift	Toggles orthogonal mode

Crosshairs in 3D

If you're planning to do any 3D modeling—and you should be, if you're using AutoCAD 2007—set up the crosshair cursor for 3D so you'll know which way is up. Use the Options command, and click the 3D Modeling tab.

Select Show Z Axis In Crosshairs. Doing so adds the third "up" dimension to the crosshairs; it appears in blue. There is a method to the madness of color coding. Anyone who knows computers knows that monitors use RGB color space. Painters often get confused because they learned that yellow is a primary color, and it is—at least, for the *subtractive* color you see with reflected light (as in paint on a canvas). Computer monitors shine light in your eyes, so they use *additive* color, which is an entirely different animal. But we digress.

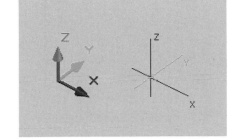

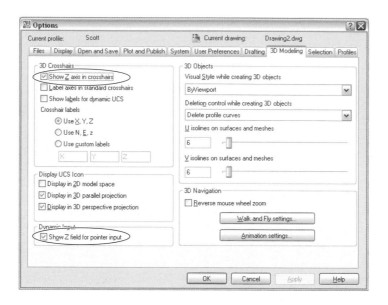

The mnemonic, or way to remember it, is *RGB=XYZ*—red represents the X axis, green for Y, and blue for Z. The UCS icon is fatter and has conical arrowheads on the axis tips by default, but observe that it follows the same hard and fast color-coding rules.

You might choose to label the axes on the crosshairs (in Options), but once you get the color mnemonic, doing so will be overkill. Before closing the 3D Modeling tab of the Options dialog, select Show Z Field For Pointer Input. This option is helpful if you ever want to key in Z coordinates on screen using dynamic input, but point input must also be enabled in Drafting Settings.

As the Wheel Turns

Tell us that you have a wheel on your mouse. If you don't, what are you thinking? Go out and buy a wheeled mouse ASAP—have a bake sale or a carwash, whatever it takes! The mouse wheel is one of the best productivity boosters. A few important system variables control the behavior of the mouse wheel:

MBUTTONPAN MBUTTONPAN is the system variable that controls whether the middle buttons pans or displays the object snap menu (which isn't quite as useful). Panning with the wheel button is so intuitive that most of us take it for granted. It's on by default, but if someone turns it off, you'll probably go crazy—so, this tip will make your day. Set MBUTTONPAN to 1 for panning, and set it to 0 to display the object snap menu. There's no need to use the scroll bars on the screen or key in PAN anymore when MBUTTONPAN is on—just use the wheel button. Those of you who still have an ancient three-button mouse will prefer setting MBUTTONPAN to 0, because you won't be able to pan anyway.

ZOOMWHEEL The ZOOMWHEEL system variable controls the direction you rotate the wheel to zoom. AutoCAD has forever been set to zoom in when you rotate the wheel away from you (forward direction). You're moving the camera toward the objects on the screen by scrolling forward and away from the objects by scrolling backward. It's now possible to reverse that behavior by setting this system variable to 1.

Why would you want to do that? To make it easier on your visual cortex as you switch between AutoCAD and Autodesk Inventor, Google Sketchup, and/or Google Earth. All these apps (and probably many others) use the reverse mouse-wheel zoom direction, so that rotating the wheel forward (away from you) zooms out. The objects are moving away from the camera and vice versa. Now power users will be less disoriented as they switch between 3D programs (although old habits are hard to break).

ZOOMFACTOR ZOOMFACTOR controls how quickly your mouse wheel zooms in and out when it's rotated. The *zoom factor* is a number that represents a percentage of the maximum possible speed. Set ZOOMFACTOR to a number between 1 and 100 to govern zooming speed. Lower speeds give you finer control, but it can take all day rolling the wheel to get anywhere. This is a personal setting that you'll need to choose for yourself.

Customize the Right Mouse Button

If you've been using AutoCAD for a long time, then you'll remember how efficient it was when a right-click meant Enter. You could draft much more quickly with the mouse instead of having to use the other hand to hit the Spacebar or Enter key to end and repeat the last command.

Somewhere along the path of AutoCAD's continual evolution, a shortcut menu began to appear when you right-click instead of our good friend Enter. Although the shortcut menu often has Enter as one of its many options, it's clearly a compromise situation. Right-clicking for Enter is faster.

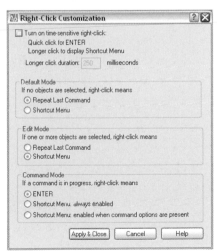

To be fair, the right-click shortcut menu has advantages, too. Some people have even grown to rely on it. We swear that there are commands in the shortcut menus that we have yet to find anywhere else! The good news is, you can customize right-click behavior so you can have the best of both worlds.

Use the Options command, and select the User Preferences tab. Click the Right-Click Customization button to bring up a dialog box of the same name. Here you can choose exactly how you want the right button to behave.

Should the right button repeat the last command, bring up the shortcut menu, or act like Enter? If you ponder it, your answer probably depends on whether objects are selected and a command is in progress. Amazingly, all these possibilities are customizable, but you'll find in practice that locking in the mouse behavior in this fashion can be a bit too constraining. What if you change your mind on occasion and want the shortcut menu to appear rather than repeating the last command?

Perhaps *the best of all possible worlds* (with deference to Voltaire) is to turn on time-sensitive right-click. Check the box at the top of the dialog, and your act of right-clicking will be timed. This isn't a test: If you click quickly—say, if the click lasts less than 250 milliseconds—that will mean Enter (or repeat the last command, if you're at the command prompt). If you take longer to complete the right-click, then the shortcut menu will appear. Give it a try; you may like leaving your options open until the moment of right-clicking.

If you're not into video games and/or you just can't stomach being timed all of the time, then disable time-sensitive right-click and breathe easier.

Drawing and Editing

DRAWING AND EDITING are your AutoCAD bread and butter. If you do a lot of drafting, this chapter is essential reading. The tidbits you pick up here will probably end up shaving off hours or days (or months?) of inefficiently spent drawing and editing time if you take them to heart.

The key to getting more done with AutoCAD is to use tools as efficiently as possible so you'll save time. If you've been using drawing and editing tools for years, chances are you're operating on automatic pilot. Use the tips and techniques in this chapter to chart a new course to increased productivity.

This chapter's topics include:

- Boosting Productivity
- Drawing and Editing Tips
- Living with Layers

■ Boosting Productivity

A lot of the marketing surrounding AutoCAD upgrades claims that they will boost your productivity. Although this may be true in theory, there are other issues to consider. Increasing productivity means getting more done per unit of time.

Assuming your boss buys into the marketing and now expects more productivity out of you after upgrading to AutoCAD 2007, here are some options: either stop yakking on the phone so you "waste" less time, or work later in the evening and spend more time to get the job done. On the other hand, you may really learn to use AutoCAD more efficiently—yak all you want—and go home early. The latter option is what this section is about.

Input Dynamically

In Chapter 1, we suggested that you hide the command line in favor of entering commands—and their options—dynamically on-screen at the cursor to increase your productivity. Maybe it doesn't sound like much to you newbies, but many veteran users are going to need therapy over this; but you're probably in therapy already if you've been using AutoCAD that long (not to knock therapy, therapists, or the therapeutic profession).

Jesting aside, sometimes dynamic input is too distracting, too Las Vegas, annoying you with its visual clutter. Maybe you just want to draw a circle, and you don't need to see the prompt, coordinates, and command options on screen. You know how to draw a circle already, right?

Press F12 or click the DYN toggle on the status bar to turn off dynamic input. Now you can draw that circle in peace. But what happens when you want to Loft something, and you aren't sure about its prompts and options? You'll be flying blind if you've taken our advice and hidden the command line and dynamic input (we can't be held responsible). Toggle dynamic input back on when you want it. It's so simple, it's transparent.

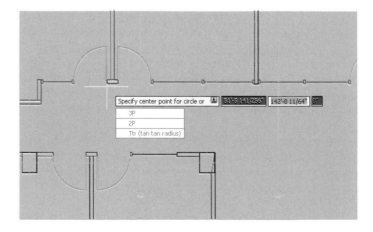

Dynamic input coordinates are relative by default. That means you don't have to preface every second or next point coordinate entry with the @ ("at sign," "petite escargot," or "monkey's tail") symbol anymore. Even little details like this can add up to big time savings in the long run. This behavior is also customizable:

1. Right click the DYN toggle on the status bar, and choose Settings from the shortcut menu.

2. The Drafting Settings dialog appears, with its Dynamic Input tab displayed. Click the Settings button in the Pointer Input area.

3. Choose Absolute or Relative coordinates and Polar or Cartesian format in the Format area. We recommend Polar and Relative for maximum productivity.

4. If you tend to get annoyed by coordinate tooltips, choose the first radio button in the Visibility area. Then, those pesky coordinate boxes will appear if, and only if, you start typing coordinates.

If you do decide to leave the Second Or Next Points coordinate entry set to Relative, you'll save time by not having to explicitly type @ to indicate relative coordinate entry. Great!

However, sometimes you'll want to enter absolute coordinates. For example, if you're aligning floor levels with respect to the absolute origin point, you need to move objects using the Second Or Next Points setting of 0,0. How will you do that if coordinates are relative by default?

The solution is the # (number sign) symbol, which forces absolute coordinate entry. Here's an example command-line transcript:

```
Command: MOVE

Select objects: 1 found

Specify base point or [Displacement] <Displacement>:

 (click a point on the object)

Specify second point or <use first point as displacement>: #0,0
```

These commands move the selected object from some arbitrary location to the absolute coordinates of the origin point. Chances are, you'll have to type # a lot less frequently than @, so this is a welcome development.

Have you noticed yet that dynamic input is kinder and gentler than the command line? If you enter an invalid command option, the dynamic prompt input box highlights in red, discreetly informing you that you made a mistake. The focus remains on the red prompt,

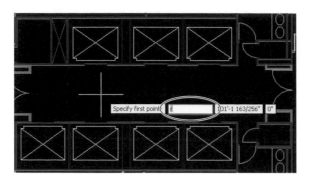

offering you instant forgiveness and a chance to redeem yourself with valid input—just type away. Sure beats the command line—which either ignores you entirely or calls you *names* (surrounding its harsh appellations with asterisks).

Tooltips Point the Way

Tooltips display extra visual information that guides you in the right direction. The advantage of tooltips is that they put information right where you need it: next to the hovering cursor. The disadvantage, should you see it that way, is that tooltips can draw your attention away from the geometry you're working on.

AutoCAD 2007 includes three kinds of tooltips: drafting tooltips, Autosnap tooltips, and dynamic input tooltips. Different settings are used to manage each kind.

Drafting tooltips appear when you hover the cursor over a toolbar button, for example. Their goal is to clue you in on the function that particular button will perform when clicked. Drafting tooltips' appearance has historically been controlled by the operating system (see "Keeping Up Appearances," in Chapter 1). The Display tab of the Options dialog box manages drafting tooltip size, color, and font. AutoCAD has a system variable appropriately called TOOLTIPS that turns drafting tooltips on and off. If you feel that you know the function of each and every button on your toolbars, consider turning off drafting tooltips. (If you know the function of each and every button, you probably need to get out more!)

Autosnap tooltips have been around a while. They inform you in writing which object snap is active when you move the cursor over an object snap location. When two different types of object snaps could be valid, the Autosnap helps you get the correct one. Autosnap also displays markers that efficiently reveal the same information in symbolic form.

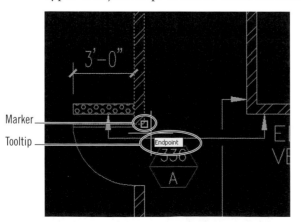

Maybe it's a bit nit-picky, but don't you think it's lame having both the Autosnap tooltip and marker tell you the same thing? Do you need to live with this visual redundancy day in and day out? We're not dealing with the Da Vinci Code symbology here—just a few basic shapes to memorize.

If you want to dispense with the Autosnap tooltips in favor of the visually more efficient markers, then you're going to have to memorize a few symbols. Fortunately, we have supplied this handy chart for you newer users to photocopy and pin up:

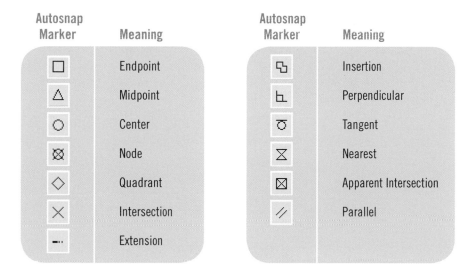

Autosnap Marker	Meaning	Autosnap Marker	Meaning
□	Endpoint	⌐⌐	Insertion
△	Midpoint	⌐	Perpendicular
○	Center	○	Tangent
⊠	Node	⊠	Nearest
◇	Quadrant	⊠	Apparent Intersection
×	Intersection	//	Parallel
---	Extension		

If you're tempted to turn off Autosnap tooltips and/or markers, here's how you can do it:

1. Use the Options command.

2. Select the Drafting tab.

3. In the AutoSnap Settings area, uncheck Display AutoSnap Tooltip and/or Marker according to your preference (but not both).

Dynamic input prompts are another kind of helpful tooltip system that offer more in the way of customization. As long as Show Command Prompting And Command Input Near The Crosshairs is checked in the Drafting Settings dialog, you may not always need the command line. Whatever would have appeared on the command line appears in the tooltip prompt near the cursor—unless an Autosnap tooltip replaces it.

Wait a minute! You don't want to memorize the previous chart, do you? If you leave on Autosnap tooltips, then the fancy new dynamic prompts and input boxes will be replaced whenever you hover over a snap location—which is just about all the time. This seriously compromises the usefulness of the dynamic input feature—say it isn't so!

Fortunately, there is a way to have the best of both worlds. You can merge the Autosnap tooltip and the dynamic input tooltips so they appear

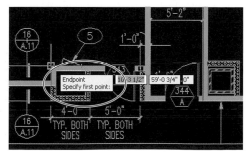

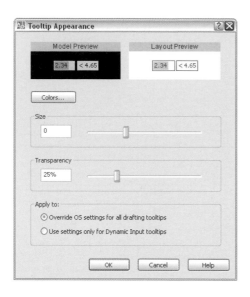

simultaneously in one big happy tooltip. To do so, set the system variable TOOLTIPMERGE to 1.

Dynamic input tooltips can be customized in more ways than the operating system allows. Control tooltip color, size, and transparency in the Tooltip Appearance dialog. Here you can also choose to override the Windows Display control panel's control over drafting tooltips with the radio buttons. (Isn't it nice when AutoCAD trumps Windows?) Access the Tooltip Appearance dialog from the Dynamic Input tab of the Drafting Settings dialog (DSettings command).

Calculate Anything Quickly

People often don't know that AutoCAD has had a built-in calculator for many years. When you pay thousands of dollars for sophisticated computer-aided design software, you might expect it to be able to add a few numbers for you, right? It better!

This old-school calculator is still available by typing **'cal** (use an apostrophe to invoke it transparently) at any command prompt. Few people used the command-line calculator because it has a terrible interface. It's so bad that the Windows accessory calculator looks fancy in comparison. Don't use either!

Fortunately, AutoCAD now has the shiny new QuickCalc, with a Graphical User Interface (GUI). QuickCalc can do more than calculate—it can convert units, act as geometry calculator, and even handle variables that persist from one drawing session to another. Furthermore, QuickCalc can pass values back and forth between itself and the Properties palette.

> Autodesk: Any plans to add Reverse Polish Notation as an option in QuickCalc? You know, so it might replace our trusty handheld HP calculators? Engineers know what I'm talking about—we want to geek out with this feature.

Invoke QuickCalc from any property in the Properties palette when you need to calculate a value that you want to enter. Try it like this:

1. Draw a circle.

2. Select the circle, and open the Properties palette.

3. Select the editable Diameter property. Notice the tiny calculator icon—click it to open the floating QuickCalc dialog.

4. The value from the Properties palette was passed to QuickCalc. Do a calculation, such as adding a value, and press Enter to calculate.

5. Click the Apply button to pass the value back from QuickCalc to the Properties palette. Slick, isn't it?

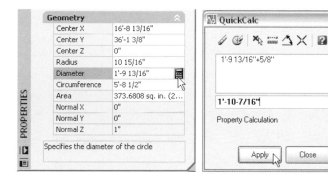

You can also invoke QuickCalc from dynamic prompts or the command line. Just be sure to do so transparently by typing **'QC** or by pressing Ctrl+8 so you don't interrupt your flow. Opening QuickCalc this way makes it appear on a palette, rather than as the floating dialog you saw before. To experiment with QuickCalc, try a unit conversion:

1. Press Ctrl+8 to open the QuickCalc palette.

2. Expand the More button if you haven't done so already.

3. Expand the Units Conversion rollout by clicking the down arrow on its title bar.

4. Choose Length as the units type. Convert from inches, and convert to millimeters.

5. Click in the Value To Convert field, and type a number. Unfortunately, all values must be decimal—no mixing of feet and inches is allowed.

6. Press Enter to convert units. Right-click in the Converted Value field, and notice the tiny calculator icon. You can click this icon to pass the converted value back to the active command.

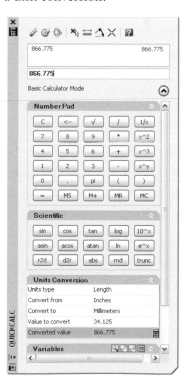

All you sacred geometry buffs will appreciate that the Variables feature in QuickCalc has Phi built-in (1.61803399) so you can easily work with the golden section.

Survey Says?

Have you ever had to deal with land-title documents that show property boundaries drawn with distances and bearings? Unless you're a civil engineer or trained surveyor, chances are the angles, or *bearings*, are in units you don't know how to use.

Did you know that AutoCAD can handle everything from nanometers (in the realm of quantum physics) to parsecs (very large astronomical units)? Check out the INSUNITS system variable or go to the Options command/User Preferences tab and view the drop-down list under Insertion Scale. It should be no surprise that AutoCAD can understand distances and bearings given in surveyor's units, which are specifically rotational units of measure.

Let's see how it's done:

1. Use the Units command, and set Angle Type to Surveyor's Units.

2. Choose the precision you need—probably degrees, minutes, and seconds.

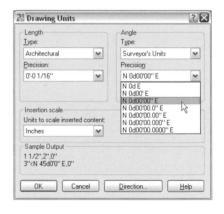

3. Draw property boundaries with polar coordinates using surveyor's jargon—for example, 120′<S15D25′32″W. It starts with a distance; then, following the angle symbol < are degrees, minutes, and seconds in a particular quadrant. The angle must be surrounded by quadrant letters—N or S precedes the angle, and W or E must follow the angle. The letter D is used to indicate degrees, the apostrophe is for minutes, and the quotation mark is for minutes.

Angles in surveyor's units can be confusing, if you aren't used to them. Angles increase positively from the North and South axes. You can use the cardinal directions to draw orthogonal lines, such as 10′<E to draw a 10-foot line horizontally to the right. Numerical angles are always acute in surveyor's units.

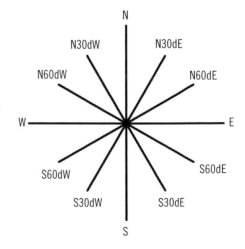

Work with Angles

If you've drawn much geometry at an angle, it gets old quickly—especially if it's some weird oblique angle that isn't easily divided into 360. Many of the drawing tools in AutoCAD assume you're dealing with reasonable, orthogonal geometry—but that's not always the way things are in the real world. In particular, snap, grid, ortho, polar, and object tracking work best when you're drawing mostly horizontal and vertical lines.

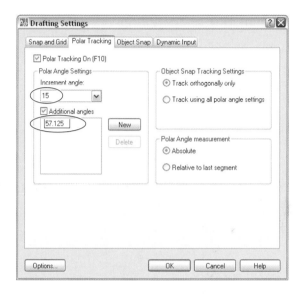

If the tilted geometry you're working with has an angle that divides evenly into 360, then set polar tracking's increment angle to that number, and that's probably all you need to do. On the other hand, if you're working with an oddball angle, add it as an additional angle in the Drafting Settings dialog.

Polar tracking is a help, but if your neck is sore because you're subconsciously tilting your head to straighten the angular geometry, then read on.

What if you're working on the wing of a building that's at an oblique angle, or something similar? You'll have a very sore neck at end of the day unless you take action to straighten things out. Here's a section of a building that would be easier to work on if it was oriented differently.

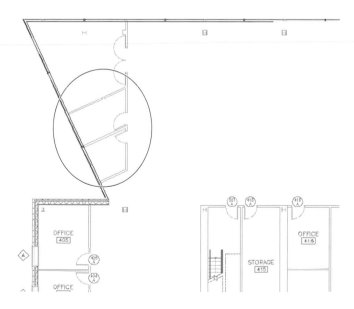

The first correction rotates the user coordinate system (UCS) about the Z axis to match the 2D geometry on screen. An easy way to do this is to use the UCS's Object option—no math required.

The second correction uses the top secret PLAN command. Follow these steps:

1. Use the UCS command, and type OB for the object option.

2. Click a line that is part of the angular geometry you want to work with. If no such line exists (for example, if everything is part of a block or Xref), draw a line first, and then align the UCS to it.

3. Type **Plan**, and then press Enter twice. Yes, PLAN is a command; it displays the plan view of a specified UCS. The second Enter accepts the default, which is the current UCS. It's like you're looking at the "plan" of the UCS you just set.

4. Save a view with the UCS so you can get back here easily.

The resulting view shows the geometry rotated and should be easier to work on. Note that lines drawn at 90 degrees go straight up, as you might expect (because of the UCS), and the drafting tools work normally. To return to the original orientation, type **UCS** Enter Enter **Plan** Enter Enter. This sequence returns you to the world coordinate system and then "plans" to it.

Set UCSFOLLOW to 1 for automatic restoration of plan view whenever the UCS is changed (the view you see will follow the UCS). This is helpful when working on 2D drawings because then you only have to change the UCS to rotate the view.

> It's best not to use UCSFOLLOW with the new dynamic UCS feature, so you can visualize what's happening in 3D from any vantage point you choose.

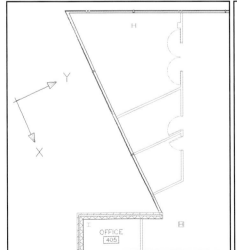
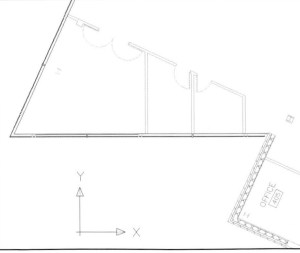

Rotated UCS about Z axis to match object   Resulting view after PLAN command is used

Sketching Tricks

AutoCAD shines at managing highly complex, structured, hard-lined information; but it isn't great at capturing looser, ephemeral, conceptual ideas. AutoCAD 2007 can make hard-edges look sketchy with the new visual style features, but the toolset doesn't inspire visual brainstorming.

A physical sketchbook and/or Google SketchUp are hard to beat, but AutoCAD offers a couple of little-known sketching techniques that you might like to use.

The first is the ancient and under-appreciated SKETCH command. This command hearkens back to the days when tablets were popular because, in case you haven't noticed, the mouse isn't exactly easy to sketch with. With some practice, though, you might get good enough to sketch with a mouse.

See what we've come to? We got rid of pencils to use computers, and now we're using computers to simulate what a pencil can do far more effectively. C'est la vie. Anyway, try it out:

1. Use the SKETCH command (keyboard entry only for this one).

2. Dynamic input is disabled while sketching, so you have to open the command line. Your "sketch" consists of short straight lines so set the record increment small enough so curves won't be too jagged. Click two points to graphically determine the segment length, or press Enter to accept the default.

   ```
   SKETCH

   Record increment <0.1000>:
   ```

3. This unusual command was designed to work with a six-button "puck" on a tablet, but it still works with a mouse. Type **P** and press Enter to start sketching. Be careful, because everywhere the mouse moves gets recorded as vector segments.

   ```
   Sketch. Pen eXit Quit Record Erase Connect .p

   <Pen down>
   ```

4. Press Enter to bring the pen up and stop sketching. The sketch is complete. You may want to trim and/or erase a few segments if your sketch isn't perfect.

> Set SKPOLY to 1 if you want SKETCH to generate polylines rather than individual line segments.

The next sketching technique we'll show you takes advantage of the power of Booleans to sketch with 2D shapes—or, more precisely, with regions. It's more like playing with construction paper, scissors, and glue than true freeform sketching, but this technique may be useful in the conceptual stage of your design process.

Before we dive in, you should first know something about regions. They're bounded 2D shapes that define an area. Unlike a closed polyline, which is only defined along its edges, a region is defined everywhere within its boundary. Boolean operations such as union, subtract, and intersect are like your scissors and glue—they work on 2D regions (and 3D solids). Give Boolean sketching a whirl:

1. Draw a few rectangles, ellipses, circles, polygons, or manually draw closed polylines. Think of these like pieces of construction paper (bear with us).

2. Make the pieces overlap by moving them around until you create a pleasing collage.

3. Use the REGION command, and select all the shapes you've arranged. Press Enter to convert them all to regions—they look exactly the same, but now they're defined with area.

4. Use the UNION, SUBTRACT, and/or INTERSECT commands to join, cut away, or yield new boundaries that combine the original shapes. Keep playing until you've formed an interesting piece of geometry that is more than a freehand sketch.

5. Explode the region, turning it into lines.

6. Use the PEDIT command's Join option to link the individual lines into a continuous edge.

7. Offset the polyline with a wall thickness, for example. Take it from here, and develop the design further using drafting tools.

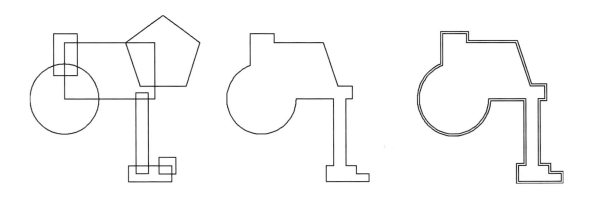

Draw As-Builts from the Outside In

This isn't so much a technique as it's a piece of advice born from experience. If you're working in a profession where you need to produce drawings of things as they were built from innumerable measurements taken in the field (sometimes called *as-built* plans), then this tip is for you. Of course, as-built plans are all too often in contrast with how things were originally designed, but that's another story.

Measurements taken in the field always include some error. Whether every measurement was a bit sloppy, or whether just one or two out of hundreds of perfect measurements were off, it doesn't matter. Chalk it up to human error or a problem with the laser or tape measure. It makes your job of putting together all the pieces in AutoCAD a potential nightmare.

Let's say you're drawing a building, but the description could just as well be a mechanical part or a garden plan. If you start drawing in one area and continue working around the perimeter, you'll inevitably end up finding measurements at the other end that seem to be wrong. This happens because all the tiny errors add up and are magnified the more you draw in a line or circuit.

Many people are tempted to sweep the "wrong" dimensions under the rug, ignoring what the field notes say. But what appears wrong may have more to do with where the plan came together as you drew it than specific incorrect measurements. Tracking down which dimension is wrong can be a tricky business. It's like putting together a jigsaw puzzle, only to find that the last pieces don't fit. Which pieces are wrong?

The solution to this vexing issue is to draw the outside perimeter or overall geometry before working your way in and adding detail. Drawing the longest measured runs first is a way of error-checking the smaller dimensions that make up a given length. This way, the problem is bounded, and you're less likely to magnify errors in one area. It will also be easier to locate bogus dimensions: You know the internal geometry must fit within its container, so inaccuracies are more easily spotted.

Snap To It

Did you know it's possible to control the magnetic strength of snap, so you don't have to bring the cursor as close to geometry for markers (or tooltips) to appear? It's like turning up the juice flowing to an electromagnet, giving the cursor a wider target to attract snap points.

The system variable responsible for the size of the snap target is APERTURE. It ranges from 1–50 pixels with a default of 10. Before adjusting it, temporarily turn on APBOX (set it to 1) to turn on the aperture box—this makes Autosnap's magnetic field visible. Now, adjust APERTURE, and test out the new setting in a crowded drawing to be sure it meets with your approval. When you're satisfied, turn off APBOX to hide the visible aperture box.

A large aperture setting makes it easier to snap in most drawings but can make it harder to snap to what you intend in a crowded drawing. Pressing the Tab key repeatedly when acquiring a snap point cycles through all the possibilities that fit within the aperture—but this doesn't work if dynamic input is on (tabbing cycles through dynamic input fields instead). Therefore, press F12 to toggle off dynamic input, and then tap the Tab key to cycle through possible snaps.

The benefit of working with a small aperture is you don't have to toggle off dynamic input and cycle through all possible snap points to get what you want, saving you some time. However, you have to accurately target what you want in order to snap with a small aperture, which means you need better eyesight and concentration. It's up to you.

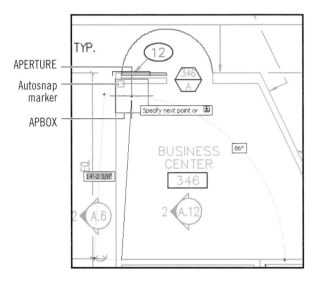

A more geeky snap tip has to do with bitcodes. Each running object snap mode has a *bitcode*—a unique counting number associated with it. Bitcodes are added up to determine the overall running object snap combination.

Why do we care? If you have a favorite combination of running object snaps, isn't it painful to always have to open the Drafting Settings dialog to check and uncheck every setting the way you want it? A quicker way is to add up your magic number and set it using the OSMODE system variable. Follow along:

1. Right-click the OSNAP toggle on the status bar, and choose Settings from the context menu to open the Drafting Settings dialog.

2. Check and uncheck individual running object snaps to arrive at your favorite combination. Click OK.

3. Type **OSMODE**, and press Enter.

   ```
   Enter new value for OSMODE <255>:
   ```

   The current bitcode is displayed in angled brackets. Write it down—this is your magic number.

Now, whenever the combination of running object snaps gets out of whack, just set OSMODE to your magic number, and you're back in business—or better yet, write a macro and assign it to a button (see Chapter 10). No more tedious checking and unchecking in the Drafting Settings dialog.

The final snap tip we'll leave you with introduces you to Mid Between 2 Points, which turns out to be a super-useful single-use object snap. This snap has been around for a while, but it's almost top secret because it doesn't appear in the Drafting Settings dialog. Access it instead by Shift+right-clicking when you want to snap.

On the other hand, keyboard aficionados can type **M2P** (or **MTP**—they both perform the same function) to force a single use of Mid Between 2 Points while in a running command. Snap midway between two points on the fly, and avoid making (and deleting) construction lines. From and Temporary track point snaps also help you avoid making construction lines.

> If you're one of the few people who know about the MEE variable in the geometry calculator, use the snap Midway Between 2 Points (M2P) instead—it does the same thing in fewer steps.

Affect Visual Effects

AutoCAD comes with some nifty visual effects that may be a little over the top for some of you. If objects thickening and appearing with dashes as you hover your mouse over them is a bit too Las Vegas, you can tone it down or even turn it off. Your inner curmudgeon may also disapprove of the transparent color-coded crossing and window selection marquees that appear when selecting multiple objects. Here's how to affect the visual effects:

1. Use the Options command, and click the Selection tab.

2. The Selection Preview area has two check boxes and a button. Uncheck When No Command Is Active to tone down the visual effects so they occur only when a command is active.

3. Click the Visual Effect Settings button to open its namesake dialog.

4. If you're in a mood to further tone down visual bedazzlement, choose Dash or Thicken, but not both. Advanced Options offers finer control over where the selection preview effect occurs.

5. Uncheck Indicate Selection Area on the right side of the Visual Effect Settings dialog to revert to classic selection marquees without transparent color overlay. If you don't mind this effect, leave it on, and pick your favorite colors for the window and crossing selection. Unfortunately, your favorite color must be one of the classic 255 index colors, not a True Color (but here is your chance to match your windows to your outfit!).

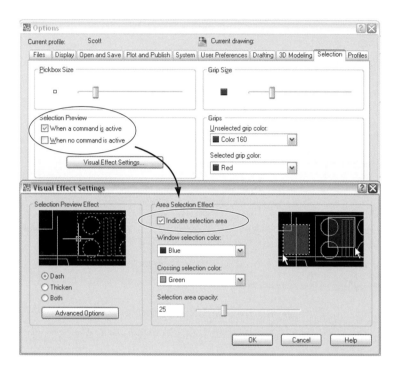

Select Like a Pro

There are probably more ways to select objects in AutoCAD than the number of Inuit words for snow. Real pros are fluent in all object-selection methodologies because selecting is a big part of what they do every day. You'll be more productive when you learn to select like a pro.

Selection Basics

You must select before you can do, right? Not necessarily—with noun/verb selection enabled, the cart can come before the horse. Set PICKFIRST to 1, if it's not already, so nouns can come before verbs. If commands are verbs, objects are nouns, snaps are adjectives, and command options must be adverbs. Do you speak AutoCAD?

Another basic selection feature everyone should know and use is called *implied windowing*. PICKAUTO must be turned on (default) for this feature to work. A regular window is implied when you draw a selection window from left to right, selecting only completely enclosed objects. A crossing window is implied when you draw a selection window from right to left, selecting anything crossed by the window.

See "Affect Visual Effects," earlier in this chapter, to choose colors for implied windows.

Recovering Mac users seem to always be dragging things when a click or two will do. The PICKDRAG system variable helps those suffering from this affliction. Turn it on (it's off by default), and dragging in the viewport will get you a selection window—no clicking required.

One more basic tip nugget: Locking a layer prevents the objects on that layer from being selected, even though they remain visible and snappable.

Select Previous, Last, and All

You can't call yourself a power user unless you regularly use what we call selection *buffers*, for lack of better jargon. These buffers hold various selection sets that increase productivity when you call on them—saving you from having to reselect something on screen. Power users know the difference between *previous* and *last* and perceive when to use them almost subconsciously. Selection buffers don't survive beyond the current drawing session. They're as follows:

Last This is the last object created. There is only ever one *last* object selection. It must be visible to go in this buffer, so objects created on off or frozen layers don't count (but you don't draw that way, do you?)

For example, let's say that for one reason or another, you need to draw a line directly on top of an existing line. It's hard to say which line would be selected if you were to pick directly on the two overlapping lines. An implied selection window gets them both. If you want to subsequently move the line you *just* drew, type **L** at the Select Objects prompt to grab the object in the *last* buffer.

Previous This means the selection set of objects and/or subobjects (hold Ctrl) that was selected immediately before the present moment, during the last command. The previous selection can include more than one object.

Another common situation cries out for use of the previous buffer. Whenever you want to perform more than one action on a selection, like move a bunch of objects and then rotate them, use *previous*. Start the second action (rotate), and then type **P** at the Select Objects prompt to grab what you were just working on.

All This is what is says—it selects *all* objects, but only in the current space. Type the full word **all** at a Select Object prompt, or press Ctrl+A. All won't select objects on frozen or locked layers.

A quick way to get rid of everything in a layout is to go to that layout, use the Erase command, and use *all* at the Select Objects prompt. Rest easy that your precious geometry in modelspace won't be touched. Need to convert a drawing from Imperial to metric? Go to modelspace and scale *all* by 2.54; you get the picture.

Did you know that SELECT is also a command in its own right? The output of the SELECT command is placed into the *previous* buffer. Use SELECT when you want to be explicit about what you select. SELECT is always used prior to deciding what to do with that selection. It's a kind of formal cart-before-the-horse situation. Here's how it works:

1. Use the SELECT command.

2. Make a selection, and press Enter. The command ends, and you're left scratching your head about the point of it all, right?

3. Perform an action such as using the MOVE command again. At its Select Objects prompt, type **P** and press Enter to grab the output of step 2.

4. Press Enter again to exit select objects mode, and continue with the rest of the command started in step 3.

Add and Remove from the Selection Set

If you've ever been stumped as to why your selection is replaced when you select additional objects, it's due to the obscure system variable PICKADD. If you've never heard of it, chances are you inadvertently clicked its toggle button at the top of the Properties palette.

Trying to sort out the PICKADD dilemma is especially confusing because one of the icons for this toggle displays a 1 but corresponds to the PICKADD setting of 0. Why the deliberate obfuscation, you ask? At least the icon designers meant well, because they were going for meaning—rather than the value of the system variable.

When PICKADD is set to 1 (default), you can keep adding to your selection until the cows come home. Thus its icon shows a tiny plus symbol with a couple of outlined selections (cows).

On the other hand, when PICKADD is set to 0, its icon shows a 1 because you may only have one selection at a time, even though this one selection can contain multiple objects.

> If you like being constrained to one selection at a time (PICKADD set to 0), drawing an implied selection window in a blank portion of the drawing area will quickly clear the selection set. Use this as an alternative to hitting the Esc key to clear a selection.

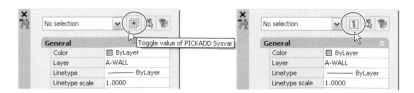

Remove objects from the selection set informally by holding down the Shift key and picking. This works no matter what PICKADD is set to, although we recommend leaving its default setting of 1 (on).

More formally, type **R** and press Enter at a Select Objects prompt to turn it into a Remove Objects prompt. Now, anything you select gets removed from the set. To go back and add some additional objects, type **A** and press Enter:

```
Select objects: 28 found

Select objects: R

Remove objects: 1 found, 1 removed, 27 total

Remove objects: A

Select objects: 1 found, 28 total
```

You can go back and forth like this forever. Formally removing (and adding back) is useful when you're dealing with large selection sets that you want to be extra careful not to lose.

Select Multiple Objects

Aside from picking individual objects or using implied windowing to select multiple objects, there is a plethora of more explicit selection modes to choose from. Here's what the Select Objects prompt looks like:

```
Window/Last/Crossing/BOX/ALL/Fence/WPolygon/

CPolygon/Group/Add/Remove/Multiple/Previous

/Undo/AUto/SIngle/SUbobject/Object
```

The selection modes are a bit mysterious because the only time you'll ever see them listed is on the command line (sorry, dynamic prompt) and then only when you make an invalid selection (or type **?** at a Select Objects prompt). The selection modes are so under the radar that it's assumed you must know them all! We'll highlight a few choice modes in case you don't:

Crossing (C) Used to force a crossing window, overriding implied windowing. Especially helpful when you're using Stretch—this allows the crossing selection to occur from left to right.

Fence (F) Draws a series of connected line segments that select whatever they cross. Selection fences are helpful in selecting a series of parallel objects, especially when they're drawn at an angle—use Fence when it's difficult to select with other methods.

Crossing Polygon (CP) and Window Polygon (WP) Two great, underused selection secrets. The objects you wish to select don't always conveniently lie within a rectangular area. Hence, rectangular windows don't always do the trick. The CP and WP options allow you to create a polygonal area with as many sides and whatever shape you'd like. Rather than creating several windows to get the desired objects, try using these two options. CP selects all the objects within or crossing the polygonal area; WP selects only those objects that fall completely within the area There is one rule that both CP and WP must follow: The polygon may not cross or touch itself. AutoCAD continually sketches in the last segment to ensure a closed polygon. You'll notice an Undo option, should you accidentally select an incorrect location for a polygon vertex.

Group (G) Selects all objects within a group (see the section "Group Selections," later in this chapter).

SUbobject (SU) An alternative to holding the Ctrl key while selecting. It lets you select vertices, edges, and face subobjects of 3D solids. SU is good for holding the phone with one hand while drawing with the other.

Select Touching Objects

It can be difficult to select objects that are touching, especially in tight quarters where a drawing looks more like the innards of the Borg (or spaghetti, if you don't get *Star Trek NG* references). There are two ways to do this: *object cycling* if you only want one object, and *fast select* if you want all touching objects selected.

Object cycling is an old feature that always seems to be news to people, perhaps because it doesn't show up in the Command Reference, because it only works at the Select Objects prompt. Object cycling used to be activated with the Ctrl key, but that no longer works; that honor has since been given to subobject selection.

To cycle through objects in a kind of preview selection mode, simultaneously hold down the Shift key and Spacebar, and then click repeatedly while holding the cursor above overlapping objects. The command line will say <Cycle on> as you click while highlighting each successive object. Press Enter when the object you want to select is highlighted. The command line will say

```
<Cycle off>1 found
```

```
Select objects:
```

Press Enter to exit selection mode and continue on your merry way. Object cycling is more effective if the selection target is larger. PICKBOX controls the size of the selection target (3 pixels by default). If you increase the size of the selection target, then you'll probably have to do more object cycling. On the other hand, if you set PICKBOX to a small value, you may suffer eye strain, because you must pick objects more exactly to select them. It's a matter of personal choice.

Fast Select is an express tool that selects all objects touching the one you select. It works best if you use it transparently at any Select Objects prompt.

For example, use the MOVE command, and type **'FS** at its Select Objects prompt (the apostrophe makes it transparent). The tooltip by the cursor then reads Select Touching Object. When you click an object, all the other objects immediately touching your selection are also selected.

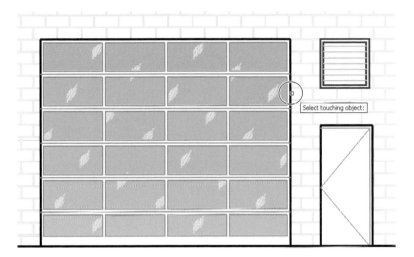

In the case of this elevation, if the outer thick vertical line of the window frame is clicked, then all the horizontal lines touching it will get selected—fast!

There is a further refinement to Fast Select called FSMODE. Turn on this mode to select the objects touching the objects that are touching the object you select. It cascades the concept of overlap outward one iteration in the chain.

If FSMODE is set to ON, then using **'fs** at the Select Objects prompt in the previous example selects all the horizontal lines in the window—plus the entire adjacent door because it's touching the base line. Here is a command-line transcript of using Fast Select:

```
Command: Move

Select objects: 'fs

Use 'FSMODE to control chain selection.

FSMODE = ON

Select touching object: 16 object(s) found.

Exiting Fastsel

Select Objects:
```

Fast Select is a powerful weapon in your selection arsenal. It's easy to use; just remember to type **'fs** at any Select Objects prompt.

Group Selections

Groups are an underappreciated feature that are worth learning about—once you get to know groups, you'll be amazed at how they can accelerate your production.

Groups are similar to blocks in the way they encapsulate information. However, groups are more flexible than blocks—the ability to select the entire group or its building blocks can be toggled at a moment's notice. As you're doubtless aware, editing blocks requires explosion and redefinition, or an edit-in-place operation.

Although groups can't be reused in other drawings, grouping objects into named selections is a great way to manage collections of blocks and objects in the current drawing. For example, take a look at this office image.

The office on the right has desk, computer, chair, and credenza blocks. It makes sense to group collections of blocks into a named selection for easy reuse:

1. Use the GROUP command, or type **G** and press Enter.

2. Type something descriptive into the Group Name text box, and click the New button.

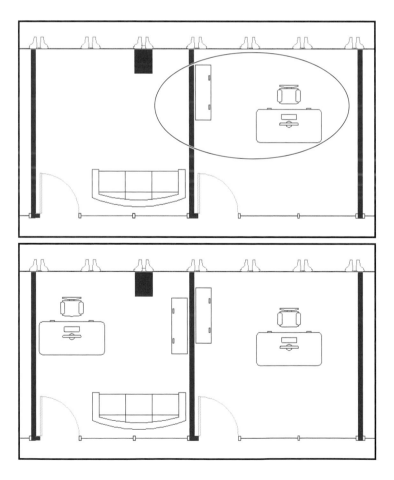

3. Select the items you wish to group. In this example, select the desk, computer, chair, and credenza blocks, and press Enter. Click OK to close the Object Grouping dialog.

The beauty of groups is how you can manipulate them and/or their contents with a simple toggle. Press Ctrl+H to toggle the system variable PICK-STYLE on and off. When it's on, clicking any part of a group selects the entire group. When it's toggled off, picking a part of a group selects only that part. Try it:

1. Copy the group by picking any part of it (PICK-STYLE is on by default). Place the copy in the adjacent room in this example.

2. The relationship between the desk/computer/chair and credenza needs to be different in the left office. Press Ctrl+H to toggle off PICKSTYLE. Move and rotate the credenza independently as needed.

3. Press Ctrl+H, and select the chairs in both rooms—see that they remain grouped with all the other parts as before. You have the best of both worlds—individual and group selection, toggled by PICKSTYLE.

> Groups can be selected by name by using the G option at a Select Objects prompt.

Get Selections Quickly

Slow down and read this. With all the hype about having commands that are in some kind of race, it's important that you understand how to make selections efficiently—no matter how long that takes.

Found in the Selection tools portion of the Express menu, GETSEL (Get Selection Set) is an express tool that selects faster than AutoCAD's core QSELECT (Quick Select) command. If you have your druthers, use GETSEL when you want to get all the objects of a particular type on a given layer—for example, if you'd like all the text objects on the Notes layer. Here's how it works:

1. Type **GETSEL**, and press Enter.

2. Pick an object on the layer you want to constrain your selection to—or press Enter if you want to search all layers.

3. Pick an object of the type you want to constrain the selection to—like a line, lightweight polyline, 3D solid, and so on. Press Enter at this prompt only if you want to get all the objects on the layer you selected in the previous step. Here's the command-line transcript:

```
Command: Getsel

Initializing...

Select an object on the Source layer <*>: (pick an object)

Select an object of the Type you want <*>: (pick an object)

Collecting all LWPOLYLINE objects on layer A-EXST-WALL...

8 objects have been placed in the active selection set.
```

Perform some action, and select the output of GETSEL by using the previous selection buffer of P (see the earlier discussion of Select Previous, Last, and All). Get Selection Set is useful in myriad ways, such as moving all the lines on the A-Wall layer to the XY plane, or deleting all the leaders on the annotation layer, or selecting anything specific to an object type and/or layer.

Master the FILTER Command

Use the FILTER command when Get Selection (see the previous section) isn't specific enough. Not to be confused with layer filters, FILTER is a command in its own right. FILTER has been in AutoCAD since the digital Pleistocene—and it remains one of the most arcane, powerful, and least understood commands.

FILTER is the granddaddy of selection tools, and it isn't intended for the faint of heart. You can build an arbitrarily complex selection program by adding filters sequentially to the list. For example, let's say you want to select all the lines on the A-CORE-WALL layer that don't have their color property set to ByLayer. Here's how it's done:

1. Use the FILTER command. It can be used transparently, but let's rely on the previous buffer to be more explicit.

2. Choose Line in the Select Filter drop-down. Click the Add To List button. This is the first filter in the selection program.

3. Choose Layer from the Select Filter drop-down, and click the Select button. Pick a specific layer from the list (A-CORE-WALL in this example), and then click OK. Click the Add To List button to add the second filter to the selection program.

4. Choose Color in the Select Filter drop-down. Click the Select button; the Select Color dialog box appears. Click the ByLayer button—this corresponds to color 256—and then click OK. Click the drop-down just below the Select Filter drop-down list, and change the operation to !=, which means "not equal to." Click the Add To List button.

5. You can optionally save the selection program you've just built as a named filter that will be saved with the drawing. Click the Apply button to dismiss the dialog.

6. Select Objects is still the current prompt. You must now select the objects to which you wish to apply the filter program. Press Ctrl+A, and press Enter twice to filter everything.

7. Perform whatever action you had in mind before you designed the elaborate filter program. In this example, you might open the Properties toolbar and change color to ByLayer, but the sky's the limit.

Note that objects are already selected when you exit the FILTER command, so there's no need to use the previous buffer when noun/verb selection will usually do. However, if the command you want to use doesn't work with noun/verb, then use the Previous buffer (see Select Previous, Last, and All, earlier in the chapter).

We could devote an entire chapter to the many different capabilities of the FILTER command—dive in and give it a try. Join the AutoCAD gurus that always have the command hiding up their sleeves!

Drawing and Editing Tips

What follows is grab bag of tips and tricks that we hope you'll enjoy. Maybe you'll learn a few helpful tips about commands you use every day, or some novel tricks that you'll use occasionally when the need arises.

Arc More Effectively

Arcs are some of the most complex 2D objects you can make in AutoCAD. At last count, you can draw an arc 11 different ways. Many of these methods have in common the unwritten rule—and here we go writing it—that arcs must be created in counterclockwise fashion.

Even if this rule has beaten you into submission over your years of using AutoCAD, you must harbor some resentment at the sheer inflexibility of said rule. We've come to announce a way out, a secret method to subvert the rule and draw arcs the way you've always wanted to—clockwise. Follow along if you dare to be different:

1. Use the UCS command. Yes, you must trick AutoCAD into drawing backward to successfully draw arcs clockwise. Sad but true.

2. Use the Y option to rotate the coordinate system about the vertical axis. Type **180**, and press Enter again to complete the transformation.

3. Draw your arc with the Center option, and then click Start and End points in a clockwise relationship. The arc follows as you want it to—perfect for door swings!

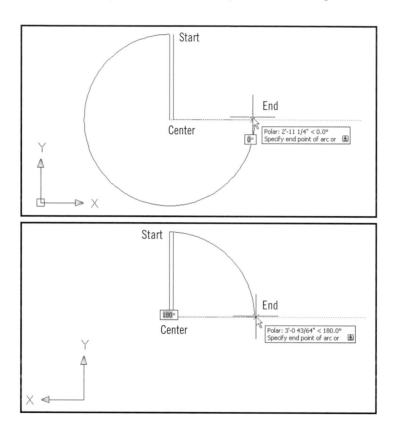

Don't forget to set UCS back to World if you want to draw "normally" again. These steps are suitable for incorporation in a macro, lisp, and/or automation program of your choosing, but that's up to you. If you use this technique frequently, it would serve you well to add it to a toolbar button for easy access.

Here's a convenient way to set an existing arc's length to any angle. Use the LENGTHEN command's Total and Angle options. Here is a command-line transcript for you to study:

```
Command: Lengthen

Select an object or [DElta/Percent/Total/DYnamic]: t

Specify total length or [Angle] <0'-1">: a

Specify total angle <0.0>: 45

Select an object to change or [Undo]: (pick arc)
```

If you've ever tried to close an arc into a full circle, you've undoubtedly met with frustration. Why can't this be done? Because AutoCAD can't accept an arc that has 360 degrees in it (that's breaking the official definition of an arc). Even if you don't like this answer, we know of a solution—that is, other than drawing a circle and erasing the original arc, which is the solution you've probably used in the past (and that lacks in elegance but gets the job done).

A better way is to use the new JOIN command option: close. Don't ask us why the capitalized option letter is L, when it's the only option. There are some things we're better off not knowing:

```
Command: Join

Select source object: (pick arc)

Select arcs to join to source or [cLose]: L

Arc converted to a circle.
```

The arc goes full circle, at last. Checking the Properties palette reveals that the object undergoes conversion to a circle—it isn't an arc any longer. Hallelujah!

Polyline Tips

The first polyline tip we have is all about respect. Respect for you, the user—who we know is an intelligent human being. When you use the PEDIT command, you presumably want to edit polylines, are we right? Of course you do. Otherwise you wouldn't use the PEDIT command. Maybe you too have been irked when AutoCAD asks the following:

```
PEDIT Select polyline or [Multiple]:

Object selected is not a polyline

Do you want to turn it into one? <Y>
```

The PEDITACCEPT system variable is responsible for this pernicious question. Set it to 1, and you'll never again be asked if you want to turn an object into a polyline, because this system variable is saved in the system registry and persists between sessions.

The next tip concerning polylines is a way to create them automatically using the BOUNDARY command. One of the most common uses of polylines is tracing an existing boundary—to calculate an area, to make a ceiling grid, to create a loft path, or what have you. Creating a polyline automatically is a lot easier than clicking each and every vertex manually. This is the process:

1. Arrange what you plan to find the boundary of, so it's entirely visible on screen. This is a must because the BOUNDARY command uses an outdated version of the hatch engine (it doesn't have gap tolerance, either).

2. Use the BOUNDARY command. Select Polyline as the object type (it's the default).

3. Click the Pick Points button, and click a point anywhere inside the boundary. Press Enter, and a polyline is generated on the current layer.

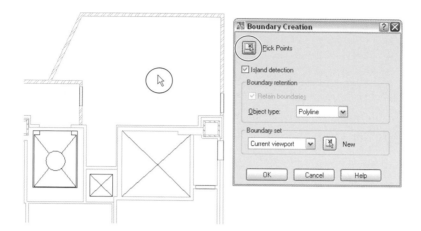

If you get an error stating that the boundary can't be found, there are two possible reasons: the boundary isn't entirely visible on screen as we told you in step 1, or there is a gap in the boundary. Finding gaps can be tricky, especially if they're microscopic. Try filleting all the lines together with a 0 radius to fill in any potential gaps. Then, run the procedure again.

We'll leave you with this thought: Do you really want a polyline? If you plan to eventually make a 3D model, the POLYSOLID command is like a supercharged 3D version of polyline. Check it out if you're using AutoCAD 2007 or later (see Chapter 6). 3DPOLY is another older and related command, although it's less useful and more like an outdated SPLINE command than anything.

Neat Cloud Revisions

Revision clouds indicate an area of a drawing that has changed since the drawing was last submitted. You want to draw attention to the change, not your sloppily drawn cloud. REV-CLOUD can help, but all too often the connected series of arcs drawn with this command appear haphazardly placed, almost like they were drawn by a child willfully defacing your precise work. Here are a couple of tips that ought to keep your clouds nice and tidy, and looking a bit more professional:

1. Draw a rectangle around the area of the drawing you wish to indicate as a revision.

2. Set the fillet radius (FILLETRAD) to a reasonable size, which obviously varies with the scale you're working in. Then, use the FILLET command's Polyline option to evenly round out the corners of the rectangle.

3. Use the REVCLOUD command. Press A to set its arc lengths. You can set minimum and maximum arc lengths, but doing so makes the resulting cloud look more hand drawn. Make these values equal if you want more uniform clouds.

4. Use the Object option of REVCLOUD, and pick the rounded rectangle.

5. Do you want fluffy clouds or prickly ones? Some people intentionally differentiate between the two to indicate different revision phases; for others, the choice is purely aesthetic. Answer **Y** when asked if you want to reverse direction, and you'll get prickly clouds—which is arguably more of an attention grabber. Here's the sequence of steps we followed, shown on the command line:

```
Command: Revcloud

Minimum arc length: 1" Maximum arc length: 1" Style: Normal

Specify start point or [Arc length/Object/Style]<Object>: A

Specify minimum length of arc <1">: 8"

Specify maximum length of arc <1">: 8"

Specify start point or [Arc length/Object/Style]<Object>: O

Select object: (pick rounded rectangle)

Reverse direction [Yes/No] <No>: Y (it's up to you)
```

This sequence is begging for automation. CAD managers—make it so! Then, you'd be able to draw a rectangle and get an instant neat revision cloud.

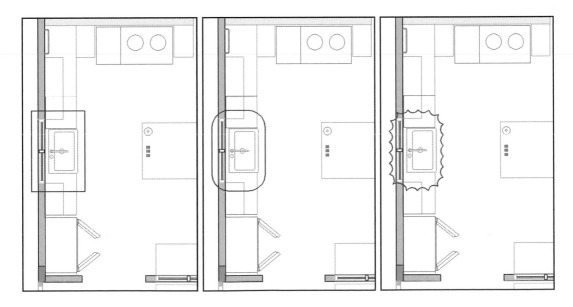

Control Overlap

Question: What is *overlap* in a 3D program like AutoCAD? Doesn't it mean that some objects are literally above others in the Z axis? Answer: Not really. Although you technically could move objects in the Z axis to "stack" them, doing so is strongly discouraged. In fact, never do that, because it will mess up your file, should you ever decide to make it 3D.

Overlap refers to an entirely 2D phenomenon—it's how you control display and plotting order in the XY plane, and it isn't spatial as you might assume.

Many users are familiar with the DRAWORDER command, which is used to manually order objects for display and plotting. You can use DRAWORDER to move objects to the back or the front of the stack on screen. What you see on the screen (after a REGEN) is just how it should look when plotted.

Most of us only care about overlap when something we want to see gets obscured by another object. Using DRAWORDER will fix it, but using the command can be a pain if you have a lot of fixing to do. This brings us to our tip: Use the TEXTTOFRONT command when you want to bring all the text and/or dimensions to the front all at once. It's a hassle-free experience.

WIPEOUT is more than what surfers do—it's a way of overlapping objects with a mask that displays the background color. Use WIPEOUT as an alternative to erasing; when you don't want to explode an underlying hatch pattern; to block, bind, and explode an Xref; or to just hide a geometrically busy area. Draw a wipeout manually, or convert a polyline into one. Either way, you'll be able to edit the shape of the wipeout object with its outer frame.

To go totally covert, turn off the Frame option of WIPEOUT. Then, what is obscured remains so—but you'll have no way of telling what's obscuring the objects. WIPEOUT is a bit dangerous when used covertly because it's guaranteed to mystify the uninitiated. Consider writing a visible note on a nonplotting layer, warning your compatriots about the hidden danger. Use the TFRAMES command to toggle the frames on and off.

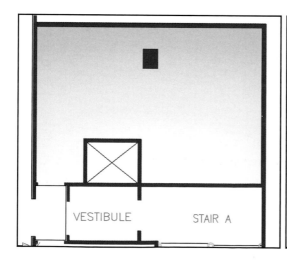
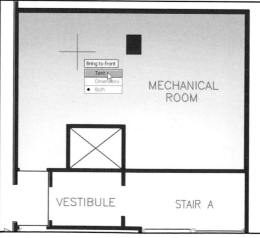

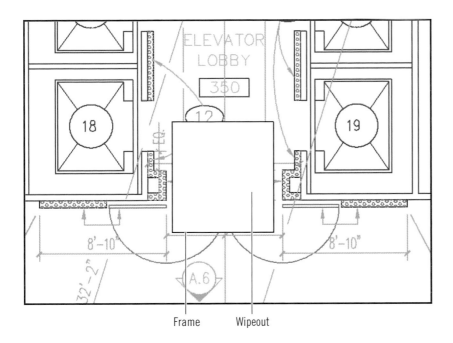

Frame   Wipeout

Make a Mark with UNDO

Do you ever feel like you're climbing a wall with AutoCAD? When a difficult modeling procedure involves many steps, sometimes you go down the wrong road and have to retrace your steps and try again. After all, there are usually several ways to model the same forms, and trial and error is often the path to success. Thank goodness for UNDO!

There is more to the UNDO command than meets the eye. First of all, U is different than UNDO—U is a subset of UNDO. In other words, typing **U** and pressing Enter or clicking the Undo button on the Standard toolbar just takes you back one step in the command history. The UNDO command gives you more options:

```
Command: Undo

Current settings: Auto = On, Control = All, Combine = Yes

Enter the number of operations to undo or

[Auto/Control/BEgin/End/Mark/Back] <1>:
```

Unless you're exceptionally good—or just plain lucky—you won't finish complex 3D modeling procedures without having to retrace your steps a few times. Think of AutoCAD as technical climbing. Using the Mark option of the UNDO command is like putting a piece of hardware into the wall you're climbing. When you fall, you drop back as many steps as it takes to the safe foothold where you set the last mark. Then you can try again.

When you reach a milestone and are feeling good about what you've accomplished, set an undo mark. It's easy to do—type **UNDO** Enter **M** Enter. Now your piton is firmly hammered into the ice waterfall.

Go about your business with impunity, trying out a dangerous and experimental modeling technique. If you make a mistake and want to try again, typing **UNDO** Enter **B** Enter will take you back to when you set the mark. You can place as many marks as necessary to provide a sense of security, but don't see it as false security—remember to back up your data!

> Don't use the Back option of UNDO if you haven't set any marks, because that would take you back to the start of your AutoCAD session, and you'd lose all your work. Better to close the file without saving, if that's your intent.

Drag to Move and Copy

Forget commands, forget grip editing—the most intuitive way to quickly move and copy objects is to select and drag. What could be more direct? Mind you, this is still a two-step dance. First, select one or more objects by clicking them so that they highlight. Then, drag them across the screen to move the selection.

Sounds straightforward, right? You'd be surprised how many people get hung up on this. After compiling the research and combing over the statistics, we believe grips to be the stumbling block. Grips are an alternative editing interface to drag-to-edit—not better, not worse, just different.

Don't drag from grips; drag from any highlighted object edge. In fact, you may want to turn off grips so you're not tempted. Set GRIPS to 0, and you can drag without distraction. Of course, the downside to all drag-to-edit techniques is that they sacrifice accuracy for convenience. You can't enter coordinates or angles when dragging, so it's not for everything. But dragging tags around is just about perfect.

A further refinement of the dead-simple drag-to-edit technique is to hold down the Ctrl key *after* you start dragging. Doing so copies what you drag, leaving the original version behind.

> Don't hold down Ctrl before you drag, or AutoCAD will think you're trying to make an additional subobject selection; it will change the cursor to a select objects pickbox.

Even more sophisticated is the right-drag-to-edit technique. This is top secret—it's hard to find documentation anywhere on this feature. That's right, select objects as you've done before and, while holding down the right mouse button, drag the selection across the screen.

You'll be rewarded with a tiny shortcut menu with three options (plus Cancel): Move Here, Copy Here, and Paste As Block.

Paste As Block sounds good, but realize that this makes an anonymous block with an automatically chosen block name such as A$C3F637FDA—not especially descriptive or useful, but good for one-off situations. You're better off copying blocks using other methods if you want to preserve their block names, or renaming the block to something logical after the fact.

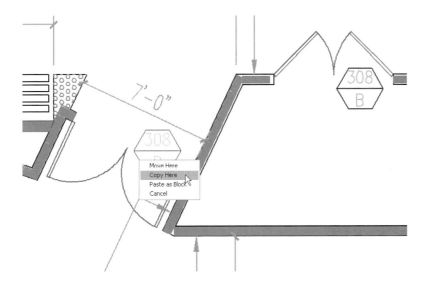

Changing and Matching Properties

The sands of time have hidden many ancient AutoCAD commands from the light of day and public awareness, including a few that edit object properties. To our utter astonishment, we dusted off these commands and—they still work! Who knew? Nowadays we all use the Properties palette to change object properties. But here are a few old gems that you may find useful.

The CHANGE command existed before the dialog box and way before the palette. Use it to change object properties faster than any other method—if you like entering things on the keyboard, that is:

```
Command: Change

Select objects: 1 found

Specify change point or [Properties]: P

Enter property to change

[Color/Elev/LAyer/LType/ltScale/LWeight/Thickness/Material/Plotstyle]
```

The CHANGE command must have been secretly updated to handle Materials and Plot Styles, which are relatively newer in the AutoCAD command archaeology.

Bonus: The CHANGE command allows you to set the 3D elevation of an existing object, which is something that still isn't possible on the Properties palette. Use ELEV to set the current elevation of all future objects.

CHPROP is slightly more streamlined than CHANGE. Change Properties lacks the Elevation option present in the CHANGE command; otherwise, they're identical.

The CHANGE command has a few other tricks up its sleeve. If you want to quickly lengthen a series of lines to a specific point, you can use the Change Point option of the CHANGE command. Select the lines, press Enter, and then select the point to which you want to extend the lines. Turn on Ortho to ensure you get horizontal lines (otherwise they will meet at a point):

```
Command: CHANGE

Select objects: Specify opposite corner: 5 found

Select objects: (enter)

Specify change point or [Properties]:
```
select the point you want the lines to be extended to.

CHANGE has many hidden capabilities, including the ability to change the radius of a circle as well as modify aspects of existing text strings.

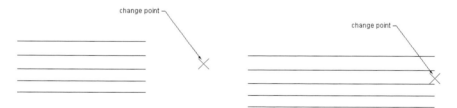

Match Properties is another blast from the past, but it's one that every AutoCAD guru has in their pocket. Use it to match the properties gleaned from a single source object to a destination object or set of objects. MATCHPROP can be activated from its paintbrush button on the Standard toolbar. Here's what it looks like on the command line:

```
Command: Matchprop

Select source object: (pick one)

Current active settings: Color Layer Ltype Ltscale Lineweight Thickness PlotStyle Dim
Text Hatch Polyline

Viewport Table Material Shadow display

Select destination object(s) or [Settings]:
```

Use the Settings option to select exactly what you want "matched" or copied from source to destination objects. There are a lot of possibilities.

You may only want to match dimension styles, or perhaps hatch patterns, but not layers. Check the appropriate boxes in the Property Settings dialog. Match Properties is really many tools in one.

Hip Grip Tips

True AutoCAD gurus are wizards when it comes to grips. Grips display after objects are selected. Grips themselves are selected only when you click them individually—then

they're known as *hot grips* (and are red by default). However, clicking an additional grip deselects the previous hot grip. Would you do more grip editing if you could select more than one hot grip at a time? The key here is to *hold down the Shift key before clicking individual grips*—selecting now makes them all hot. Yowza!

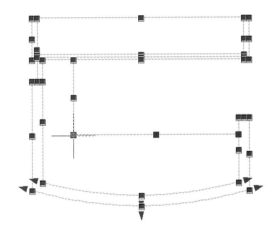

After you've built up a meta-selection of hot grips, then let go of Shift, and click one of the hot grips to act as base point for your editing operation. Now, press the Spacebar to toggle through stretch, move, rotate, scale, or mirror operations. Welcome to this new vista of editing possibility! This tip comes in handy when you're trying to stretch out two corners of a rectangle.

Clear grips quickly by holding down the right mouse button for a second or two instead of pressing Esc.

Master TRIM and EXTEND

It pays to master TRIM and EXTEND, because these are two of the most popular editing commands. TRIM and EXTEND are like the opposite sides of the same coin. They're so similar that you may only need to use one command in practice. If you have to pick, choose TRIM, because it has one option that EXTEND lacks—the ability to erase stray lines:

```
Command: Trim

Current settings: Projection=UCS, Edge=None

Select cutting edges ...
```

```
Select objects or <select all>:

Select object to trim or shift-select to extend or

[Fence/Crossing/Project/Edge/eRase/Undo]:
```

For years, only a few of us knew about the top-secret option of "select all" when selecting cutting or boundary edges. Gurus would enter the TRIM (or EXTEND) command and immediately press Enter to turn everything into a cutting edge. Although this option wasn't documented, it was alive and well. AutoCAD 2007 now displays this as an actual option, thus clueing the entire world in on this great timesaver.

You'll find that when you press Enter to select everything as a cutting edge, nothing highlights, which is counterintuitive. Just have faith, go with the Force, and it will work (we promise).

Most of the time, when you need to trim and extend, use the default option of Select All to select all the cutting or boundary edges. Then, each time you trim or extend, the active edge will move to the next available boundary, which is extremely efficient.

> When you have only one specific edge to trim or extend to, it's faster if you select it, instead of using the default Select All.

When you go on a trimming and extending binge, haven't you noticed that there are often stray lines around? These strays are the result of trimming off either end of a formerly whole line of which they were once a part. Now, you don't have to delete the strays as a second step because that option is built into the one-stop-shop TRIM command.

If you're using the TRIM command, you can switch to EXTEND by holding down the Shift key, and vice versa. This saves a lot of planning and allows you to decide on your course of action at the last possible moment.

Fence-selection mode used to be the killer secret for trimming or extending multiple segments quickly. Eventually, fence-selection mode found a permanent home as formal options of TRIM and EXTEND.

Now that you can select what you want to trim or extend by an implied selection window, you don't need the Fence option as much. However, there still are some good reasons to use Fence. For example, if you want to trim off a bunch of segments that project beyond a wall, your first thought should be to use a crossing window. But if these segments are at an angle with respect to the vertical or horizontal, Fence is the best option.

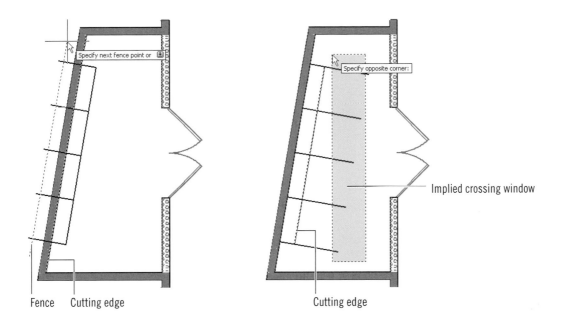

Fence   Cutting edge   Cutting edge

Implied crossing window

Have you ever wanted to trim or extend something that doesn't intersect a boundary or cutting edge? Shyeah! Don't think it's possible without drawing construction lines or extending one of the objects first? Try the Edge option. Here's how it works:

1. Use the TRIM command (works equally well with EXTEND).

2. Select a single cutting edge, and press Enter.

3. Use the Edge option by typing **E** Enter. You must make one more choice: Extend or No extend. Use Extend unless you're trimming a hatch pattern.

4. Click the objects where you wish to trim them. They will be cut by the extrapolated edge selected in step 2.

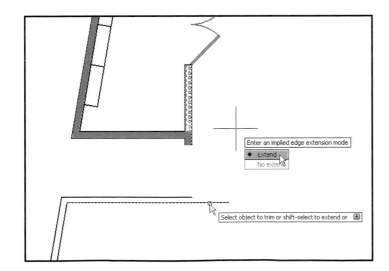

> Set EDGEMODE to 1 if you always want to trim with imaginary extensions (we won't tell anyone).

Sometimes, we find ourselves in a situation where we'd like to trim some objects that appear to intersect on our screen due to our current view—but in reality, if we look at them in 3D, don't. But we need to trim them anyway. What do we do? We use the Project option in the TRIM command. The Project option has three different settings:

None The default. The TRIM command will work only on objects that truly intersect.

UCS If the objects in question were projected onto the current UCS (or XY plane) and an intersection would occur, the TRIM command declares these legal and lets you trim them.

View This is the option we use the most. If the objects appear to intersect in the current view, the TRIM command works on them—plain and simple.

If you can't seem to trim polylines when using a block as a cutting edge, then it's not you—it's officially a problem with polylines. You see, there are two kinds of polylines: light and heavy (go figure). Only the heavies can be trimmed by blocks acting as cutting edges. Obviously, the lightweight polylines are too fluffy for this kind of serious trimming.

Use CONVERTPOLY to convert an existing polyline to a heavy version of itself—whatever that means. Then, trim part of it away using a block as a cutting edge. If you run into this issue often, make a macro out of it and stick it on a toolbar button for easy access.

> PLINETYPE controls what kind of polylines are generated and converted when a drawing is opened. Light polylines are the default.

How Do You Say Fillet?

Fillet isn't a French word. So, why do most Americans pronounce it "fill-A," ending as in the letter *A*? At least the British and Australians have come to their senses and pronounce it "fill-it," which is often what we do with the command in AutoCAD—fill in the spaces between lines that don't cross, joining them into a corner.

FILLET does more than fill in lines; it can produce arcs between 2D lines as well as radiused transitions between two 3D surfaces. Did you know you can fillet all the vertices of a polyline at once by using the aptly named Polyline option?

```
Command: Fillet

Select first object or [Undo/Polyline/Radius/Trim/Multiple]: P
```

Even more astonishing, if you select two separate polylines when using the FILLET command, the command will not only place a fillet between them—it will also join them into one polyline. It's like having two commands in one.

As nice as filleting with a radius can be, we all know that 99 percent of the time, people cheat and set FILLETRAD to 0 to get crisp corners without transitions. You almost need two commands: one that joins lines together, and another that adds radiused transitions between lines and/or surfaces. Almost, but not quite.

Once you know about this next tip, you'll be happy with FILLET for all your corner-joining and curved transition needs. Set a fillet radius, and leave it in there—there is absolutely no need to set FILLETRAD to 0 every time you want to make a corner. Instead, hold down the Shift key while picking the second object to apply a corner (equivalent to a 0 radius). This override is temporary, and FILLETRAD retains its value. Sometimes it pays to read the command line:

```
Select second object or shift-select to apply corner:
```

Power OFFSET

OFFSET may be the most useful drawing tool in the universe. It lets you draw new geometry based on what's already there, a fact not lost on the lazy. You've probably been using this command for years, unaware of important refinements that make OFFSET even better.

Don't be a doofus—learn to harness all the power of OFFSET, and you'll see an immediate jump in your productivity. We'll give you three tips regarding OFFSET that we hope you'll take to heart.

First, stop offsetting an object only to go back later and erase the original object from which you offset the new geometry. Sound like a familiar drawing situation? The Erase option within the OFFSET command handles this more elegantly. Here's how it works:

1. Use the OFFSET command. Read the command line (assuming you haven't turned it off), and notice that several modes are listed with their current states—Erase Source, Layer, and OFFSETGAPTYPE. This is for your information only:

   ```
   Command: Offset

   Current settings: Erase source=No Layer=Source OFFSETGAPTYPE=0
   ```

2. Type **E** Enter to set the Erase option. Choose Yes to set Erase Source to Yes—this mode will stay the same until you change it:

   ```
   Specify offset distance or [Through/Erase/Layer] <1.00>: E

   Erase source object after offsetting? [Yes/No] <No>: Y
   ```

3. Set an offset distance by pressing Enter to accept the default, typing a number, or clicking two points in the drawing window.

4. Select the object to offset and then a point on the side to offset. The source objects apparently move the offset distance, because the source object is erased.

> Set up O as the command alias for OFFSET, rather than OPEN. Chances are, you'll do a lot more offsetting than opening drawings. Check out the ALIASEDIT express tool to make this change.

Next, you often find yourself offsetting objects and then changing the new geometry to another layer afterward, don't you? It sure beats drawing a new object on the correct layer using the confusing "from" object snap, doesn't it? We lazy AutoCAD users will try anything to avoid having to draw something. A better solution is to use the Layer option of OFFSET. Check it out:

1. Set the current layer to the one you want new objects to be on. This is different from the layer the source objects are on that you'll be offsetting.

2. Use the OFFSET command. Read the command line, and notice the current states of its modes. If Layer=Source, then you need to change it.

3. Type **L** Enter to set the Layer mode. Type **C** Enter to set Current as the Layer option:

   ```
   Enter layer option for offset objects [Current/Source] <Source>: C
   ```

4. Set an offset distance by pressing Enter to accept the default (controlled by OFFSET-DIST), typing a number, or clicking two points in the drawing window.

5. Select the object to offset and then a point on the side to offset. The offset object miraculously appears on the current layer.

Finally, there is a system variable to know about when it comes to offsetting polylines: OFFSETGAPTYPE. Notice that the state of this variable is given on the command line every time you use OFFSET. Why, you ask? Because it has a dramatic effect on the way polylines look post-offsetting.

Technically speaking, polylines shouldn't be allowed to be offset at all, because gaps have to open between supposedly ever-connected segments. We want to be able to offset polylines though—and we can. The OFFSETGAPTYPE system variable was invented to address this issue, and it controls what happens in the gaps. Here's what is filled into the gaps in polylines according to the three possible values of OFFSETGAPTYPE:

Value	Polyline Gaps Closed With:
0	Extended straight-line segments
1	Filleted arc segments
2	Chamfered line segments

The most accurate representation of a polyline offset would be achieved with filleted arc segments, because they preserve the offset distance. However, the default is to extend straight-line segments, and, as you can see from the table, chamfered segments are also a possibility. OFFSETGAPTYPE is stored in the registry, so it affects all drawings and persists between drawing sessions. If you forget the name of this important variable, its value is always listed on the command line when using the OFFSET command—so no worries (once again, as long as you have your command line displayed).

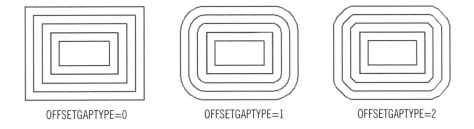

OFFSETGAPTYPE=0   OFFSETGAPTYPE=1   OFFSETGAPTYPE=2

DIVIDE and MEASURE with Style

DIVIDE is used to divide an object perfectly into a specific number of sections. MEASURE divides an object into sections of a specific length, often leaving a remainder less than the measurement increment.

Some users are mystified by the DIVIDE command. What does it do? Apparently not much, for the uninitiated. However, DIVIDE is an extremely useful command.

It doesn't act directly; DIVIDE outputs *points* that mark strategic locations. This is getting more obscure—what are points? Points are geometric entities that technically have no size, orientation, or any other feature except location, at least according to Euclid. Fine; points are location markers—but by default, points are almost invisible in AutoCAD because they're represented by single pixels. Hence, if you use the DIVIDE command right out of the box, you won't be able to tell that anything happened.

The key to dividing successfully is point style—it controls how points appear. Choose Tools → Point Style, and select an icon other than the single pixel or the blank icon. You'll be able to see (and print) points on the screen. To be speedy, set PDMODE to 3 (which turns those pesky points into easy-to-see Xs).

Use DIVIDE, select the object to divide, and then enter the number of equal segments you want the object to have. Equally spaced point objects are placed along the length of the selected object.

Use the DIVIDE command's Block option to evenly space blocks along a path, perimeter, or circumference. You can even tell the block to retain its orientation or to follow that of the path—very cool!

For example, dividing a segment into three parts yields two points that mark off three segments. Understand that the original object isn't broken; the segments are virtual.

You can also snap additional geometry to points. Point entities use the Node object snap. Select Node snap in the Drafting Settings dialog to snap to segments laid out with DIVIDE.

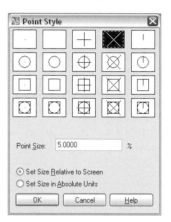

After you snap objects to the points created by DIVIDE, it's generally a good idea to delete the points. You can use GETSEL to delete all point objects efficiently (see "Get Selections Quickly," earlier in the chapter). Go ahead—divide and conquer.

Of equal value is the MEASURE command. This command works similarly to the DIVIDE command but allows you to specify distances along an object to place markers. For example, suppose you want to place 10 blocks in your drawing along a polyline, and you'd like them to be 6 feet apart. The MEASURE command makes it easy to do exactly that.

Although it also uses points as a default, you can easily indicate a block. MEASURE starts at the end nearest to where you selected the polyline (unless it's a circle, in which case MEASURE starts at 0 degrees and works its way around counterclockwise). It isn't unusual to have an extra section left over at the end, unless you magically select a value that fits evenly along the object.

Is It Overkill?

Is it overkill that we keep foisting off Express Tools on you as tips? We don't see it that way—the Express Tools are some of the finest and most useful tools ever to run in Auto-CAD. I (Lynn) remember panicking when I heard the Express Tool Team had been disbanded, because never had such great tools been added to AutoCAD.

There is nothing worse than duplicate copies of entities—maybe that's overstating it, but it's bad. For example, coincident lines, arcs overlapping circles, duplicate lines atop polylines—they all need to go. Remember the old days of pen plotters, when overlapping objects could lead to a hole in your final plot? The trouble is that these redundant entities are hard

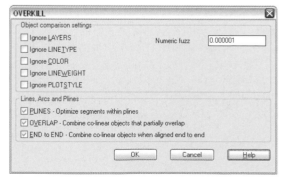

to perceive, let alone select. They can and do get in the way from time to time, so it's nice to be able to tidy things up with the Express Tool OVERKILL.

OVERKILL is a command, we kid you not. Type it on the command line, and select all. The Overkill dialog box allows you to select exactly what redundant geometry you want hunted down and killed.

The Ignore check boxes are used to gloss over certain criteria in the selection of duplicates. For example, checking Ignore Layers will allow objects on different layers that overlap to be deleted and/or combined.

Numeric Fuzz controls whether OVERKILL wipes out entities with surgical precision or with an indiscriminate blast. Set the fuzz higher to cause more similar entities to be considered identical and thus redundant and scheduled for termination. Be careful with fuzz (use low values), or you'll wipe out more than you bargained for.

The Lines, Arcs, And Plines area contain three interesting check boxes. OVERKILL can act as a polyline optimizer when PLINES is checked. Overlap and End To End act much like the new JOIN command, combining co-linear objects when partially or completely overlapping. The advantage of combining segments in this method is that the whole drawing can be processed automatically, rather than the objects being processed one at a time with JOIN. Add this tool to your arsenal, and you'll save lots of valuable time.

Living with Layers

Layers must be the most ubiquitous organizing tool in AutoCAD. Unfortunately, what is simple in concept (layers) doesn't always translate to what is simple in execution (layer handling). Many tools and techniques make layer handling easier—and once you know them, your job will be easier as well.

Make Use of Nonplotting Layers

This tip is kind of a one-liner, but here it is: Use nonplotting layers to document your drawing. You have at your fingertips the world's most sophisticated computer-aided design software, and yet you print out a copy and paste a sticky note on it for your colleague to read. Are you crazy?

Make a layer for internal documentation purposes, and write text, draw pictures, paste in spreadsheets, whatever—just get the point across within the drawing file. That way, your colleagues can immediately know your mind the next time they open the drawing. You're guaranteed that whoever opens the drawing will see your documentation.

If you heed this simple advice, remember that it's likewise essential that this information remain "for eyes only"; put it on a nonplotting layer. Internal documentation isn't to be printed.

In the distant past, proto-drafters had to use the DEFPOINTS and/or ASHADE layers to ensure their primitive markings would never appear on the cave wall. They knew these layer names were and are special because they never plot, by definition. DEFPOINTS was created automatically for dimensions, and ASHADE was created for lights.

But that was ancient history, and you're going to eschew obfuscation! Indulge yourself, and make a brand-new layer with a descriptive name—don't use DEFPOINTS or ASHADE; that confuses the issue. Toggle your new layer's Plot icon to make it nonplotting, and annotate, annotate, annotate!

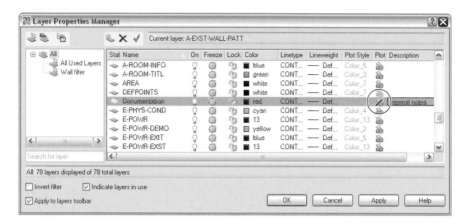

Use Layer Tools

Layer tools that were once part of the Express Tools have grown up and become core tools in AutoCAD. If you've held back all these years, there's no sin in learning how to use these firecrackers now—Autodesk has given its blessing. You could say there is an amnesty in effect.

Many of the layer tools are based on the philosophy that it's easier to manipulate objects on screen than to fuss with layers in the layer drop-down menu or in the Layer Properties Manager dialog box. The layer tools allow you to click an object and manipulate the layer on which the object resides.

The beauty of this visual approach is you may never have to learn layer names to get the job done—a fact that's greatly appreciated by those who regularly deal with dozens, if not hundreds, of layers in a typical drawing.

> This philosophy of the object-based layer tools depends on steadfastly assigning properties ByLayer. Otherwise, you may assume a particular object on screen is representative of a certain layer—only to be fooled when you turn off its layer, for example.

The object-based layer tools are accessible from the Format pull-down menu or the Layers II toolbar, and they're also available in the following command forms:

Icon	Command	Function
	LAYOFF	Turns off the layer of the selected object
	LAYFRZ	Freezes the layer of the selected object
	LAYLCK	Locks the layer of the selected object
	LAYULK	Unlocks the layer of the selected object

There are two more companion tools that don't have icons because they aren't used directly on objects. Instead, these tools affect all layers:

LAYON Turns on all layers. This can conveniently follow up some work done after turning a bunch of layers off with LAYOFF, for example.

LAYTHW Thaws all layers. This is useful for those who prefer to freeze, rather than selectively turn off, layers to clean up the screen while working.

Anyone who's used 3ds Max and/or Autodesk VIZ knows how useful the Hide Unselected and Unhide All commands are in those programs. These commands provide a way to visually isolate what you're working on and then restore the visibility states to what they were previously after the work is done. In a way, it's a lot easier than fussing with layers, because you aren't required to remember any layer names or states. AutoCAD 2007 provides similar functionality in its core toolset with the following commands:

LAYISO Isolates the layers of selected objects. All the other layers in the drawing are turned off. Note that you can select multiple objects (and layers) with this command. It's great for reducing visual complexity on screen so you can focus on specific work that needs to be done.

LAYISO can be used differently in a layout with its VPFreeze mode. When VPFreeze is on, LAYISO freezes all other layers in the current viewport (it doesn't turn off any layers), leaving the other viewports in the drawing unchanged.

> LAYVPI is a more specialized tool for freezing viewport layers. It works only when two or more viewports exist in a layout. Use LAYVPI to isolate layers in the current viewport, in the current layout, or in all layouts. It's a real braintwister, but may be just the ticket if you make heavy use of viewport layers.

LAYUNISO Reverses the On/Off changes in layer status made since isolation. It turns on all the layers that were turned off with the last LAYISO command. However, LAYUNISO can't be used recursively to restore earlier or nested isolated layers.

For example, start by isolating some layers with LAYISO. Then, as you're working, turn off a few more layers using LAYOFF. LAYUNISO turns on all the layers as they were set before using LAYISO—including the ones that were turned off subsequently with LAYOFF. LAYUNISO won't thaw any layers, however.

The final layer tool we'll recommend is COPYTOLAYER, which is more like a supercharged COPY command. Use this tool when you want to copy and deal with layer assignment in one fell swoop. This tool is available on the Layers II toolbar and the Format menu (under Layer Tools) as Copy Objects To New Layer.

COPYTOLAYER can't copy objects to a brand-new layer, as its tooltip suggests. Instead, the layer must already exist. A better name for this command might be Copy Objects To Another Layer (or COAL for short)—but COPYTOLAYER is good enough. Here's how it works:

1. Issue the COPYTOLAYER command.

2. Select the objects you wish to copy, and press Enter.

3. Pick one object on the destination layer. The objects you copy will end up on this layer.

4. Copy as usual, picking a base point and then a second point of displacement.

5. Here's how it looks on the command line:

```
Command: CopyToLayer

Select objects to copy: 2 found (Enter)

Select object on destination layer or [Name] <Name>:

1 object(s) copied and placed on layer "A-CORE-WALL-EXTR".

Specify base point or [Displacement/eXit] <eXit>: (pick point)

Specify second point of displacement or

<use first point as displacement>: (pick point)
```

> You can use COPYTOLAYER to simulate having the same objects look different in different viewports. Copy the objects to a different layer, freeze the other layer in the viewport, and make the desired changes (color, linetype, and so on) to the new objects.

Search Layers

If you've got layers coming out of your ears, then chances are you have trouble keeping track of them in the Layer Properties Manager. Fortunately, a search engine is now built into the Layer Properties Manager dialog box. Enter filter criteria in the search box, and you'll be able to find what you're looking for in the layer list.

You can use wildcard characters in the search box to sort layers by name. Most people know that asterisk * means all—it matches any text string and can be used anywhere within the string. So, a search for *CORE* matches all layers that have the word *CORE* in them.

Here are a few lesser-known wildcards:

Wildcard	Matching Effect
*	Any string of any length
~	Anything but the pattern (logical NOT)
?	Any single character
#	Any number
@	Any alphabetic character

If you want to search for layers that aren't in an XRef, then your clever search criteria will search for all layers that don't have the pipe symbol in them because it denotes an externally referenced layer.

To get all the layers with the pipe symbol, type *|* into the search box. To get anything but that pattern, preface it with a tilde character, like this: ~*|*. Now, you'll get all layers that aren't part of an XRef listed in the Layer Properties Manager.

In older versions of AutoCAD, sometimes layers wouldn't sort alphabetically in the Layer Manager because the MAXSORT system variable was set lower than the number of layers in the drawing. Now it defaults to 1,000, which should take care of you. If you ever exceed this number of layers, then it may be time to rethink your layer strategy.

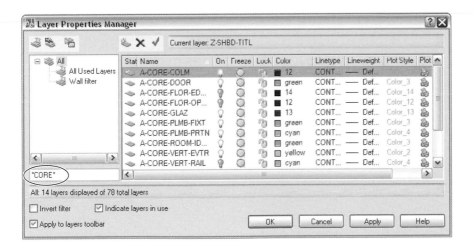

Layer Filter Tips

Layer filters are like formalized layer searches that can be saved with a drawing file. They can be based on properties, or they can group a bunch of layers together for organizational purposes. If you deal with zillions of layers every day, then it pays to learn to use layer filters.

Property filters can search for more than just layer names. Armchair scientists will want to try this thought experiment:

1. Open the Layer Properties Manager by typing **LA** Enter.

2. Press Alt+P to create a new property filter.

3. In the Layer Filter Properties dialog, set On to the lit bulb symbol and Color to Cyan. Title the filter **Cyan and On**. The sky's the limit for how specific you want to make your filter criteria. You can add multiple lines to the filter—they act like logical OR statements.

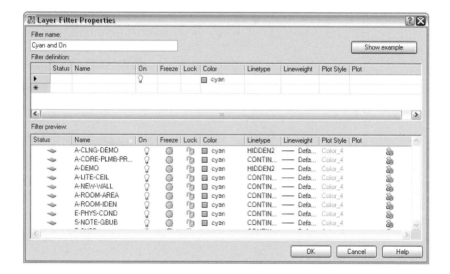

4. The Filter preview in the bottom half of the Layer Filter Properties dialog reveals what this filter does. Only layers that are on and have a cyan color are shown. Click OK.

5. Notice that the filter you just made resides in the left pane of the Layer Properties Manager. Right-click Cyan And On, and choose Isolate Group ➔ All Viewports from the shortcut menu.

6. Check Apply To Layers Toolbar at the bottom of the Layer Properties Manager if you also want the drop-down to show the current property filter. Invert Filter is also an interesting option—check it if you want all layers that are off and not cyan, in this example.

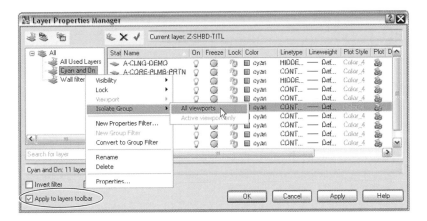

Group filters are used to lump a bunch o' layers together. This kind of filter sure is easy to use, because you don't have to figure out complex filter criteria—just drag and drop. This is the way to go when you want to work on a group of layers that may not have much in common, property-wise. We'll walk you through it:

1. Open the Layer Properties Manager by typing **LA** Enter.

2. Press Alt+G to create a new group filter.

3. Give the filter a descriptive name; use **Grab Bag** here.

4. Click the All node at the top of the filter tree, so no filtering is happening.

5. Drag any selection of layers from the list in the Layer Properties Manager, and drop them in the Grab Bag.

6. Select the Grab Bag group filter node in the filter tree, and see what the cat dragged in. Notice the group icon is different from the property filter icons—it shows a hand grabbing (or pointing to) a stack of layers. Apropos, don't you think?

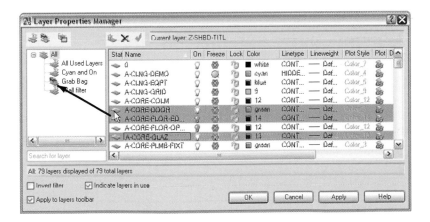

FILTERS lets you delete unused or unwanted layer filters (not to be confused with the FILTER command, which is completely different). LAYERFILTERALERT is a system variable that lets you decide when to get warned about having too many layer filters—they can seriously bog you down.

Take a Layer Walk

Layer Walk (LAYWALK) is an unusual and massively useful command (also formerly an Express Tool)—it's like AutoCAD's own set of Ginsu knives. First, you can use it to set layer states visually, by walking through layers dynamically. The resizable LayerWalk dialog lists all the layers in the drawing. Hold down Shift to select contiguous layers, or hold down Ctrl to select individual layers in the list (it's a Windows thing). Whatever is selected is turned on, and whatever isn't is turned off.

Layer Walk is fantastic because you see changes on screen immediately as you select and deselect layer names. It's a great way to get to know the layer structure of an unfamiliar drawing. This command comes in especially handy if you're working on someone else's drawing—someone who didn't get that whole "standards" deal. Select the layers in the list one at a time, and AutoCAD displays only the objects on that layer.

But wait, there's more! Use Layer Walk not only to familiarize yourself with layer structure, but also to set layers. If you want Layer Walk to set layers, then uncheck Restore On Exit.

In the upper-left corner of the dialog is a Select Objects button that allows you to select one or more objects; then, LAYWALK will highlight the associated layers for you. You can't do this with the LAYER command!

The Purge button is enabled in the LayerWalk dialog when any of the selected layers is unreferenced, so you can go for a walk and take out the trash.

How much would you pay for an excellent tool to freeze dynamic viewport layers? Now that LAYWALK is part of the core, it's absolutely free (price of AutoCAD notwithstanding). LAYWALK turns layers on and off in tiled modelspace but freezes and thaws layers in the current viewport in floating modelspace—that's inside a viewport on a layout, for those in the know.

It slices, it dices, it will fix your car—LAYWALK can even save layer states. Right-click the layer list, and you'll see a shortcut menu with Save Layer State as an option. Uncheck Restore On Exit, and you can quickly restore layer states in the drawing by selecting them from the drop-down list at the top of the LayerWalk dialog. Amazing!

Translate Layers

Have you ever imported a drawing from <insert competing CAD program here>? Did something get lost in translation? Layers are often garbled or not up to your standards when you open a non-"Autodesk Trusted DWG" in AutoCAD. Microstation layers are particularly heinous, using color numbers as layer names in AutoCAD.

Enter LAYTRANS. It's a godsend for translating layers from one convention to another. It's such a hassle doing them one at a time in the Layer Properties Manager.

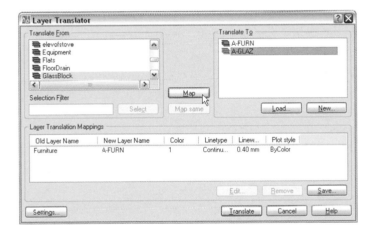

The method is simple. LAYTRANS loads the current layer names into the left side of the dialog. You set up the desired layer names by selecting New and assigning the appropriate properties. Then, it's as simple as selecting layers on the left and the right and clicking Map. A sequence of layer translation mappings is built up in the list below, and all are executed when you click Translate.

> You can map multiple layers from the old layer convention to a single layer in the new one with LAYTRANS.

The real power is the ability to save this setup for future use (in a .DWS file). Do the work once, and use it over and over for quick translation of multiple drawings. If your goal is to do this procedure only once, then you may as well use the LAYER command. But if you find yourself tediously faced with this scenario often, then you'll love the Layer Translator.

LAYTRANS can optionally translate layers nested in block definitions—something that is hard to do manually. Use the Settings button in the Layer Translator dialog box to use this feature.

Layers: The Good, the Bad, and the Ugly

It's amazing that we can work the title of a famous spaghetti western into something as mundane as layers, but we hope it gives you something to chew on.

The Good

You definitely want to keep good layers and the objects they contain, but there are plenty of times when you don't want to see them on screen. Freezing a layer is more serious than turning it off for the simple reason that freezing takes that layer out of the regeneration queue. That's right: Frozen layers don't regenerate, so your regens happen faster.

The Bad

When layers go bad, you can try to delete them in the Layer Properties Manager. If they go gentle into that good night, then count yourself among the lucky. If they won't delete, then you'll probably see a warning like this:

That doesn't sound too bad, but layers that are nested inside block definitions also count as layers containing objects. They're much harder to track down. If you find yourself with a stubborn such layer, try PURGE. Purging can get rid of a lot more than layers, so be careful. Check Purge Nested Items in the Purge dialog box to get rid of layers trapped in definitions. You may even have to run purge a few times to get rid of layers upon layers of digital sedimentation.

If you can't beat them, then join 'em, right? If purging doesn't work, try merging. LAYMRG is the command to use to merge selected layers onto a destination layer. It's one way to get rid of bad layers, but you must realize that you're only moving the bad stuff around, which brings us to our next topic.

The Ugly

We all know what it's like to have a layer that refuses to purge—it's downright ugly. We turn off all the other layers and zoom around trying to find something on the militant layer, but alas, there is nothing to be found! Why won't AutoCAD let us delete it? There are many possible reasons.

The brilliant Bill Fane once sent me (Lynn) an e-mail with an entire page of possible reasons why a layer won't delete. It may be that the layer is referenced in a block definition or used for dimensioning at one time, or it can be something as frustrating as someone having placed on the layer a text string consisting of just a space (I hope we don't give anyone any ideas!).

You don't really care why the layer won't delete—you just want to remove it from your CAD life. Here is the silver bullet: The awesome LAYDEL will come to your rescue. This command doesn't care what is on the layer; it's happy to vanish it into oblivion. Even if that layer is referenced in a block definition, LAYDEL is smart enough to open the block definition, remove the offending layer from the block, and then delete the layer—now that is raw power. But remember, where there is power, there is danger! Be careful what you ask for, because the layer doesn't have to be empty to be removed with LAYDEL. Your drawing could incur some serious damage if you aren't paying attention.

Annotation

A DRAWING ISN'T finished without some form of annotation. In AutoCAD, annotation takes the form of hatch patterns, text, dimensions, attributes, fields, and tables—meta-information that clarifies and documents drawing geometry. Although it may not be as engaging as drawing a design, documenting the design is just as important.

There are a lot of subtleties to hatch patterns—we discuss them in plain language and offer strategies for getting the most out of hatches. This chapter gives you what you need to have an optimal experience with the interconnecting world of attributes, fields, and tables. In addition you're offered life-saving techniques for taming the complex beasts that are text and dimensions.

3

This chapter offers you a plethora of annotation tips, organized into the following categories:

- Hatches
- Text and Dimensions
- Attributes and Fields
- Tables

■ Hatches

Hatch patterns and gradient fills are wonderful window dressing. If used correctly, hatches can make a drawing readable and pleasing to look at. Aside from the aesthetic, hatches visually annotate areas in ways that would be difficult to depict in any other way.

On the Origins of Hatch Patterns

Anthropologists have finally uncovered the true origins of hatch patterns, successfully tracing them back to the HPORIGIN system variable. In what is considered an "astounding" find, the unearthed HPORIGIN blows away the deprecated SNAPBASE system variable that experts say held the hatch origin before AutoCAD 2006.

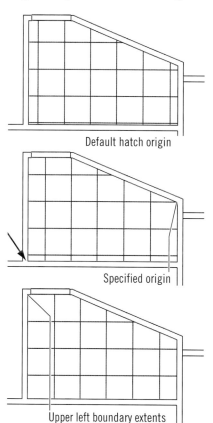

Default hatch origin

Specified origin

Upper left boundary extents

Being able to set the hatch origin point easily from the Hatch And Gradient dialog is tremendous; this capability makes hatch patterns much more useful. For example, if you're laying out ceiling grids, chances are you want to register the origin point of the grid with one corner of the room it's suspended above. That way, you won't have to cut little slivers of ceiling tiles all around the edges of the room where less than a full tile fits in the available space.

In the Hatch And Gradient dialog, two radio buttons appear in the Hatch Origin area. Select Specified Origin, click the button, and then set the new origin point on screen—full tiles now emanate from this hatch origin point.

An alternative way to specify the hatch origin is to default to one of five boundary extents points—top left, top right, bottom left, bottom right, or center. When you think about it, most rooms are more or less rectangular, so chances are one of these points will work for you as a hatch origin. Check Default To Boundary Extents in the Hatch Origin area, and choose one of the five options from the drop-down list.

HPORIGINMODE controls whether the point stored by HPORIGIN is used as hatch origin (set it to 0) or whether any one of five boundary extents points is used instead (values 1–5). These values are set by the drop-down in the Hatch Origin area of the Hatch And Gradient dialog box.

The default hatch origin always starts out coincident with the origin point of space—that is, until you store a new default 2D point with HPORIGIN. Once stored, HPORIGIN becomes the common point of origin for all subsequent hatch patterns you make. Check Store As Default Origin at the bottom of the Hatch And Gradient dialog box to save the specified point in HPORIGIN.

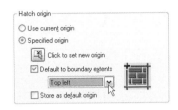

Along with being able to alter the common point of origin for subsequent hatch patterns, you can reuse in a new hatch an origin point from an existing hatch pattern you made some time ago. To accomplish this feat, follow these steps:

1. Double-click an existing hatch pattern to edit it. PICKSTYLE must be set to either 0 or 1 in order to edit the hatch pattern by double-clicking. Otherwise, use the HATCHEDIT command explicitly.

2. In the Hatch And Gradient dialog, check Store As Default Origin in the Hatch Origin area. You've just saved the origin of the existing hatch pattern in HPORIGIN. Click OK to close the dialog box. Otherwise, you can use the HPORIGIN command and enter the 2D coordinates directly.

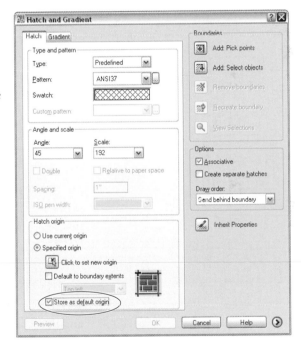

3. Type **H** and press Enter to create a new hatch pattern (or select Draw → Hatch from the menu). Choose the Use Current Origin radio button in the Hatch Origin area. Now you're using the value you put into HP-ORIGIN in the previous step.

4. Continue creating the new hatch pattern. That's it.

Set the Default Pattern

We find it annoying to be presented with the ANSI31 pattern in the Hatch And Gradient dialog box in every new drawing.

How often do you use this most basic of all conceivable patterns—maybe never? Perhaps you have another favorite hatch pattern, or at least one that you use most often.

Fortunately, you can set the default hatch pattern so it greets you in the Hatch And Gradient dialog. Type **HPNAME**, and then type the name of your favorite hatch pattern—for example, **SOLID**. The next time you create a hatch pattern, this pattern will appear by default in the Hatch And Gradient dialog box.

Unfortunately, the value of HPNAME is never saved. That's right; it's saved neither in the registry nor in the drawing file, so you can't add it to your template. That means you'd have to set HPNAME manually in every drawing, thereby destroying any productivity gains you might realize. What's up with that?

We have another tip you can use to set the default hatch pattern once and for all. Yes, you must use arcane knowledge to make this happen, but it's well worth it. Here's what to do:

1. Type **VLIDE** and press Enter to open the Visual LISP Integrated Development Environment. Don't panic if you've never done any Lisp programming. What you have to do here is super basic.

2. Click the New File button in the toolbar to create a new file. A blank window appears in the Visual LISP IDE.

3. Type the following in the new Lisp window:

   ```
   (setvar "HPNAME" "SOLID")
   ```

   Substitute your favorite hatch pattern name for SOLID if you wish, such as ANSI37, ISO12W100, BRICK, AR-HBONE, or whatever.

4. Save the file in the Visual LISP IDE as acaddoc.lsp. You must use this exact name because this file loads with every drawing you open. Save this file in the root AutoCAD support folder, which is the default location in the Visual LISP IDE:

   ```
   C:\Program Files\AutoCAD 2007\Support\acaddoc.lsp
   ```

Definitely don't save your file as acad2007doc.lsp—this file exists and has lots of code that AutoCAD needs. Both acad2007doc.lsp and acaddoc.lsp are loaded with every drawing. Add custom code to the latter file only.

Close the Visual LISP IDE, and you're done. Now, every time you open a drawing, the hatch dialog will be preset with your chosen pattern—annoyance removed.

To Fill or Not to Fill?

That is the question. Display performance can be adversely affected if your drawing contains lots of hatching. Although massive hatch patterns are generally handled as single objects so they're easy to manipulate, AutoCAD still has to draw the zillions of tiny lines that make them up on the screen and in plots.

Use the FILL command (FILLMODE system variable) to turn off hatches when you don't need them—whenever displaying the patterns on screen is distracting or gets in your way. Follow FILL with REGEN, and the display updates. Simplifying the display by turning off hatch patterns accelerates performance while you're working. When plotting, what you see on the screen is what you get for output.

> Hiding fill is possible only in the 2D Wireframe visual style. All other visual styles show fill no matter what.

If displaying the myriad lines within hatch patterns is the problem, one mitigating solution is to limit the number of lines that can be created within a hatch pattern. The MaxHatch system registry variable controls the maximum hatch pattern density.

By default, MaxHatch is set ridiculously high at 1 million. Every hatch pattern you create can have up to 1 million lines—no wonder display performance gets bogged down.

Altering MaxHatch is perhaps the geekiest thing you'll ever do (if you do worse, don't let it be known). It isn't a command, nor is it a system variable. MaxHatch is a system registry variable—so it's deep, deep within AutoCAD, almost at the operating-system level. Here's how you do it:

1. On the command line, type exactly the following (case matters):

   ```
   (getenv "MaxHatch")
   ```

   This tells you the number of lines MaxHatch is set to. If you've never changed the value, then it will say "1000000"—that's one million.

2. To change MaxHatch, type the following on the command line:

   ```
   (setenv "MaxHatch" "1000")
   ```

   This sets the maximum number of hatch lines to 1,000, which should be enough for you.

Now, whenever you try to create a hatch pattern that calls for more than 1,000 lines, it won't happen. Instead, you'll see the following message:

```
Hatch spacing too dense, or dash size too small.
```

Try increasing the scale or choose a different pattern to stay within the threshold set by the MaxHatch system registry variable.

Another vexing hatch issue has to do with waiting for the HATCH command to locate a boundary from a point that you pick. The number of objects the hatch engine has to consider affects the time it takes to find a boundary. The system variable HPOBJWARNING controls

how many objects are searched to locate such a boundary before a warning is issued. Its default value is 10,000. Set this number lower (say, 1,000) if you like to be warned before embarking on a lengthy calculation—at least then you'll have a good excuse for a coffee break.

Disable Snap for Hatches

Does it drive you crazy when your object snaps keep grabbing your hatch patterns instead of the desired geometry? Let's face it—how often do you need to snap to a hatch pattern? Never in a million clicks.

The Drafting tab of the Options dialog lets you tell AutoCAD to ignore your hatch patterns whenever you're using any object snap.

Incidentally, the Ignore Hatch Objects check box sets a *bitcode* (equal to 1) in the OS-OPTIONS system variable. The Ignore Negative Z Object Snaps For Dynamic UCS check box sets bitcode 2 for this same system variable. When both check boxes are selected, the bitcodes add up to 1+2=3. That's why OSOPTIONS is 3 by default, in case you were wondering (we knew you weren't, but it was a good opportunity to educate you about bitcodes). For those of you using AutoCAD 2005, you'll find that the now-obsolete OSNAPHATCH system variable is set instead.

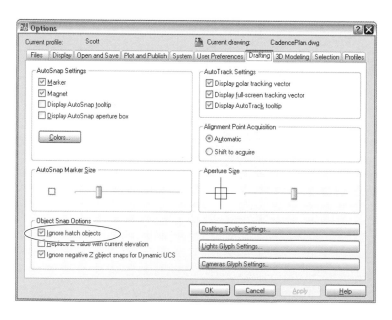

Tolerance Is a Good Thing

Aside from promoting social diversity and fostering more interesting culture, tolerance is also a good thing for hatches. In the old days, AutoCAD hatch boundaries were *intolerant*—AutoCAD either found them worthy or kicked you out. Nowadays, you can set just how tolerant you want AutoCAD to be.

The Hatch And Gradient dialog box has a right-facing arrow button near the bottom that expands the dialog with more options. Enter a number in the Gap Tolerance area to set the maximum size of gaps that can be ignored when objects are used as hatch boundary.

Enter a small tolerance value to gloss over small gaps so you can more easily find a hatch boundary from a selection of objects. Few things are more frustrating than not being able to find a hatch boundary due to a microscopic gap. In the past, fixing this problem required tedious filleting of edges (with a zero radius); but given tolerance, this is no longer necessary.

> It's faster and more direct to enter a gap tolerance value using the HPGAPTOL system variable—no hunting through the huge Hatch And Gradient dialog box.

You might be tempted to make HPGAPTOL large, to ensure against running into this painful issue in the future, but we suggest against doing so. If you set the value too large, it won't work—especially if the value is larger than either of the adjoining edges. Set it to something reasonable, and hatch away!

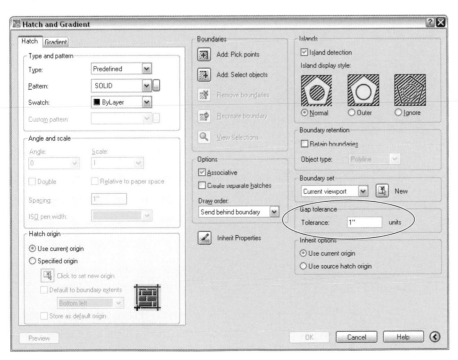

Separate Patterns for Flexibility

Have you ever hatched a bunch of boundaries all at once and later discovered that there was a problem with one of them? For example, the design evolves, one of the rooms changes shape, and now the hatch patterns that fill it need adjustment. Fixing any one of the boundaries normally requires you to reselect all of them—what a royal drag. Most people erase the hatch pattern and start over.

The savvy among us figured out one way around this problem: Use the HATCH command separately each time you want to make an individual boundary. This too is kind of a drag, especially when you have many hatch patterns to make (a row of ceiling grids in identical offices, for example). You have to use HATCH, pick a single boundary, set its parameters, click OK, and repeat this sequence for each boundary. Yawn.

Now there is a more elegant solution to the question of hatch-boundary independence: Set HPSEPARATE to 1 prior to selecting several boundaries, and they'll all be independent from the get go. HPSEPARATE is also available as a convenient check box in the Hatch And Gradient dialog box.

Separate boundaries can be edited independently, so when there is a problem with one of the patterns, you can fix it without affecting all the other patterns you made at the same time.

CREATING A BOUNDARY ON THE FLY

Wouldn't it be nice if you could quickly create a boundary and hatch it at the same time? Most of us create a boundary first, perhaps using the PLINE command, and then enter the HATCH command. Both these steps can be combined into one if you use the command-line interface for the HATCH command, which can only be accessed by keying in a dash before the word HATCH: −HATCH (which, incidentally, is how you access the command-line interface for any command). Here you'll find the groovy option Draw Boundary, which lets you draw an impromptu polyline boundary and then hatch it. You can even tell it to delete the boundary when it's finished hatching, leaving only your shiny new hatch pattern behind.

Pick Your Selection Style

PICKSTYLE is a system variable that has to do with selecting groups and/or associative hatch patterns. What do groups and hatch patterns have in common, you ask? Nothing, really. PICKSTYLE is a relic of AutoCAD's convoluted evolutionary history. What should really be two separate system variables have been confusingly lumped together.

It's possible to select both a hatch pattern and its associated boundary simultaneously by properly setting PICKSTYLE. And while that is going on, you can also toggle group selection on and off with PICKSTYLE. In a nutshell, here's how it works.

From the perspective of hatch patterns, when PICKSTYLE is set to either 0 or 1, you can select hatch patterns separately from their associated boundaries. This is the default behavior.

Set PICKSTYLE to 2 or 3 (it doesn't matter), and hatch patterns and their associated boundaries are selected together. This can be useful if you want to select and/or manipulate a hatch boundary that may be difficult to get at any other way.

If a hatch pattern was created from a selection of objects (rather than a picked point), moving the objects moves the associated hatch pattern regardless of the value of PICKSTYLE.

However, when PICKSTYLE is set to either 2 or 3, double-clicking hatch patterns no longer triggers HATCHEDIT. Instead, the Properties palette opens, showing multiple objects selected. This happens because both the hatch and its boundary are picked together in this selection style. However, you can still edit patterns by using the HATCHEDIT command explicitly.

Pressing Ctrl+H toggles group selection no matter what. If PICKSTYLE is set to 0, Ctrl+H toggles PICKSTYLE to 1 and vice versa. If PICKSTYLE is set to 2, Ctrl+H toggles PICKSTYLE to 3 and vice versa. Got that? Here is a table for your reference:

PICKSTYLE	Effect
0	No group selection or associative hatch selection
1	Group selection
2	Associative hatch selection
3	Group selection and associative hatch selection

Just remember to press Ctrl+H whenever you want to toggle group selection, and you can forget about the actual value of PICKSTYLE as far as groups are concerned.

Pick Points for Hatches and Boundaries

Pay attention to what is visible on the screen prior to picking points for hatches and boundaries. HATCH and BOUNDARY both automate the tedious process of selecting objects to include in a boundary by employing an algorithm to do the job for you. BOUNDARY gives you just the boundary, and HATCH fills it with a pattern or a gradient.

This algorithm goes fishing for boundaries by casting rays out from the point you pick. Whenever these rays catch objects, the objects are added to the boundary. Mostly this works under the hood. You can specify the direction in which the rays are cast using the command-line version of –HATCH. Not that you'll need to, because AutoCAD 2007 is much better than previous releases at finding hatch boundaries.

However, you still have to pay attention to what's on the screen when casting about for boundaries. AutoCAD is smart but lacks common sense. For example, let's say you want to fill a room with a gradient. At first, you may be tempted to use HATCH and just pick a point inside the room—but you then realize that the door layer is on. The door and its swing arc will become part of the boundary if you pick a point inside the room, and that's not what you want.

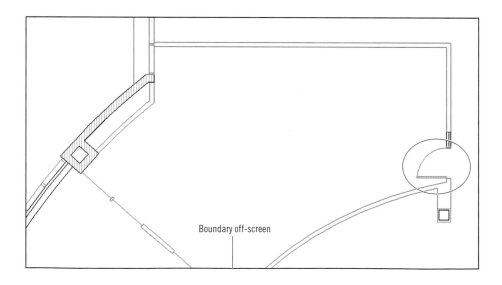

Boundary off-screen

Common sense tells you to turn off the door layer. By the same token, it should also dawn on you to turn on the header layer—showing lines closing the gap in the wall where the door is located. Then a boundary has a good chance of being found.

See the earlier section "Tolerance Is a Good Thing" for help in closing small gaps in boundaries.

We're told that in AutoCAD 2007, the HATCH pick-points algorithm takes in an area nine times the size of the screen when fishing for boundaries. It no longer matters if part of the boundary you're trying to hatch is off the screen. Hurray!

That wasn't the case with HATCH in previous releases—and it does still matter what is on screen when you're using BOUNDARY. Why did Autodesk upgrade one ray-casting algorithm but not the other? We aren't sure. Remember that BOUNDARY is a bit more fussy than HATCH. Just make sure that what you're trying to bound is completely visible on screen when using BOUNDARY.

It's smart advice to zoom in as close as possible to the area you wish to hatch. Doing so reduces the boundary set, so the ray-casting algorithm has less work to do, saving you time.

If you're trying to create a boundary polyline over a particularly large area (like the shell of a large building), try splitting it into a few zones. Draw bulkheads across the space, and it will be easier to create smaller compartmentalized boundaries that can each fit on the screen. Then, isolate, explode, and join compartments into a super-boundary, if that's your object.

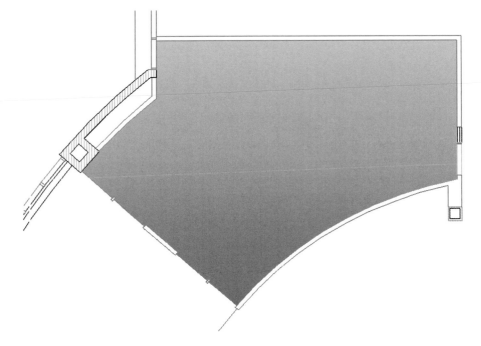

Find Areas with Hatches

AREA is the obvious command for finding areas of enclosed boundaries, right? Obvious, yes; but wise, no. The AREA command is passé. Hatch patterns are all the rage now that they have an Area property. Why this changing fashion?

See "Display Area in a Field," later in this chapter.

Perhaps in the past you created boundary polylines to measure the area of spaces. Consider the elegance of hatch patterns:

- Hatch patterns that fill spaces are easier to select than boundary polylines.

- Hatching can intentionally exclude islands to avoid calculating unwanted areas. Areas must be subtracted separately with polylines.

- Selecting multiple hatches tabulates their cumulative area automatically. The AREA command works one object at a time.

Not only are hatch islands considered when calculating area, but overlapping hatches are, too. Overlapping hatches don't increase cumulative area when added to a selection of hatches. Use the Properties palette to find the area of one hatch object or the Cumulative Area property when several hatch objects are selected.

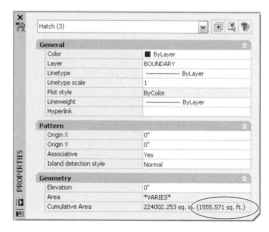

If you're concerned with picture-perfect accuracy, set HPGAPTOL to 0 before creating any hatch patterns. However, if you have trouble getting hatch boundaries to close (due to small gaps), setting a tiny value in HPGAPTOL probably won't throw off your area calculations too far. It's only when people use a large gap tolerance that they risk calculating bogus areas.

Customize Hatch Patterns

If the hatch patterns that ship with AutoCAD leave you feeling a bit underwhelmed, the good news is that you can use custom patterns. Developing a hatch pattern definition requires knowledge, practice, and patience.

That's clearly out for most of us. The faster route to pattern Nirvana is to buy ready-made custom hatch patterns from a vendor. Here are a couple of sources:

- http://www.autocadhatchpatterns.com

- http://www.hatchpatterns.com

There are even a few tools on the market that automate the tedious coding of hatch patterns. We haven't tried these, but they sound good in concept. If you're up to the challenge, read the entry on creating hatch patterns in the AutoCAD Customization Guide, and try making your own patterns. Here's some sample hatch-pattern code:

```
*TRIANG, Equilateral triangles

60, 0,0, .1875,.324759526, .1875,-.1875

120, 0,0, .1875,.324759526, .1875,-.1875

0, -.09375,.162379763, .1875,.324759526, .1875,-.1875
```

There is obviously some logic here, but we don't have what it takes to figure it out. We do know that this code resides in the AutoCAD pattern library, which lives in a text file in the following location:

```
C:\Program Files\AutoCAD 2007\

UserDataCache\Support\acad.pat
```

You can append user-defined hatch patterns to this file—good luck!

IT'S A BIRD. IT'S A PLANE. IT'S … SUPERHATCH

If you have the Express Tools loaded on your computer, then you'll find the SUPERHATCH tool makes it easy to create your own hatch patterns. The process is simple: You draw the hatch pattern of your dreams and then make a block out of it. SUPERHATCH allows you to hatch with blocks, images, Xrefs, and wipeouts.

You can get clever with the SUPERHATCH command. Imagine hatch patterns with different colors, linetypes, or lineweights, all defined within your block. You can also control the visibility of the layers making up your hatch patterns. Use images as hatch patterns to get a rendered look. There's no such thing as a 3D hatch pattern, but with SUPERHATCH, you can create a 3D block and use that to hatch. So many possibilities!

Text and Dimensions

AutoCAD text and dimensions are your opportunity to spell out your design, both literally and figuratively. It pays you to get the most out of these essential forms of annotation.

The Height of Style

STYLE controls all text subscribing to its particular fashion. The power of text styles is their ability to globally control text objects. However, not all text obeys the rules of style. The multiline text command MTEXT allows you to override anything defined in a text style on a per-letter basis. Even so, text styles have strategic advantages.

The best strategy is to employ a few styles and use them to format all your text objects so you retain global text control. Use MTEXT's superior formatting abilities to override any formatting inherent in a style only in exceptional circumstances.

Warning: The height of a style should not be defined. Leave the text style's Height setting at 0. Only then will you have the right to set Height to any value when you create text objects.

You may be tempted to ignore our warning, but do so at your own peril—styles with fixed heights can't be scaled when dimensioning. Using a style with a fixed height is like throwing a monkey wrench into the dimension machine. Clank, crash, boom! If you like to live on the edge, go ahead and fix the height of your styles, but only for styles never destined to be included in dimensions.

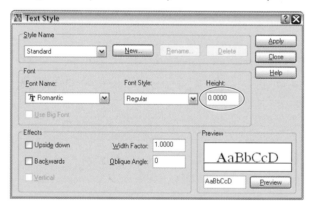

Use TEXTSIZE to set the default height for new text objects. It has no effect if the current style has a fixed height.

Why must we suffer the aesthetic abuse of this font? TXT is AutoCAD's default text style—there is no known way around it. Well, actually there is one way—but we don't like it because it's like cheating. You could select another font file and rename it txt.shx, replacing the original. Be aware that this substitution only works on your local machine where you've overwritten the original font file—not a robust solution.

TXT is the most hideous font in the universe.

Believe it or not, the TXT font was designed to optimize the pen motion in early plotting devices. Why we are using it today is one of AutoCAD's greatest mysteries.

The first thing you should do when designing a template is to change the default font to anything but TXT. ROMANS is a nice, simple SHX font. Why not use it as the font for the Standard style?

AutoCAD can handle two flavors of fonts: SHX and TTF. The former are compiled shape definition files, and the latter are TrueType fonts. SHX fonts are primitive; they ship with AutoCAD, and they're free of intellectual copyright restrictions. TrueType fonts generally have a much nicer appearance and can access any of the fonts installed on your Windows machine.

Although it's tempting to use TTF over SHX—because TrueType fonts can be very attractive—we must sadly recommend against doing so. No fonts can be saved in a drawing due to intellectual property issues. It's hard enough maintain drawing files without having to track down font files as well.

Text made with TrueType fonts may not be usable on other computers that lack the specific font file. It's possible to open a drawing and not be able to edit its text because of issues with missing TTF fonts. If you use SHX fonts, you can rest assured that everyone in your office and others down the line will be able to read your fonts well into the future. There will be no font substitution—in short, no worries!

> Use eTransmit (or Pack'n Go in earlier versions of AutoCAD) to send drawing files that contain TrueType fonts to others. Be sure to include fonts in the Transmittal setup options; the referenced TTF files will be included in the ZIP archive you send. Remember, it's illegal to transmit fonts that the receiving party doesn't own.

If you get tired of the default text strings that appear in the Style Manager dialog box and in the MTEXT prompt, you have the power to change these messages. In the Text Style dialog box, type a brief message (such as your name), and click the Preview button.

Click the Font Name drop-down list, and select a font—giving focus to this particular drop-down list in the Text Style dialog box. Now, press the Up and/or Down Arrow keys repeatedly to cycle through fonts. Each time you cycle, the preview text changes, giving you a quick feel for what that font looks like. There is no better way to preview fonts in AutoCAD.

It's also possible to change the boring MTEXT sample text string to something other than *abc*. Use MTJIGSTRING to set any 10-character message. Put a period (.) into MTJIGSTRING, and there will be no sample string (but what fun is that?). What's the word of the day?

Change CASE

How many times have you started typing, only to realize later that you had Caps Lock off? Many people prefer to use ALL CAPS in their drawings' annotations. Typing in the wrong case usually means you have to type the text all over again. No longer!

Use the fabulous TCASE express tool to tweak the case of any text. Just execute, select, and choose an option from the TCASE – Change Text Case dialog box. This works on both single-line and multiline text or any combination. Most significantly, TCASE works on multiple objects, so you can fix a whole drawing at once.

It's also possible to change the case of individual words from the comfort of the MTEXT editor. Highlight the text in question, and click the Down Arrow button on the Text Formatting toolbar (or right-click to display the shortcut menu). Choose Change Case → UPPERCASE (or lowercase) from the menu. Note that you can more quickly press Ctrl+Shift+U for UPPERCASE and Ctrl+Shift+L for lowercase.

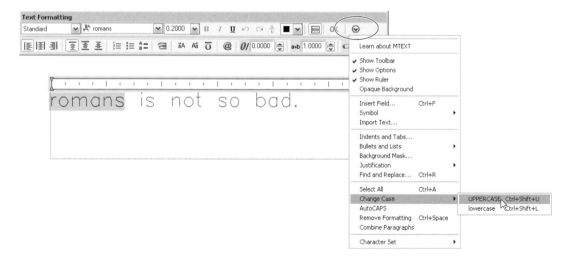

Spell Czech!

How many of you regularly use a spell checker in Microsoft Word but haven't thought to do the same in AutoCAD? It's about time to start! Nothing destroys the professionalism of a drawing faster than misspelled text.

If you're linguistically challenged or are having a little difficulty with the lexicon, SPELL may be your savior. Issue the command, and select the text you want to interrogate. The Check Spelling dialog alerts you to each potential blunder and gives you a chance to remedy the situation.

Pardon the pun, but we're checking the string *Spell czech* for an educational purpose. You see, SPELL is dead stupid. It merely checks each word against a database of correctly spelled words and can't help you with grammar or diction—that's word choice. Running SPELL on this string recommends that we capitalize *Czech*, but SPELL is perfectly willing to let this blunder through the net. There is no substitute for proofreading, as our editors will heartily agree—but spell-checking is still a great help.

Chances are good that you often use abbreviations and technical jargon in your drawings. SPELL won't like that. Instead of jettisoning SPELL, start adding your jargon to a custom dictionary, and SPELL will progressively become more useful to you.

Click the Add button in the Check Spelling dialog box to add the current misspelled word to the current custom dictionary. Click the Change Dictionaries button and then click the Add button to be proactive and add all your approved jargon at once. Why not save the custom dictionary on the server so everyone in the office can share in building a real-world lexicon?

Click the Browse button in the Change Dictionaries dialog box to specify where you want to save the fruits of your linguistic efforts.

Find (and Replace) Words

It's a word processor, it's a spreadsheet, no wait—it's a computer-aided design program. AutoCAD now functions just like any good word processor; it lets you globally find and replace text.

Issue FIND, click the Select Object button, and select any and all text in the drawing. Type the string you're looking for, and then click the Zoom To button if that's all you're interested in. Alternately, type replacement text in the Find And Replace dialog box if you want to exercise this ability. Click Replace and/or Replace All as required.

Did you know that FIND supports wildcards? This means you can now use wider searching criteria to find and replace text that may only differ by a few characters.

> Use the asterisk (*) and question mark (?) to represent any string of characters and any one character, respectively.

Trivia: Before the FIND command came into existence, AutoCAD old timers used the arcane FILTER command to perform text searches. Be thankful for progress!

Enlarge Text While Editing

This simple tip may not occur to you unless you hear it, and it may prevent unnecessary eye-strain. It's often convenient to edit multiline text while zoomed out so you can see more of the drawing. When you're in the MTEXT editor, zoom in by turning the mouse wheel. The text you're editing enlarges, along with the rest of the drawing.

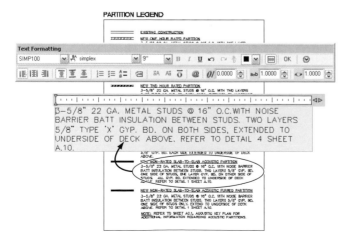

The system variable MTEXTFIXED also helps in this regard. Set it to 2 to automatically display text that is too small or large to read at legible size on screen for editing. In addition, text that is oriented vertically is automatically rotated back to horizontal, saving you from having to tilt your head uncomfortably to read it.

Control MTEXT Width

The only annoying thing about MTEXT, in our humble opinion, is the fact that you have to click two opposite corners to estimate the width of a paragraph prior to typing text. When you use a text tool, you want to get down to typing, right? Maybe you don't know how wide you want the paragraph to be beforehand, either.

Here's the good news: You don't have to set the paragraph width prior to typing if you make a macro that does this seamlessly for you. Yes, it requires "programming," but only in the most rudimentary form. If you have any reservations about using MTEXT, this should cancel them. Follow these steps:

1. Open the Text toolbar.

2. Right-click the first button, which is the Multiline Text tool. Choose Customize from the shortcut menu.

3. In the giant Customize User Interface dialog box that appears, select the Multiline Text command in the Customizations In All CUI Files list.

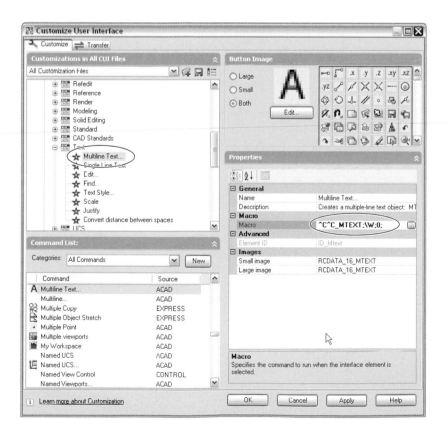

4. Look at the macro that's listed in the Properties list:

   `^C^C_mtext`

   ^C^C means to press Esc twice to cancel any running command. The underscore means to translate the following word into the language under which AutoCAD is installed. If you're speaking English, then this doesn't do anything. The command executed is MTEXT. Easy as pie.

5. If you want to avoid clicking two points to set the paragraph width, then you have to make the macro pause for you to click once before programmatically setting a zero width. All text needs an insertion point at the least. Type in the following macro:

   `^C^C_MTEXT;\W;0;`

   Analyzing this macro, it begins where the original macro left off. Semicolons mean Enter. The backslash means to pause for user input. So, this macro waits for you to click an insertion point, issues W to specify a width, and then assigns the width of zero, quick as lightning.

6. Click Apply, click OK, and try out your new Multiline Text tool. Click a point and start typing, just like single-line text.

   What could be better? Now you have multiline text with the simplicity of single-line—but jam-packed with all the editing features of a full-fledged word processor. Before you consider using MTEXT for all your textual needs, one other issue needs your attention.

   If you start making multiline text with zero width, you'll eventually discover that it has only a single grip—just like single-line text. Hey, wait! What happens when you want to give width to zero-width MTEXT? Here's what:

1. Double-click some multiline text that you made with the previous macro. This brings up the Text Formatting toolbar.

2. Notice the arrows just above the zero-width text. Drag the arrowhead on the right to the right. Doing so gives the paragraph width. You can see the words wrap dynamically to fit the paragraph width.

3. When you're satisfied with the state of the word wrap, click OK on the Text Formatting toolbar. Case closed.

> You can also alter paragraph width on the Properties palette, but it's not as intuitive as dragging the ruler.

Edit MTEXT the Way You Want

In case you haven't noticed, all you have to do to edit text is double-click it. In fact, you can double-click just about anything and trigger the appropriate editing command automatically. No more racking your brain for DDEDIT, PROPERTIES, EATTEDIT, HATCHEDIT, or whatever editing command is appropriate for the selected object.

> Turn DBLCLKEDIT on if double-click editing doesn't work for you (on by default).

Here's another mini-tip that makes working with MTEXT that much faster. When you're finished writing some MTEXT, click anywhere outside the on-screen editing window to close the editor. There is absolutely no need to click the OK button on the Text Formatting toolbar or to press Ctrl+Enter. Terminally lazy people the world over will appreciate this one (ourselves included).

Not happy with the bloated MTEXT editor? Do you long for the good old days? Well, those days aren't gone (yet). The MTEXTED system variable allows you to choose which text editor you want to use. MTEXTED has three possible values:

Internal The default MTEXT editor built into AutoCAD 2007. Use this choice to edit text in place with the behemoth Text Formatting toolbar.

Oldeditor The old editor from the good old days (circa the 20th century). Why you'd want to use this is anybody's guess—midlife crisis perhaps? We won't tell.

:lisped The Lisp editor (don't forget the preceding colon). This is an interesting choice because it's like two editors in one. When you're editing text with 80 or fewer characters, a simple text dialog box is displayed. If the text has more than 80 characters, the massive internal editor is displayed. Why 80 characters, you ask? That's all that fits on a punch card (no joke).

We like the Lisp editor because it presents a streamlined interface when you're editing brief notes but delivers the full-blown extravaganza when you're editing paragraphs. Plus, you can elect to go for the full editor with the click of a button.

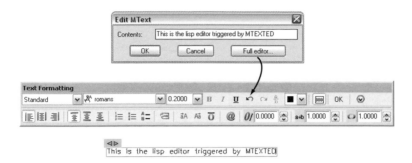

Single-Line Text Tips

For all multiline text is cracked up to be, it will never match the cool efficiency of single-line text. Single-line text gets the job done fast, without much fuss.

The Dynamic Text Editor Saga

This just in: The DTEXTED system variable has a new option that will make many of us die-hard techies happy. Let's recap and catch everyone up with the continuing saga. Before Auto-CAD 2006 came out, you could easily put multiple strings of text all over your drawing while in the DTEXT and/or TEXT commands. After keying in the first string (and without leaving the command), you moved the mouse to another location and picked. The text prompter moved to the new location, and you could key in more text—very cool! This is one thing that doesn't work with MTEXT.

Along came AutoCAD 2006 with the new in-place text editor. Unfortunately, the new text editor broke the functionality just explained—what was up with that? Picking in the drawing to start a new text string at a new location terminated the command! Oh, the pain of it all. The only way to get the old functionality back was to set DTEXTED to 0 (which essentially turned off the new text editor).

Enter AutoCAD 2007, with a new setting for DTEXTED that gives us the best of both worlds—the ability to place text strings in multiple locations within the TEXT/DTEXT commands and the ability to use the new text editor too. Just set DTEXTED to 2. This makes it super easy to knock out many text strings in the same command.

> TEXT is now identical to DTEXT for all intents and purposes—permission granted to drop the *D*.

Make Text Fit

If you ever need to make text fit within a box, you can squeeze (or stretch) it by adjusting the text object's width factor property. By default, text has a width factor of 1. Anything less than that squeezes the text, and values greater than 1 stretch the text. If you've ever tried fitting text into a box, it can be tedious trying to come up with a width factor value that results in the text fitting as precisely as you want it to—it's pure trial and error.

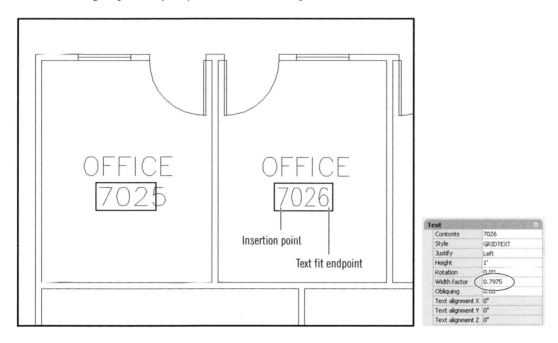

Enter the Express Tool TEXTFIT. The way it works is simple. Just execute, select a single-line text object, and click an endpoint. The text is squeezed or stretched as needed to fit between its insertion point and the text fit endpoint you choose—implying that you'll carefully justify the text prior to trying to fit it in somewhere. Once the text in question has been manhandled into the box, it's left with a weird width factor—whatever was needed to make the text fit. It sure beats finding the winning width factor by trial and error.

Upgrade Single-line Text Format

If you're completely sold on the superiority of multiline text over single-line variants—as you should be—you'll like this tool. The Express Tool TXT2MTXT does what its acronym suggests: It converts TEXT (and DTEXT) objects to the much-improved MTEXT object.

It's not uncommon to come across drawing files that use single-line text—derived from either the TEXT or DTEXT commands—throughout the drawing, even for paragraphs. Typically this occurs when the drawing file is old (before the MTEXT days) or when it was drawn by someone who wasn't a fan of the MTEXT command. Adding words to or removing words from single-line text often requires reconstructive surgery that involves manually "wrapping" words by editing each and every line. Argh!

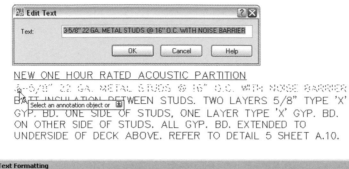

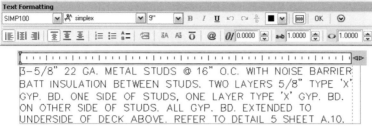

Editing paragraph text in the MTEXT dialog is easy—and it supports word wrap! TXT-2MTXT asks you to select the single-line text objects, and then it converts them into one big happy MTEXT object for you. It doesn't even matter what order you select the single-line text objects. Super simple!

Super Subtext

It can be confusing to try to figure out how to make superscripts and subscripts with MTEXT. The caret (^) is the key, but it isn't enough. You must also access the elusive Stack Properties dialog box to properly control supertext and subtext. Here's how to do it:

1. Issue the MTEXT command, and click an insertion point on screen.

2. Type **W** and press Enter to set a zero width, or click the opposite corner of the paragraph rectangle to set a width if you prefer. The Text Formatting toolbar appears (use the full editor if MTEXTED is set to :lisped).

3. Type some text, for example **E=mc2^**. The caret character indicates that something extraordinary is about to happen.

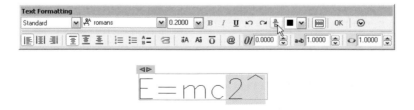

4. Highlight both the caret and the numeral in the in-place editor. Click the Stack button on the Text Formatting toolbar. The numeral is lifted if it precedes the caret or depressed if it follows the caret. If you see a subscript when you want a superscript (or vice versa), don't despair—help is a step away.

5. Highlight the superscript or subscript character, and right-click. Choose Stack Properties from the shortcut menu.

6. Congratulations! You've discovered the elusive Stack Properties dialog box. Text appearing in the Upper box becomes a superscript, and text in the Lower box becomes subscript. The Style option should be Tolerance to avoid having a slash or horizontal line (used for fractions) between possible superscripts and subscripts. Set Position and Text Size, and click OK. Click outside the in-place editing window to end the MTEXT command. Whew!

Now, sit back and appreciate your superscript—Einstein would be proud. Let's hope you don't have too many of these, because creating them does take a while!

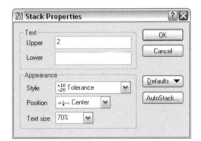

$$E = mc^2$$

Clever Alignment via the Clipboard

Anyone who has used Adobe Illustrator knows how nice it is to be able to align text with the click of a button. AutoCAD can do something similar, although it requires you to do a little manual copy 'n paste job.

Each text object has a location in space, and every location is split up and stored as X, Y, and Z position components. Aligning text objects is as simple as copying and pasting position coordinates between text objects. Choose whether to align in X, Y, or Z based on which coordinates you copy.

Single-line text objects store their position coordinates in two different sets of properties, depending on how they're justified. Only one of these sets of properties is editable at a time—those with the white background.

Justification plays a major part in alignment. Remember, you're aligning text objects from their *justification points*; these are what the coordinate properties locate.

You can paste a position coordinate into more than one text object at a time. Paste a value previously stored on the clipboard into any *VARIES* text field.

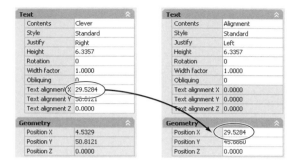

Renumber Text without Losing Your Mind

If you've ever had to manually renumber a large number of text objects, we feel for you. It's a tedious job editing one at a time. Isn't this the kind of mindless task computers were supposed to relieve us from doing?

Maintain your sanity by using the awesome TCOUNT Express Tool. It adds sequential numbering to text objects. Each time you select a text object, the next number in the sequence is entered. You can use TCOUNT both to add numbers to alphabetic strings and to replace existing numbers already present in the text objects. Bonus: You can add numbers either as prefixes or suffixes to text, so no worries, mate. This thing really works!

What is most impressive about TCOUNT is how you can tell it to sort according to the X or Y axis. If you have a bunch of text arranged in a column—for example, sheet notes—TCOUNT starts at the top and works its way down the list (in the Y direction), incrementally renumbering. You don't even have to click each item in sequence—sweet. Here's an example command-line transcript:

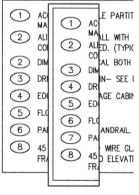

```
Command: TCOUNT

Initializing...

Select objects: 45 found

Sort selected objects by [X/Y/Select-order]

  <Select-order>: Y

Specify starting number and increment

  (Start,increment) <1,1>: (Enter)

Placement of numbers in text

  [Overwrite/Prefix/Suffix/Find&replace..]
```

```
<Prefix>: Overwrite
```

```
45 objects modified.
```

Create Logos with Text as Linework

Occasionally, you may need to draft a logo design that treats text not as text, but as a drawing. This is necessary if you want to play with the geometry of the letters. Of course, once text is converted to linework, there's no going back.

An Express Tool called TXTEXP explodes text into geometry, but in practice we have found that it doesn't work quite as well as another top-secret method. If you have the security clearance, then proceed with this preferred method for turning text into perfect linework:

1. Use the PLOTTERMANAGER command to open a folder containing your printer drivers.

2. Double-click the Add-A-Plotter Wizard.

3. Advance to the second page of the wizard, and select My Computer. Click Next, and select AutoCAD DXB File. Complete the wizard accepting all defaults.

4. Create some logo text using any font you want. Don't worry about not using TrueType fonts, because these letters' days as text are numbered.

5. Turn off fill by setting TEXTFILL to 0. This produces cleaner results because the letters are outlined, not filled with innumerable lines.

6. Print the text using the DXB plotter driver you just set up. Save the output as a .dxb file.

7. Use the little-known DXBIN command. Select the .dxb file you created in the previous step. The letters appear as microscopic line segments; they're no longer text objects.

8.   Join lines together to manipulate the letters more easily as individual entities. Trim, extend, hatch, or what-have-you to make a pleasing logo design.

> If DXBIN doesn't bring in letters as expected, either try another font, or try TXTEXP instead. Neither method is perfect, but both are better than drawing letters by hand.

Reassociate Fudged Dimensions

Sometimes we work with designers or consultants who prefer to fudge the dimension text value rather than create the drawing the correct size to begin with—bad, very bad!

When you look at an AutoCAD drawing, there is no way to visually discern which dimensions are accurate and which ones aren't. If you find yourself in doubt, a wonderful Express Tool can check your drawing for you and even reset dimension text to its actual values.

DIMREASSOC is responsible for keepin' it real—or, more accurately, for policing the scene. Select the offending dimensions, and AutoCAD highlights all that differ from their real measurements. You can also key in the word **All** to select all the dimensions. An additional Enter returns the dimensions to their actual values—and then you can go have a friendly chat with the renegade designer. Here's how it works:

```
Command: DIMREASSOC

Select dimension objects with non-associative text.

(select any/all of the dimensions in the drawing

 and AutoCAD will highlight the offenders)

Select objects: Specify opposite corner: 16 found

Select objects: (Enter)

16 objects modified.
```

> Don't be a dimension fudger. If you get an incorrect dimension value, change the drawing, not the dimension text!

Easily Flip Dimension Arrows

Sometimes, AutoCAD puts dimension arrows on the wrong side of its extension lines. Which is the wrong side? That depends on the situation, doesn't it? It usually happens when there isn't quite enough space to fit both text and arrows between the extension lines. But there are times when forcing the arrows inside makes for a more readable drawing.

Fortunately, you can easily flip dimension arrows without having to fuss with dimension styles. Select a single dimension that you'd like to flip (on the side you intend to flip), and right-click. Choose Flip Arrow from the shortcut menu, and voila—instant flippage. Flip Arrow is a toggle, so choose it again from the shortcut menu to go back if you don't like the result.

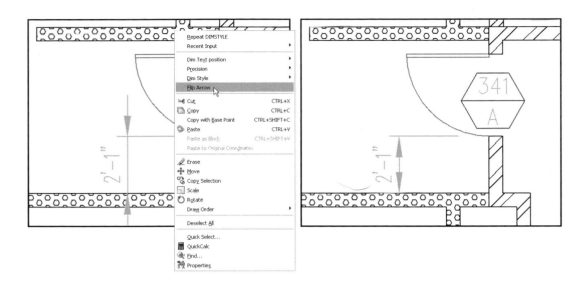

Attributes and Fields

Most people are a bit confused about how attributes differ from fields. In a nutshell, *attributes* are static data attached to blocks. *Fields* are like magic text that updates automatically when whatever they point to changes. Fields can be placed inside attributes, making the situation more complex. We hope the tips you read here will clear up these issues for you.

Define, Insert, and Burst Attributes

Attributes don't exist on their own—they're qualities attached to blocks. Typical attributes are manufacturer, price, room name, part number, or any other piece of data you want to have carried by a block.

More precisely, attribute definitions are saved within blocks, and their data is carried by block references in the drawing.

Here's an executive summary of attributes. The command you use to create an attribute definition is ATTDEF. Every attribute definition has a tag, prompt, and default value.

The *tag* is a name that you, the attribute designer, keep track of. The *prompt* is what users of the attributed block see when they give data to the attribute to hold. The *value* is any optional default value you want to give to the attribute definition. Typically, we set the default value to be the most prevalent value (so you don't have to key it in).

Define Attributes within Blocks

If you've been designing attributed blocks for years, then you probably start by creating the attribute definitions, draw some geometry, and then use the BLOCK command; are we right?

The Block Editor is a better environment in which to create blocks. Use BEDIT (or select Tools → Block Editor from the menu) to open the Edit Block Definition dialog box. You're prompted to name your creation and click OK before you begin designing. Click the Define Attribute button in the block editor, and you can forget the ATTDEF command. Draw geometry, and add some parameters and actions while you're at it (see Chapter 5). Save and exit; you've defined an attributed (and possibly dynamic) block.

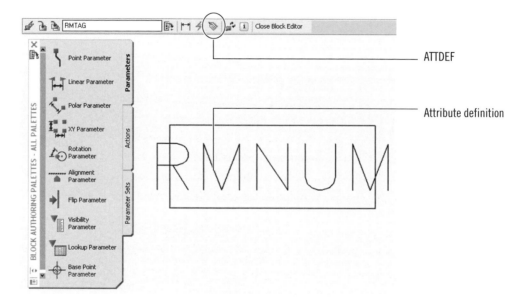

ATTDEF

Attribute definition

If you've defined several attributes in one block definition, the order in which the user of the block reference sees the attributes is important. Traditionally, savvy users have been aware that the order in which you select the attribute definitions when defining the block sets the prompt order in the block reference.

Changing the prompt order used to be nearly impossible because it required block redefinition and the consequent loss of attribute data stored in existing block references. This is no longer a problem—BATTMAN to the rescue! The block attribute manager (BATTMAN) can change the prompt order without breaking a sweat. Give it a whirl like this:

1. Execute BATTMAN (without killing him).

2. Select the block definition that has the disordered prompts from the Block drop-down list in the Block Attribute Manager dialog box. BATTMAN has global scope.

3. Click one of the attributes from this block, and click either the Move Up or Move Down button, as you prefer. Click OK. The prompt order is redefined.

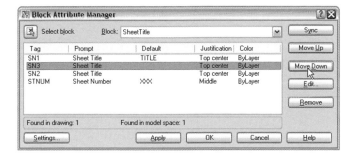

Do You Want to Be Prompted?

Sometimes, being prompted for attribute values can be annoying, especially when you want to accept the defaults. Other times, prompting is essential to enter data into blank attribute values. You can control whether you want to be prompted and how you want to be asked. Well, isn't that nice?

ATTREQ controls whether attribute values are requested. By default, ATTREQ is on (on is 1, off is 0). If you turn it off temporarily to insert a bunch of blocks whose attribute defaults you're willing to accept without prompting, remember to turn ATTREQ back on before you leave the drawing. Otherwise, there is a good chance the next designer—obviously less well informed than yourself—will be stymied as to why they aren't being prompted. And we don't want to stymie.

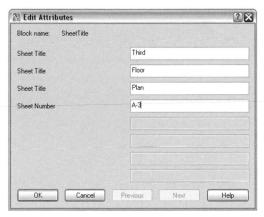

ATTDIA controls how you're asked when prompted for attribute values. If you're old school, you'll probably want to leave ATTDIA set to its default off position so you're prompted on the command line. More progressive folks, who prefer dialog boxes, set ATTDIA to 1. But you're prompted for attribute values in a dialog box only when you insert blocks with the INSERT command; dragging and dropping from the DesignCenter (or other drawings) doesn't count. It's funny that ATTDIA is off by default—old-school wins out.

Burst, but Do Not Explode

What happens when you explode an attributed block? It reverts to its definition, which means you're left with geometry and attribute definitions. The values stored in the attribute reference are irretrievably lost.

An explosion usually isn't what someone has in mind when they want to take an attributed block down a peg or two. BURST is a kinder, gentler way to pop an attributed block. There are no options to BURST, so it's as idiot proof as EXPLODE. The difference is that you're left with text containing the former attribute values, rather than empty attribute definitions. Oh, happy day.

See Invisible Attributes

We must come clean and disclose that invisible attributes need not remain hidden forever. You can bring them into the light of day with ATTDISP. Turning on ATTDISP makes all attributes visible, regardless of whether they're flying the invisible flag. This can help you visually spot inaccuracies quickly. Set ATTDISP back to Normal to return to the status quo—visible attributes are shown, and invisibles are hidden.

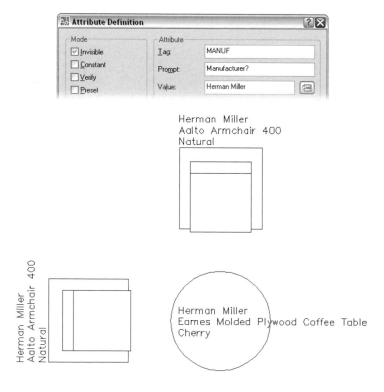

Setting ATTDISP to Off makes all attributes invisible. If you're in a rush with no time to input attributes, you may also find this setting useful. Later, you can restore the attributes' visibility and edit them to have the proper values. ATTMODE is an equivalent system variable with values of 0 (Off), 1 (Normal), and 2 (On).

Do Something with Invisible Attribute Data

We're willing to bet that there was a reason you created invisible attributes—other than deliberate obfuscation, that is. Use invisible attributes honorably whenever you want to carry a piece of data with a block, but you don't want to see it on the drawing. Eventually, you must realize that you have to do something with all those invisible attributes if they're ever to serve a higher purpose.

The "something" that all invisible attributes aspire to is to be *extracted*. Yes, ripped away and collated into a table, external spreadsheet, or database.

For example, let's say you went to the trouble of including an invisible COST attribute in all your equipment blocks. Use the Attribute Extract Wizard (EATTEXT command) to extract this data into an .XLS file which you can take into Excel. On page 4 of the Attribute Extraction wizard, you can specify to output to an external file (and you're given several filetypes to choose from). Open your extract file; you can easily tabulate what all that equipment will cost your client.

You can also use EATTEXT to extract attributes into a table in AutoCAD. See "Generate Tables from Attribute Data," later in this chapter.

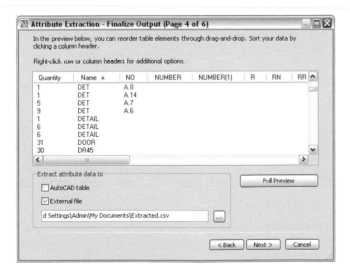

Attributes: Think Local

It's hard to keep all the attribute-editing commands straight in our minds, so we thought it would be valuable to give you a visual reference. First, let's consider the commands that have local scope—meaning they affect only one attribute at a time.

Editing Attribute Definitions Locally

DDEDIT is the command that edits attribute definitions. Remember, ATTDEF is the command used to create attribute definitions (but you already knew that). Of course, if you follow our previous recommendation and use Block Edit, you get to forgo the ATTDEF command altogether. By the way, DDEDIT is a hard-working command; in addition to editing attribute definitions, it can edit such disparate things as single-line text, dimension text, and feature control frames for geometric tolerances.

Editing Attribute Values Locally

Here you have two choices: the streamlined ATTEDIT or the fancy EATTEDIT. Use ATTEDIT when you want to get right down to business and edit attribute values only.

The Enhanced Attribute Editor allows you to edit attribute values—plus you can edit the definition's text formatting and layer properties. The cool thing is that you can edit these additional properties in real time, without having to go into the block editor and redefine the block. Anything you do with EATTEDIT affects the current block only (it's a local command). Double-clicking a block with attributes launches the EATTEDIT command by default.

> ATE is the default command alias for ATTEDIT. Make EAT the alias for EATTEDIT using the Express Tool ALIASEDIT. Ready for lunch?

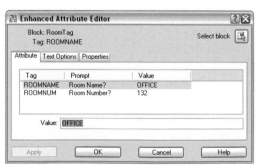

Attributes Go Global

If editing attributes one at a time seems too provincial for you, try these international editing commands with global scope. There are two such global commands: one for editing definitions en masse and one affecting values across the board.

Editing Attribute Definitions Globally

BATTMAN (Modify menu → Object → Attribute → Block Attribute Manager) works on all blocks in the drawing, so you have to start by selecting which block definition you want to edit from its drop-down list. As we already mentioned, BATTMAN can change the attribute prompt order (see "Define, Insert, and Burst Attributes").

In addition, BATTMAN can do another something EATTEDIT can't: It can change the mode of an attribute, such as setting its Invisible, Verify, and/or Preset flags. All of this is possible without having to explode and redefine blocks, so attribute values are preserved. Changes affect all blocks in a drawing by default (see "Synchronize the Old with the New (or Not)," later in this chapter).

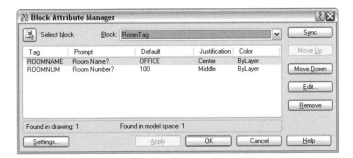

ATTREDEF is an obsolete command that redefines a block and updates its associated attributes. We caution you against using it. It will mess up changes you make with EATTEDIT, it deletes XDATA, and it may affect dynamic blocks, so watch out.

Editing Attribute Values Globally

The Express Tool GATTE (which, incidentally, isn't listed in the Express menu) is the global attribute editor; it affects values only, not definitions. This tool can come in handy if you need to change a bunch of attribute text all at once. For example, use GATTE if you need to change all the myriad room tags that currently display *Cubicle* to the new and more politically correct value of *Office*.

Unfortunately, GATTE still has a command-line interface. When you're selecting with GATTE, click directly on an existing attribute value within a block reference, and you'll be editing all such values in the drawing. Here's an example of how it works:

```
Command: GATTE

Select block or attribute [Block name]:

Block: RoomTag Attribute tag: ROOMNAME

Enter new text: Office

Number of inserts in drawing = 57 Process all of them?

  [Yes/No] <Yes>: Y

Please wait...

57 attributes changed.
```

Synchronize the Old with the New (or Not)

If you make changes with BATTMAN, they affect all attributed blocks by default—both existing and new. This amounts to an automatic synchronization happening throughout the drawing. But wait: What if you don't want to autosync? Is there a way to turn off this feature? In short: Yes.

When you're not synchronized, changes you make to existing block definitions don't have any bearing on existing block references. Come again? Changes you make with BATT-MAN affect only *new* blocks you insert. It's a bit dangerous to run with two different versions of the same block, but there it is—live dangerously.

> Synchronizing never affects the values assigned to attributes in the blocks, only their properties and formatting.

To turn off what we're calling autosync, click the Settings button in the Block Attribute Manager dialog box. Then, uncheck Apply Changes To Existing References. When this is unchecked, anything you do with BATTMAN affects new blocks only—existing blocks be damned.

If, on the other hand, you decide that maintaining two different versions of the same block is foolhardy, click the Sync button in the Block Attribute Manager. Sync updates all instances of the selected block with the attribute properties as currently defined—enough of this tomfoolery.

Playing in the Fields

The values appearing in fields are expected to change, whereas values in attributes remain more static over the lifecycle of a project. Visually, fields are just text displayed against a gray background.

If you want to hide the fact that some of your text objects contain fields, set FIELD-DISPLAY to 0. But this isn't a great idea, because the gray background doesn't plot and is helpful in identifying where the fields are. Therefore, we recommend strongly that you set FIELDDISPLAY to 1 if it's not already.

Fields work across sheet sets and are often used in the attribute values of callout tags (see Chapter 4 to learn more). To edit such a field, double-click the attributed block to open the Enhanced Attribute Editor. Notice that the attribute value is shown against a gray background—this identifies that the value is controlled by a field.

Double-click the attribute value to edit the field. See how nice this is? When in doubt, double-click, and you'll get to deeper editing levels. The Field dialog box appears whenever you edit a field. Use it to select which category, type, and format of field you want to use. Don't be scared by the field expression—it's not editable, and we're not sure why it's there. It just looks impressive in a geeky sort of way.

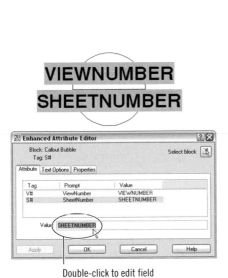

Double-click to edit field

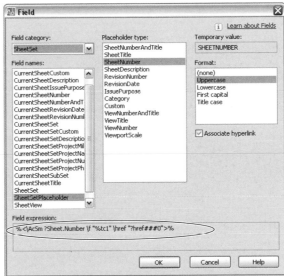

Display Area in a Field

One of the coolest things you can do with fields is display the area of a hatch pattern dynamically. If you ever change the boundaries of the hatch pattern, then the area stored in the field will automatically change.

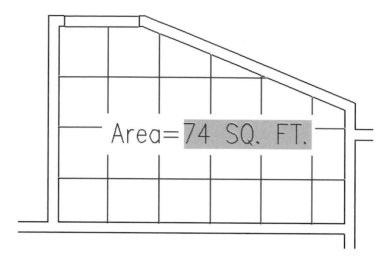

The slickest way to display the area of a hatch pattern is in a field placed inside a text object. One additional refinement we'll throw in is how to include a background mask that hides the surrounding hatch pattern, giving the text a little breathing room. Follow these steps:

1. Create an MTEXT object with zero width in the middle of the space you plan to fill with a hatch pattern. Make the text say **Area**=. This is only a prelude to adding the field.

2. Hatch the space by picking a point somewhere within its boundary. Make sure that Associative is checked in the Hatch And Gradient dialog box.

3. Go back and double-click the text object you made in step 1. Place the cursor after the equals sign in the in-place editor by pressing the End key. Press Ctrl+F to insert a field at this location within the text object.

> Use the FIELD command to insert a field that isn't part of any other object.

4. In the Field dialog box, select Objects from the Field Category drop-down list. Click Object in the Field Names list. Click the Select Object button, and click the hatch pattern you created in step 2. Select the Area property in the Field dialog, and select a format. Click OK to close the Field dialog box.

5. Select the field in the text editor, and right-click. Choose Background Mask from the shortcut menu. Check Use Background Mask in the Background Mask dialog box (incidentally, you can do this for any MTEXT object). Also check Use Drawing Background Color, and click OK. Finally, click outside the editing window to close the text editor. Whew; you're done!

6. Stretch the boundary you hatched in step 2. Unfortunately, the field doesn't update automatically. Use REGEN or UPDATEFIELD (if you get paid by the character) to show the new area value.

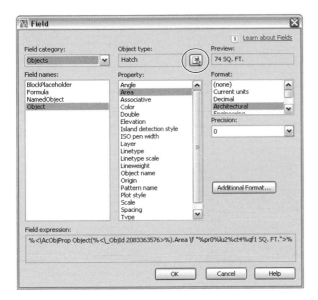

Convert any existing field to text by right-clicking the field and choosing this option from the shortcut menu. Fields converted to text lose their dynamic functionality, however.

Use Fields Inside Attributes

A smart way to use fields is inside the values of attribute definitions. When you insert a block whose attributes have field values, all kinds of important dynamic data can be displayed in a drawing. For example, we'll show you how to create such a block that shows the following information:

- Date and time of the last save
- Plot date
- File size

Last saved: 2/15/2006 6:17 PM
Last plotted: 7/1/2006 6:15 PM
Filesize: 70.63 KB

Fields inserted into attribute values should be used in preset attributes. That way, you won't ever be prompted to enter the attribute value when inserting the block reference—after all, you want the value to be preset by the field instead. Here we go:

1. Use the BEDIT command to open the Edit Block Definition dialog. Give the new block the name **Date-n-Size**.

2. Click the Define Attribute button. Check Preset in the Attribute Definition dialog box. Give the attribute definition the Tag Name **SAVEDATE**. Type **Save Date** as its Prompt, even though you'll never see it. For Value, type **Last saved:(space)**.

3. Click the Insert Field button. In the Field dialog box, select SaveDate from the Field Names list. Select an example format from the list, and click OK.

4. Repeat steps 2 and 3 twice more, adding PLOTDATE and FILESIZE attribute definitions with corresponding fields in the attribute values.

5. Draw a frame of linework around the attributes if you wish.

6. Close the block editor, and save changes.

7. Insert the Date-n-Size block, and enjoy. Save it in a block library and use it in all your drawings, or add it to your title block template.

> The BlockPlaceholder field can only be created within the block editor. See Chapter 5 to learn how this field can be used.

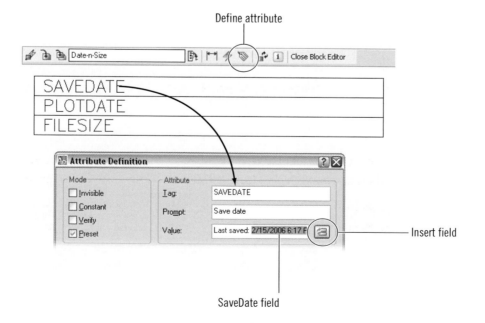

Hyperlink Text with Fields

Drawing callout bubbles are traditionally used to reference one drawing with another. Why not hyperlink text in callout bubbles? Doing so will make it that much more efficient for you to work with a set of drawings.

> The Sheet Set functionality in AutoCAD provides automatic hyperlinked callouts with the SheetSet-Placeholder field. Use the following procedure only if you don't plan to use sheet sets (see Chapter 4).

When you see a callout in a plan, Ctrl-clicking a hyperlink immediately opens the relevant detail drawing—and can even zoom right to the appropriate view. Here's how it's done:

1. Draw a callout bubble manually, or insert the bubble geometry as a block.

2. Add two MTEXT objects inside the bubble: one above for the drawing number (23 in this example) and one below for the sheet number (S# here). The sheet text will be overwritten by the hyperlink shortly.

3. While you're editing the sheet number text in place, highlight the text and press Ctrl+F.

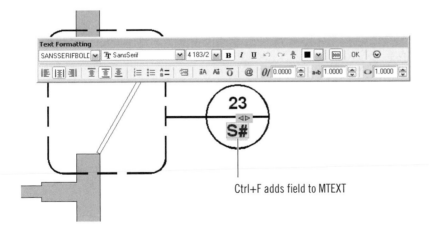

Ctrl+F adds field to MTEXT

4. In the Field dialog box, select Linked as the Field category. Select Hyperlink as the Field Name, and type the actual sheet number in the Text To Display box (A-03 in this example).

5. Click the Hyperlink button. In the Edit Hyperlink dialog box, select the Existing File Or Web Page button, and then click the File button. Browse for the drawing file you want to link.

6. Click the Target button if you want to select a named view from the hyperlinked drawing you want to zoom to when the hyperlink is followed. In this case, select view 23. Click OK in each dialog box to complete the procedure.

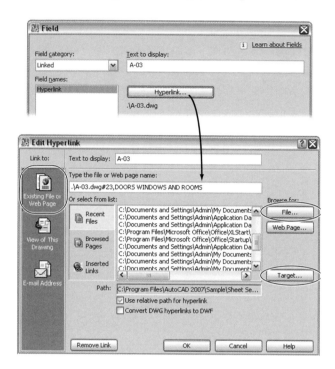

To follow the hyperlink, Ctrl-click the field text in the callout bubble. The linked drawing immediately opens and zooms to the referenced view—it's a beautiful thing. There is some overhead up front to hyperlinking with fields, but you'll save loads of time throughout the lifecycle of your project.

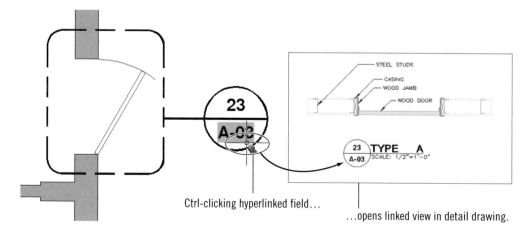

Ctrl-clicking hyperlinked field…

…opens linked view in detail drawing.

Tables

Tables are a godsend for all who need to list objects in their drawings. Not only is AutoCAD a drafting program and a 3D modeler, but it's become a full-featured calculator, database front-end, word processor, and now a spreadsheet too. What'll it be next—a web design program? We'll have to wait and see.

Import/Export Business Is Booming

For all the good that native table functionality brings to AutoCAD, it still doesn't quite stack up to Excel. Advanced Excel users may prefer to import and/or export tables to and from Excel for more sophisticated processing and formatting options.

Bring It In

Importing a table from Excel is easy, but you must know one piece of information to avoid the heinous Object Linking and Embedding (OLE) functionality that's built into Windows. OLE may sound good in concept, but in fact it has all manner of problems that are best avoided.

Instead of pasting a selection of cells copied from Excel into AutoCAD, choose Edit → Paste Special. This gives you the chance to avoid pasting the table as an OLE object—which happens if you paste with Ctrl+V. Instead, convert the copied cells into a native AutoCAD table, where you have the power to edit individual cells and control formatting in AutoCAD. In the Paste Special dialog box, choose to paste the contents of the clipboard as AutoCAD entities.

> Formulas are transferred into AutoCAD when you specially paste a spreadsheet as AutoCAD entities.

You can also perform basic arithmetic functions and input formulas in the table cells. Right-click, and select Insert Formula from the shortcut menu. Here, we can easily let Auto-CAD do the math for us and add up the square footage of the first and second floors.

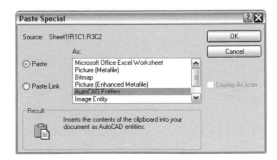

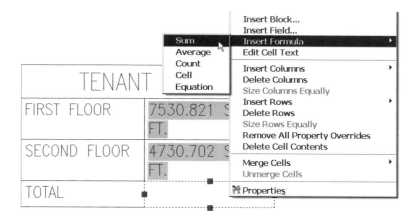

Push It Out

What good would the import/export business be if there wasn't a balance of trade? You can now export your AutoCAD tables directly to Excel, preserving their inherent table-ness. The top-secret command-line-driven command TABLEEXPORT does the trick!

TABLEEXPORT extracts your table to a .csv (Comma Separated Values) file. This .csv file can in turn be taken into Excel, Access, or any program that understands a bunch of data separated by zillions of commas. You can also get to this command by right-clicking your table and selecting Export from the shortcut menu.

Generate Tables from Attribute Data

Generating tables directly from attribute data is one of the best reasons to use attributes. EATTEXT is a wizard at extracting attribute data! Now there is an automated way to create a Bill of Materials and just about any schedule you want to design.

Using EATTEXT brings up an interface that you page through. Select the blocks, or extract the whole drawing. Page 3 allows you to rename tags with friendlier-sounding display names—tags are usually cryptic and in ALLCAPS, so this is nice. Display names become column labels in the extracted table. Page 4 gives you a preview of your table; right-clicking the headers lets you re-sort in ascending or descending order. You need to select a Table Style for your table; if you don't have one, the EATTEXT command even allows you to create one on the fly.

After you successfully extract attributes to a table, any subsequent changes you make to data stored in the referenced block attributes make the table out of date. Fortunately, a balloon will come out of the status bar tray and tell you what's up. Click the hyperlinked text in the balloon to refresh the table data. Right-click the table icon in the status bar tray to enable notification or to update tables manually.

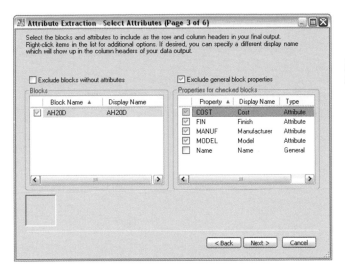

Furniture Schedule				
Quantity	Cost	Finish	Manufacturer	Model
2	$1250	Beech	Steelcase	4G5A
4	$1000	Cream	Herman Miller	123

You may be tempted to add rows or columns to an extracted table, and that's fine. Just be aware that any changes you make to an extracted table will be blown away, should you ever update the table. Additions to extracted tables are best done in the eleventh hour, after the data in the table is pretty well locked down.

Speaking of making an addition to an extracted table, consider adding a Symbol column that shows block icons. It's good to make a visual connection between the text in the table and the drawing geometry. To do so, select a cell in the table, and choose Insert Columns → Left (or Right) from the shortcut menu. Then, choose Insert Block from the same menu. Select a cell alignment in the Insert A Block In A Table Cell dialog box, and you've made a pleasant addition.

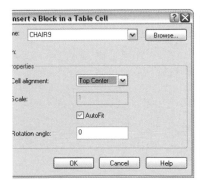

Layouts and Sheets

LAYOUTS ARE THE modern *paperspace*—a separate 2D space whose scale is based on the actual size of your paper output. You can have as many layouts (and thus "paperspaces") as you want in a drawing file. Think of layouts as sheets of paper—in fact, *layouts* and *sheets* are practically synonymous. AutoCAD has evolved from having one paperspace (years ago), to multiple paperspaces in the form of layouts, and then most recently to sheets in the Sheet Set Manager.

The original 3D space where your model resides—*modelspace*—has a scale matching the real-world size of whatever it is you're drawing. Viewports relate the scale of modelspace with what you see drawn to a 1:1 scale on a sheet.

The scale of what you're looking at through the viewport is adjustable, so you can be sure it will fit on any sheet you care to lay out. Sheets are further organized into sets, subsets, categories, and model views. We'll open this veritable can of worms later in this chapter, as we discuss the following topics.

4

This chapter's techniques are
organized into the following topics:

- Laying It Out
- Looking through the Viewport
- Lost in Space
- Nice Clean Sheets

Laying It Out

Formatting output all starts with laying out your drawing on virtual paper. Layouts typically include a title block and at least one viewport. In addition, every layout has a default *page setup*, which brings together the plot device driver, the paper size, the plot scale, the plot style table, and numerous plot options. This section has a few tips that make working with layouts less taxing and more rewarding.

Make Layouts the Easy Way

Use the LAYOUTWIZARD command, found under Tools → Wizards → Create layout, to make quick work of creating a layout, viewport, page setup, and title block, all in one go. The wizard interface takes you step by step through the process, so it can't be any easier.

This wizard offers an eight-step program to layout nirvana. Choose a name, a printer, the paper size, an orientation, a title block template, the viewport options and scale, and the location for the viewport within the title block, and you're done.

On the Title Block page of the wizard, you're presented with a list of templates. If you have a blank list, set your drawing template file location with OPTIONS, and then repeat LAYOUTWIZARD. Select a template, and notice that you have the option to insert the title block as a block or as an Xref in your new layout.

The folder where the title-block templates are stored is buried so deeply in the file system that you might never find it. This location is the only place the wizard looks, so assuming you're using AutoCAD 2007, place your custom title blocks in the following folder:

```
C:\Documents and Settings\Admin\Local Settings\Application Data\Autodesk\AutoCAD 2007\
R17.0\enu\Template
```

> You'll need to set up Windows Explorer to show hidden files and folders (or type in the whole path exactly) to access the obscure title-block templates folder.

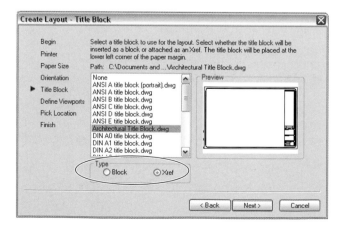

The Define Viewports page allows you to create a single viewport, standard 3D engineering views, or any array of viewports that you want. Notice that you have the option to set the viewport scale—this scale applies to all viewports that are created.

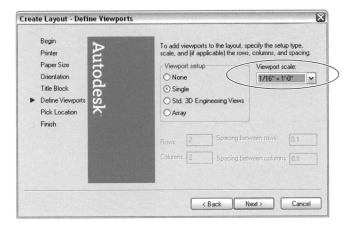

After you've completed the layout wizard, you may still need to enter some additional information into the default page setup—such as which plot-style table or color table to use. Unfortunately, the wizard isn't perfect, and it doesn't cover every possible setting. But it delivers quick results without too much fuss, so we can't complain.

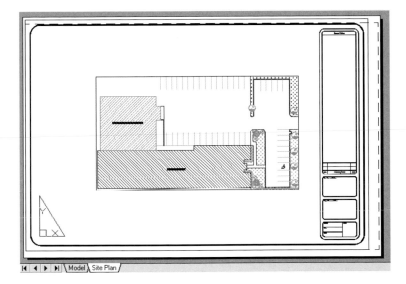

Name Your Page Setups

Every layout has a default page setup associated with it. Think of the page setup as the prepopulated contents of the Plot dialog box—it brings together all the relevant details necessary to create a successful plot.

Default page setup

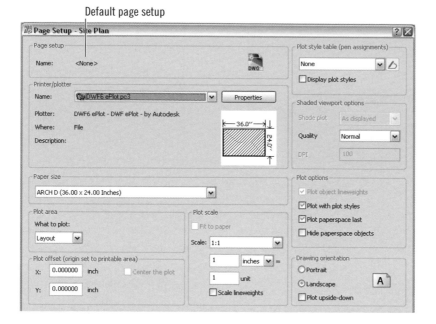

How many times do you enter data into the Page Setup and/or Plot dialog boxes? If you use default page setups, then you probably enter this stuff every time you create a layout, are we right? You're wasting your time—there is a better way.

Named page setups to the rescue! By naming a page setup, you can reuse it and thus save time. You can reuse a page setup multiple times in the same drawing, or reuse it in every drawing you create. If you do this right, you may avoid having to tediously enter data into a page setup ever again.

Think about it—a page setup brings together a plot device driver, a paper size, and lots of little details. Sit down and make a list of all the plot devices you use and all the paper sizes that ever spit out of these devices. The combinations you list are all the named page setups you need to make.

> You'll learn more about how to override page setups in the "Nice Clean Sheets" section, later in this chapter.

For example, let's say you have two plot devices—an HP Designjet and an HP LaserJet printer. Your firm seems to create only two sizes of output on the Designjet (Arch D and Arch E) and one on the LaserJet (Letter). So, you need to make three named page setups; we'll call them LittlePlot, BigPlot, and Letter. Here's how it works:

1. To make a named page setup, use the PAGESETUP command, which can also be found under File → Page Setup Manager.

2. Click the New button, and name this first example page setup LittlePlot. Click OK.

3. Enter all the relevant details in the Page Setup dialog box. In this case, choose the HP Designjet plotter and Arch D–sized paper. Set the plot scale to 1:1 for all layouts. Choose the monochrome plot-style table while you're at it, and click OK to close the Page Setup dialog.

4. When you return to the Page Setup Manager dialog box, you'll have a named page setup called LittlePlot. In addition, you still see the default page setup—it's the layout name surrounded by asterisks. But you're not done.

5. After all that work, you still need to set the named page setup as current. Select Little-Plot, and click Set Current. Close the Page Setup Manager. Now you're in business.

So far, you haven't seen any productivity gains from creating a named page setup. If this were the end of the story, making named page setups wouldn't be worth the trouble. But they are, and here's why—you'll never have to configure the named page setup again! Just assign it to any new layouts you create, using PAGESETUP. Or better yet, save it in a template, and then import it into existing drawings.

> Named page setups are like text, table, or dimension styles. Each stores detail that someone has gone to the trouble of researching and specifying. Make named page setups part of your standards.

Save your company's named page setups in a .dwg or .dwt file for safekeeping. Then, use the top-secret PSETUPIN command (not found in any menus) to import named page setups from this file into any current drawing. Hold down the Ctrl key to select multiple page setups in the Import Page Setups dialog box. Once named page setups have been imported, they still need to be assigned to layouts—do it with PAGESETUP, as usual.

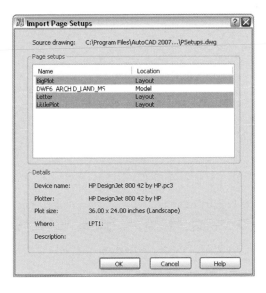

Named page setup
Default page setup

Set Layout Options

A number of layout options on the Display tab of the Options dialog box are worth review-ing. We like to hide the layout and model tabs, opting for the more streamlined new interface in AutoCAD 2007. The first option in the Layout Elements area offers you this choice.

Once your standards have been settled and you're using named page setups, seeing the dashed border on layouts that shows the printable area gets a bit stale. Uncheck Display Printable Area, and you'll be free of the dashed lines for good.

We like AutoCAD to show the Page Setup Manager for new layouts. This provides a good opportunity to set the appropriate named page setup as current.

If you don't like to have AutoCAD automatically create a viewport in every new layout, then uncheck the last option. When has AutoCAD ever automatically made a viewport to your liking anyway? Turn off this option, and you'll be the only one in charge of making viewports.

If you have multiple drawings and layout tabs that you'd like to convert from one page setup to another, you'll dread the tedious task of converting them one layout at a time. You can get around this by downloading the free software DWG TrueConvert from www

.autodesk.com/trueconvert. The goal of the software is to make it easy for you to batch-convert drawings from one release to another. A fringe benefit is that you can also use it to batch-convert layouts from one page setup to another. Give it a try!

Save and Reuse Layout Templates

LAYOUT is a command. This is news to many longtime AutoCAD pros. Not only are lay-outs the holders of little paperspaces, but LAYOUT is a command used to manipulate said layouts. In fact, you're using the LAYOUT command whenever you create a new layout, so you've used it before, even if you weren't aware of the fact.

Here we'll look at two powerful options of the LAYOUT command: SAveas and Tem-plate. These options may as well be known as layout export and layout import. You can save layouts—and anything that is in paperspace along with them—in templates for quick recall.

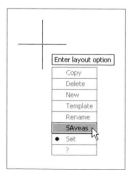

That means the layout, title block, north arrow, graphic scale, and other paperspace accoutrements go into layout templates.

Save a layout to a `.dwt` template file with the LAYOUT com-mand's SAveas option. Unfortunately, only one layout can be saved with this method.

The Create Drawing File dialog takes you immediately to the drawing template file location, which is deeply nested under Docu-ments And Settings—this is the same folder where you'll likely store your drawing templates. Save your layout template here, maybe with the word *Layout* in its title, so you can identify it later. For example, PlansLayout.dwt is a good layout template filename.

Open another drawing—new or existing—and import the layout template by using LAYOUT's Template option. This is also easily accessible from the Insert menu under Layout ➔ Layout from Template.

Select the template source, and then choose the Layout name(s) you want to import (hold down Ctrl to select more than one) from the Insert Layout(s) dialog box.

> You can't save more than one layout to a template file with LAYOUT's SAveas option. Instead, save as a .dwt file an existing drawing file that has all the layouts you want to be able to import later.

Looking through the Viewport

Layout viewports are portholes from paperspace into modelspace. Viewports are themselves drawn within the actual size of the paper they reside on, but viewports usually display real-world objects that must be massively scaled down to fit on the page. This section gives you a few tips for working with viewports.

Edit the Scale List

Do you use the metric system? Are you annoyed by all the Imperial scales you'll never use that show up in drop-down lists? Imperial unit users may be equally perturbed by metric scales like 10:1 that likewise appear in such lists. We recommend that you do something about it and streamline the scale list to suit your practice. You can also add oddball scales to the list, should the need arise—ever need to plot in $^5/_8''=1'-0''$ scale? You'll need to add that one.

SCALELISTEDIT does the trick. Delete all the scales you never have occasion to use. Doing so will simplify your AutoCAD life whenever you need to plot, create a page setup, or scale a viewport—in other words, all the time.

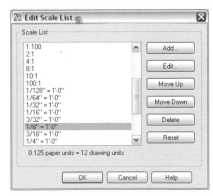

Adding or editing scales requires that you know exactly how many paper units correlate with just how many drawing units to produce the desired graphic scale. You're on your own in figuring out this potential brain twister!

Cycle through Viewports

If you ever have a viewport embedded within another viewport, you can get into a potential catch-22 situation. That is, unless you know how to cycle between viewports.

The top-secret key combination of Ctrl+R makes it easy to cycle through all your viewports until you get to the correct one. This combination used to be Ctrl+V, but we all know that's now assigned to Paste in Windows.

Consider making nonrectangular viewports so you can avoid overlapping them. This is easily done by drawing a polyline and then using MVIEW's Object option.

> When layout and model tabs are displayed, you can cycle through layout tabs by pressing Ctrl+PgUp (forward) or Ctrl+PgDn (backward). This doesn't work when the tabs are hidden—but you don't need it then anyway.

Create an Enlarged Viewport Bubble

The enlarged viewport bubble is a cool graphic effect that shows both context and detail simultaneously. You need two nested viewports to achieve this effect—one rectangular and one circular. The trick is, the objects in the rectangular viewport must not appear within the overlapping circular viewport.

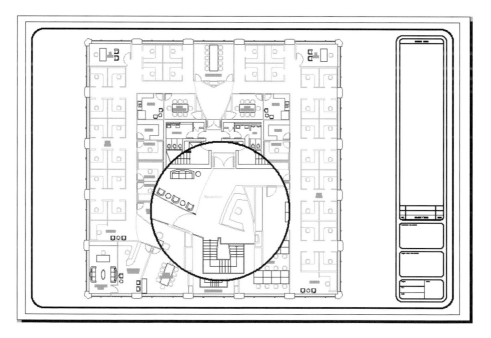

You can achieve this sophisticated effect only by creating viewports from objects, and even then the objects must be quite special. To see how it's done, follow along:

1. Create two layers to hold the viewports. Ultimately, one layer will remain on, showing the circular viewport, and the other will be turned off to hide the rectangular viewport frame. For now, create two layers called ViewportA and ViewportB, and leave them both on.

2. Create a layout, and add a title block. Draw a rectangular polyline to represent the outer viewport.

3. Draw a circle somewhere inside the rectangle you drew in the previous step. This is destined to become the enlarged bubble.

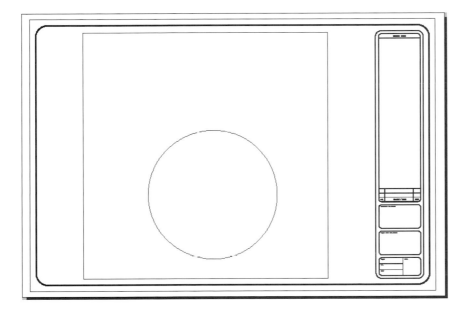

4. Duplicate the circle in place. Now you have two overlapping circles.

5. Use the REGION command, and pick the rectangle and only one of the circles.

6. SUBTRACT the smaller region from the larger by selecting the rectangular region first, pressing Enter, and then selecting the circular region. You're left with one region and one circle.

7. Convert the region into a viewport by using MVIEW's Object option. Put this viewport on layer ViewportA, and then turn it off. If you've done it right, the drawing will show up in the rectangular area but won't appear within the circle. So far so good.

8. Set layer ViewportB current so that the next viewport will be on this layer. Convert the remaining circle into a viewport. Pan and zoom as necessary to create an enlarged plan within the bubble. Voila!

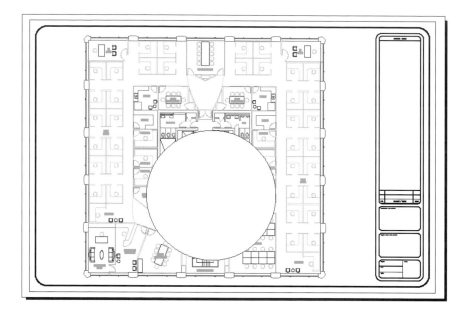

> Use PEDIT to widen two semicircular arcs that duplicate the shape of the circular viewport (because you can't convert a circle to a polyline). This effect looks better by emphasizing the enlarged viewport bubble.

Create Viewports for Viewing Solid Objects

The little-known SOLVIEW command can be used to automatically generate viewports using orthographic projection. Ortho—what was that? These are viewports at 90 degrees to what you're looking at—like top, back, left, right, and auxiliary views.

SOLVIEW is most useful to engineers who are working on solid parts. Use it to quickly lay out multiview drawings that showcase the part in question.

> SOLVIEW has a companion command called SOLDRAW that generates sections in viewports made with SOLVIEW.

Probably SOLVIEW's best option is Ortho—it creates a folded orthographic view from an existing view. Check it out:

1. Create a single viewport on a layout. Resize it so it takes up roughly one quarter of the available space. Move it to the lower-left corner of the layout.

2. Double-click inside the viewport to activate floating modelspace.

3. Issue the SOLVIEW command (Draw → Modeling → Setup → View). The following is a command-line transcript of the action sequence:

```
Command: -solview

Enter an option [Ucs/Ortho/Auxiliary/Section]: Ortho

Specify side of viewport to project:

(click right edge of existing viewport)

Specify view center: (click point off to right side)

Specify view center <specify viewport>: (Enter)

Specify first corner of viewport: (pick)

Specify opposite corner of viewport: (pick)

Enter view name: Right

Enter an option [Ucs/Ortho/Auxiliary/Section]: (Enter)
```

4. Repeat the previous step to make a viewport along the top edge of the original viewport. Call this third viewport Top.

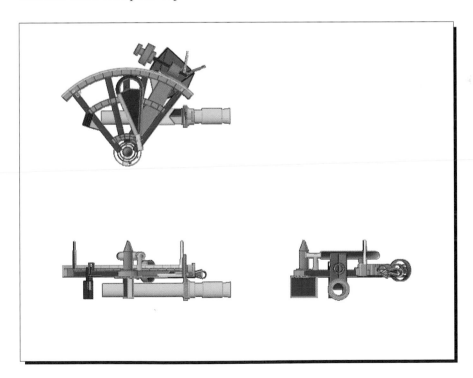

◼ Lost in Space

Do you ever get lost in AutoCAD space? Are you zoomed in to the floating modelspace within the paperspace of a layout? Or are you in the maximized modelspace of a layout viewport? Maybe you're just in plain old modelspace. Who knows? Here are a few tips that should help keep your head from spinning.

Change Space without Breaking a Sweat

Do you use trans-spatial dimensions or want to? Dimensioning in paperspace has become more fashionable lately, now that dimensions placed in paperspace can be associated with objects in modelspace. On the other hand, maybe you're completely against putting anything in paperspace save for a title block and viewports. CHSPACE works for both philosophies.

It's great to be able to move objects from modelspace to paperspace and vice versa without having to worry about scaling factors. CHSPACE changes the space of objects while perfectly maintaining their visual appearance and location.

This happens under the hood, so all you have to do is select the objects and the viewport. Best of all, no math is required—CHSPACE figures out just how much objects have to be scaled and moved. Here's what it looks like on the command line:

```
Command: CHSPACE

Select objects: (select them)

Set the SOURCE viewport active and press ENTER to continue:

14 object(s) changed from MODEL space to PAPER space.

Objects were scaled by a factor of 191.999999983437

to maintain visual appearance.
```

> CHSPACE isn't allowed from the model tab (also known as tiled modelspace). Instead, you must use CHSPACE on layouts, where you can select a viewport.

The drawing appears exactly the same as it did before using CHSPACE, but the object is in the opposite space. CHSPACE also works on dimensions beautifully, so they maintain the same appearance in either space—you don't have to fuss with DIMSCALE.

Work Safely in a Layout Viewport

The scale of what appears in a layout viewport is controlled by its zoom factor. This fact is both good and bad. On the good side, it's easy to choose a zoom factor by selecting a scale from the drop-down list on the Viewports toolbar. On the bad side, it's far too easy to zoom in to or out of an active viewport while working and thereby mess up its scale on the layout.

Perhaps the designers of this zoom-factor-viewport system thought you would always switch to the model tab (tiled modelspace) while working and never have the audacity to work on your model in a layout. They didn't anticipate people's sheer laziness about switching tabs while working—a force to be reckoned with. Plus, they didn't anticipate how often people draw in paperspace, right on top of a viewport—trans-spatial dimensions are a case in point (see the previous tip).

We're left with a couple of options for working safely in a layout viewport. As you probably know, you can toggle between paperspace and modelspace by double clicking. Double-click inside a viewport to switch to floating modelspace, or double-click outside the viewport to switch back to the layout's paperspace.

In order to ensure that you don't inadvertently zoom in a viewport whose scale has already been set, you can lock the viewport. Then, zooming in an active viewport zooms the layout, preserving the viewport's precious zoom factor. Here's how to lock a viewport:

1. Double-click somewhere outside the viewport on the layout to switch into paperspace.

2. Turn on the layer on which the viewport object resides. Select the viewport frame.

3. Right-click, and choose Display Locked → Yes from the shortcut menu. Alternatively, you can find this property under the Miscellaneous category in the Properties palette.

4. Double-click in the viewport to activate it. Zoom, and notice that the layout zooms together with the viewport—they are locked together.

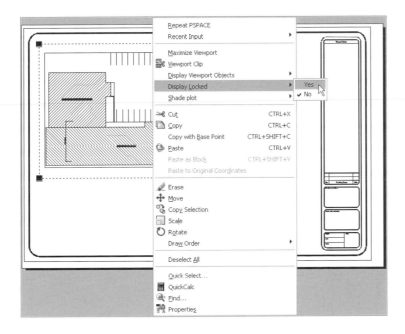

> If you selected a nonrectangular viewport, click the drop-down in the Properties palette and change it from All (2) to Viewport (1). Then, select the Display locked property, and change it to Yes.

The only liability to locking viewports is that not everyone knows it's possible. Uninformed users will be stuck, should they encounter a locked viewport that they need to unlock and adjust.

An alternative to viewport locking is to use the Maximize/Minimize Viewport toggle on the status bar. When a viewport is maximized, it fills the screen, giving you the maximum editing room. A maximized viewport has a zigzagging red border that lets you know you're working in the maximized state.

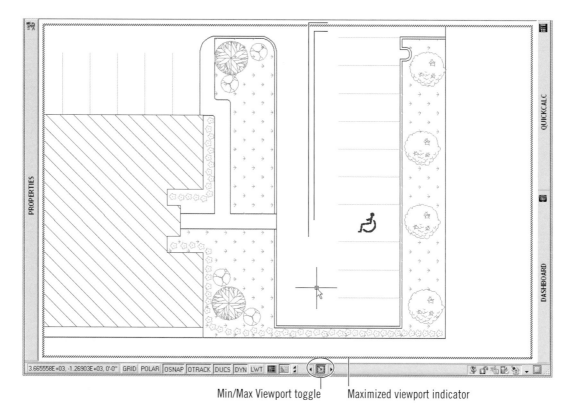

Min/Max Viewport toggle   Maximized viewport indicator

You can pan and zoom safely in a maximized viewport. When you're done working on the model, minimize the viewport to return to the layout.

> The Min/Max Viewport toggle has arrow buttons on either side that switch to previous and next viewports in the active layout.

Scale Linetypes in Paperspace

Have you ever found yourself in this common predicament? You get all your linework set up properly in model space, all the linetypes are scaled properly, and then you switch over to a paperspace layout. You insert your first viewport, assign a viewport scale factor, and then poof—your linetypes don't display properly anymore. Why not?

Understanding a little background will help immensely. Three system variables govern linetype scaling. First and foremost is LTSCALE, as you're doubtless aware. LTSCALE is what you set in modelspace—it's the global linetype scale factor. Set global linetype scale to match your drawing scale, and dash lengths should be approximately correct.

Next up is CELTSCALE (Current Entity LineType Scale), which sets the linetype scale for individual objects. Use CELTSCALE to override the global linetype scale—best used just for a particular entity or two. CELTSCALE is multiplied by LTSCALE to arrive at the displayed linetype scale.

> CELTSCALE is set to 1 by default—where it has no effect. Values between 0 and 1 decrease and values above 1 increase effective linetype scale.

When you enter paperspace, PSLTSCALE takes over controlling linetype scaling. If set to 0, PSLTSCALE has no effect, and dash lengths are based on CELTSCALE × LTSCALE, exactly as they are in modelspace. You may suppose this is copasetic, but it's not. Paperspace drawing units are massively scaled down compared to modelspace—that's why you can't see linetypes when switching over to a paperspace layout.

Setting PSLTSCALE to 1 causes the linetype display to translate over to paperspace drawing units. Even if you have different viewports, with different magnifications, linetypes display the same. AutoCAD does the math for you (thank heavens). It takes the value of the viewport scale factor and paperspace drawing units into consideration, and then scales the linetypes according to the LTSCALE × CELTSCALE settings for proper display in paperspace.

> Set PLINEGEN to 1 to have linetypes propagate continuously across 2D polylines, not necessarily generating dashes at each vertex. Doing so instructs AutoCAD to treat the polyline as one continuous object instead of multiple segments as far as linetypes are concerned.

Nice Clean Sheets

There's nothing like nice clean sheets. Even so, not everyone has fully integrated sheets into their AutoCAD practice. Sheets and sheet sets are optional in AutoCAD—you can get just as involved with them as you want.

Many people who have started to work with sheets use them to plot, publish, archive, and eTransmit entire sets of drawings but have yet to embrace their full potential. Others are seeing huge productivity gains through full implementation of Sheet Set functionality.

When fully embraced, sheet sets are the glue that holds together a drawing set. They provide automatic coordination between drawing names and numbers, with callout tags, view labels, smart title blocks, and more. Callouts can be automatically hyperlinked, providing you with an additional efficient means of electronically navigating through a sheet set. This section offers numerous tips and tricks for working with sheet sets.

Sheet-Set-Speak

To get the most out of sheet sets, you'll have to learn Mandarin. Just kidding—but you will have to absorb a lot of sheet-set jargon to understand what's going on and how sheet sets work.

The Sheet Set Manager (SSM) is the one-stop shop for working with sheet sets. Don't be afraid to mess up your drawings when experimenting with the SSM, because it saves changes in its own XML-based .dst file. The only way your drawing files will be altered is by the addition of a *hint*, which is a piece of invisible data that identifies which sheet set the drawings belong to—definitely nothing to worry about.

> SSM opens the Sheet Set Manager.

Sheets are layouts by another name. A drawing file may have multiple layouts and thus have multiple potential sheets that can be imported into the SSM. Think of a sheet as a piece of paper. Even though it may never appear on paper if you publish to DWF, physical analogies are always helpful.

The *Sheet List* tab is the first tab in the SSM. It does what it advertises—lists sheets in the current set in any order you want to arrange them in. You can add *subsets* to further organize sheets within the sheet list and provide a structure for different sheet-creation templates.

Sheet Views is the next tab in the SSM; it was formerly called the View List tab, pre–AutoCAD 2007.

Sheet List

Sheet views is another term for *layout views*, also known as *named views* in paperspace. Sheet views are used to manage drawing names and numbers. They can be organized with *categories*, each a potential repository of callout blocks that can be inserted into sheet views.

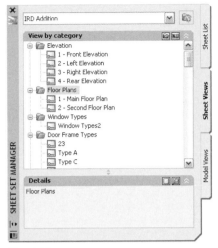

Sheet Views   Model Views

A *callout block* is a traditional bubble symbol with the drawing name and number, which calls out elevations, sections, and details referenced by the symbol. When callout blocks are defined with attributed field codes, they tie into the sheet-set system, and their values are filled in automatically.

A *label block* typically identifies a drawing name, number, and scale. Like callout blocks, when label blocks are defined with attributed field codes, their values are filled in automatically.

Model Views is the last tab in the SSM. (It was called Resource Drawings in previous versions of AutoCAD.) Use this tab to access modelspace drawings with or without named views.

If you feel overwhelmed, don't fret—using the SSM is a lot easier than it may sound. Refer back to this tip when you're confused by terminology and need to review sheet-set jargon.

Callout block

Label block

Import Sheets from Layouts or Create New Sheets?

To jumpstart working with sheets, you can import layouts from existing drawings as sheets in the SSM. Right-click an item in the sheet list, and choose Import Layouts As Sheets from the shortcut menu.

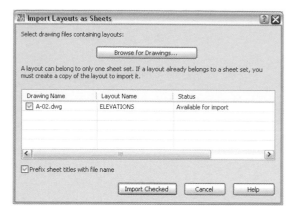

After the sheet appears in the Sheet List tab, drag and drop it into its proper location in the SSM. Use Rename & Renumber if necessary—it's also on the shortcut menu.

After you get used to sheet sets, you'll want to create new sheets directly in the SSM rather than by importing existing layouts. To create sheets efficiently, you can tell the SSM which sheet-creation template to use for new sheets.

> Use the NewSheetSet wizard to create a new sheet set. The command is NEWSHEETSET.

You can access sheet-set properties by right-clicking the top node in the Sheet List—this corresponds to the sheet set itself. Choose Properties from the shortcut menu to open the Sheet Set Properties dialog box.

Scroll down the sheet-set property list until you locate the Sheet creation template property. Click this property's more button (…), and you'll be prompted to select a template file. After you browse for a .dwt file, select which layout within that file you want to use as the official sheet-creation template—your entire sheet set can have only one. See the next tip for additional suggestions regarding the sheet-creation template.

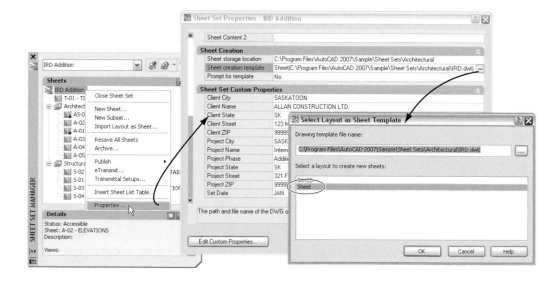

Now, you're set to create new sheets on the fly within the SSM. Just right click in the Sheet List, and choose New Sheet. After giving the new sheet a number and title, you're ready to go—and best of all, the new sheet is preregistered with the SSM.

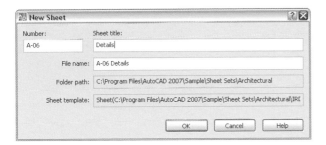

Design a Title Block with Fields as a Sheet-Creation Template

We mentioned in the previous tip that you can have only one sheet-creation template for the whole sheet set. You have to pack a lot into it, because the sheet-creation template is your opportunity to start things off right. If you plan to use sheet sets to their fullest potential, we recommend that you put the title block into the sheet-creation template.

> Put standard layers, styles, and settings in the sheet-creation template, just like any other `.dwt` file.

However, this isn't your father's title block. It's a brand-spanking-new title block that uses attribute definitions whose defaults are filled with place-holding fields that get automatic values from the SSM whenever a new sheet is created. It's pretty slick, but it takes quite a bit of setup to pull off successfully. We'll take you through the entire process by designing a sample title block.

Before we dive into designing the title block, you may want to start by creating a few custom properties that will ultimately appear on the title block. Custom properties are accessible in the SSM through the magic of fields.

1. Right-click the sheet set node in the SSM, and choose Properties from the shortcut menu.

2. At the bottom of the Sheet Set Properties dialog box, click the Edit Custom Properties button.

3. Click the Add button in the Custom Properties dialog box.

4. Give the custom property the name Drawn_By and the default value ABC. Custom properties can belong either to a particular sheet or to the sheet set. In this case, you want to indicate who drew each sheet, so choose the Sheet radio button, and click OK.

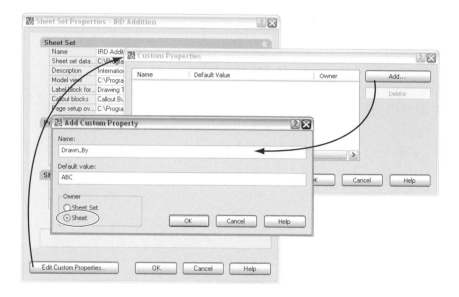

5. Continue adding the following custom properties:

Custom Property	Default Value	Ownership
Checked_By	ABC	Sheet
Sheet_Set_Date	20 Sept 2006	Sheet Set
Project_Name	My Project	Sheet Set
Client_Name	My Client	Sheet Set

Underscores are good to use with custom properties because they identify the properties as custom. Built-in properties use TitleCase (without spaces).

Now you're ready to create the title block from scratch. In order to test out the sheet-set fields you'll eventually make, it's essential to create a new sheet within the SSM so the fields will say something meaningful when you're testing. Here we go:

1. Right-click an item in the Sheet List tab of the SSM, and choose New Sheet from the shortcut menu. In the New Sheet dialog box, use a dummy number and title such as A-99 and Test Title Block.

2. Switch to a layout, and adjust its default page setup to match your intended plot device and paper size. Switch to paperspace if necessary.

3. Draw title block geometry that is positioned exactly how you want it on the layout. Add your company logo and any static text.

4. Select what you've drawn so far, and issue the BMAKE command. Give this new block the name Title. Check Open in block editor, and click OK in the Block Definition dialog box. The block-editing environment appears (you can tell by the yellow background).

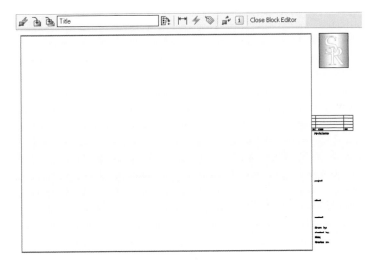

5. You'll add attribute definitions wherever you want to have dynamic text. For now, create attributes without fields in their defaults. For example, click the Define Attribute button in the block editor toolbar, and create an attribute with tag PROJECT and prompt Project. Check Preset, because you want to avoid ever being prompted to fill in a value—that's the field's job. Click a point on the screen to locate the attribute definition.

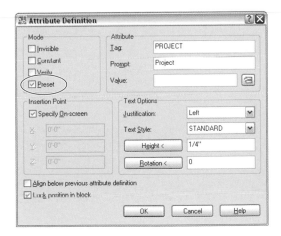

6. Create the following attribute definitions, all in preset mode with blank values:

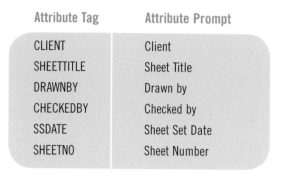

Attribute Tag	Attribute Prompt
CLIENT	Client
SHEETTITLE	Sheet Title
DRAWNBY	Drawn by
CHECKEDBY	Checked by
SSDATE	Sheet Set Date
SHEETNO	Sheet Number

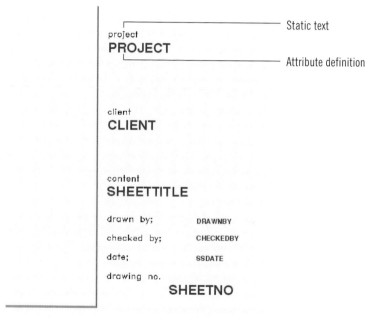

At this point, the title block is set up as a block with attribute definitions. Taking it a step further, you'll add fields to the attribute definition defaults. Let's keep on trucking:

1. Double-click the PROJECT attribute to edit its definition.

> Don't add fields to attribute values. *Values* are shown only in attributed block references, whereas *defaults* are shown in attribute definitions.

2. Click the cursor in the Default text area, and then press Ctrl+F to open the Field dialog box.

3. Choose the SheetSet field category, and select SheetSet as the field name. Select the Project_Name custom property from the Property list—you created this earlier. Click OK. In the Edit Attribute Definition dialog box, notice that the attribute default is filled in with the field's default value now—My Project. What you see in the attribute is now controlled by a custom sheet-set property.

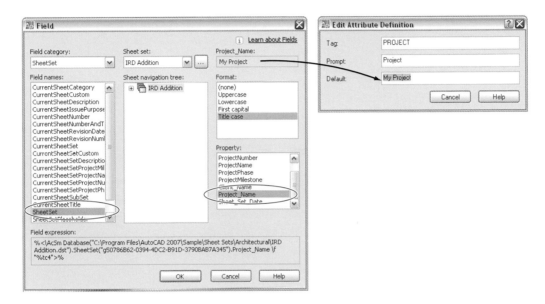

4. Continue repeating the last three steps until you've added the following fields to their corresponding attribute defaults:

Attribute Tag	Field
CLIENT	Client_Name
SHEETTITLE	SheetTitle
DRAWNBY	Drawn_By
CHECKEDBY	Checked_By
SSDATE	Sheet_Set_Date
SHEETNO	SheetNumber

Custom properties owned by sheets (Drawn_By and Checked_By) are accessed by selecting a specific sheet in the Sheet navigation tree within the Field dialog box.

5. Close the block editor, and save changes. Don't panic because the title block doesn't immediately display field values—delete the existing title block, and then reinsert it. The new block reference shows correct field values in its attributes.

Remember that you've been working on a test sheet—this is to work out any bugs. When you're ready, you can create (or overwrite) the sheet creation template:

1. You don't need the test sheet to stay in the sheet set. Right-click the current sheet in the SSM, and choose Remove Sheet from the shortcut menu. Click OK in the confirmation dialog box.

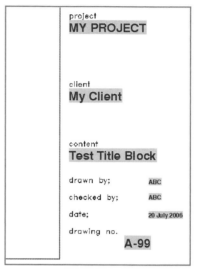

2. Choose File → Save As. Change the Files Of Type drop-down to AutoCAD Drawing Template (*.dwt). Overwrite your sheet-creation template if you already have one. Otherwise, save the .dwt file in your project folder. Optionally, enter a description in the Template Description dialog box, and click OK.

3. Right-click the sheet set in the SSM, and choose Properties in the shortcut menu. Verify that the sheet-creation template is the template file you saved in the last step. If it isn't, make it so. Confirm changes if asked.

4. Create a new sheet in the SSM, double-click it in the Sheet List, and then bask in the glory of seeing your custom title block appear automatically, filled in with the relevant data.

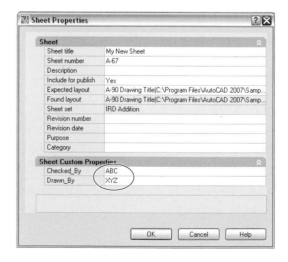

5. Right-click the new sheet in the SSM, and edit its properties. Any custom properties owned by the sheet are editable here. Go ahead and put in the initials of whoever drew and/or checked this sheet. Congratulations; you're done!

Dynamic Blocks

DYNAMIC BLOCKS ARE one of the most exciting things to happen to AutoCAD in a long time. If you haven't authored any dynamic blocks yet, let this chapter give you a kick start. Once you get going with dynamic blocks, you'll never look back—they're so useful you'll probably want to rethink your entire block library. If you have tons of similar blocks in your library, you'll be able to consolidate them into just a few powerful dynamic blocks that do it all. This makes finding things in a dynamic block library easy.

More than just static collections of objects, dynamic blocks can do all kinds of things because they have intelligence built in. Dynamic blocks can move, scale, rotate, stretch, rotate, and stretch at the same time, array, and yes, even flip, all with custom grips. In short, dynamic blocks can be programmed to do exactly what you need them to. Authoring dynamic blocks is like programming by drawing, but without any coding—that's a beautiful thing.

5

This chapter is organized into the following topics:

- Block Basics
- Way Off Base
- Playing with Parameters
- Associating Actions

Block Basics

Just like with a building, you must start with a strong foundation before getting carried away with the architecture. Dynamic blocks are based on regular, static, boring blocks. This section offers you some tips and tricks that should make working with static blocks more interesting and more rewarding.

Absolutely No Explosions Allowed

One of the age-old problems with blocks is you can go to all the trouble of designing, defining, and inserting blocks only to have some bozo (or respected colleague) explode them in a fit of drafting ignorance. The whole point of blocks is to control the many with the few—which is the essence of power, come to think of it.

The myriad block references you see in a drawing reference block definitions that are stored in the drawing's invisible block table—the place where block definitions are stored in every drawing. You gain control by being able to redefine a block stored in the block table, because the changes you make are propagated throughout the drawing to all its block references. However, when blocks are exploded, their constituent geometry loses its block-ness and becomes just some more geometry in the drawing—so you lose control. This is bad.

The good news is, you can prohibit blocks from being exploded. In theory, this protection lasts forever, but it's reversible once you know the trick. At least it stops the bozos from indiscriminate destruction.

There are two places where you can expressly deny permission to explode a block. The first is in the BMAKE command's Block Definition dialog. Uncheck Allow Exploding in the Settings area when you define a new block.

But what can you do to prohibit exploding a block once it exists? The answer is found in the block editor. Use BEDIT, and select a block definition to bring it into the block editor environment. Then, without selecting anything or using any commands, open the Properties palette. Set Allow Exploding to No in the Block area of the Properties palette.

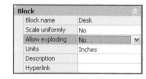

Now, when a respected colleague tries to explode one of your inflammable blocks, this is all they'll see on the command line:

```
Command: EXPLODE

Select objects: 1 found (Enter)

1 could not be exploded.
```

This will stop them unless they have the insider knowledge you've just acquired. You can always change the property in the block editor to allow exploding, should you desire that ability at a later date.

Be a Smart Bomber

We know there are times when you must explode blocks. It's always harder to create than destroy, so we hope you have a good reason for exploding a block. When you do, it pays to be a smart bomber. Instead of using EXPLODE, try XPLODE. The latter command has many options that make your job easier, whereas the indiscriminate EXPLODE has no options at all.

You know the whole trip about creating objects in blocks on layer 0 with object properties set to ByLayer, right? Anything on layer 0 in a block definition inherits properties from the current layer when in a block reference. Object properties set to ByLayer or ByBlock have inheritance issues, too.

EXPLODE blows away a block and leaves you with the original geometry from its block definition—geometry that is probably on layer 0. Not too useful, is it? Chances are good that you want the source geometry to be on the layer the block reference was on prior to explosion. If that's true, you have to Undo, select the block, *remember* what layer the reference is on, explode it again, and then change the resulting geometry to the layer that (we hope) you still remember.

XPLODE is much easier because it doesn't ask you to remember any layer names. Use XPLODE's Inherit From Parent Block option, and the block's last will and testament is dealt with; the exploded geometry inherits what is coming to it automatically. In other words, you probably won't be left with anything on layer 0 (unless the reference itself was on layer 0).

Here's what XPLODE looks like on the command line (XP is its default alias):

```
Command: XP

Select objects to XPlode.

Select objects: Specify opposite corner: 1 found (Enter)

1 object found.

Enter an option

[All/Color/LAyer/LType/LWeight/

Inherit from parent block/Explode] <Explode>: I

Object exploded.
```

The other options allow you to explicitly assign object properties to the exploded geometry. If you select more than one block, you're prompted as to whether you'd like the changes to globally change all the selected blocks, or you'd like to specify them individually. Remember to type **XP** instead of **X** to properly defrock a block.

XPLODE's Inherit From Parent Block option only works if the block definition geometry was drawn on layer 0 and its object properties were set to ByLayer or ByBlock—the most common practice.

Local Blocks Go Global and Back Again

Blocks that are defined in a drawing are considered *local* to that drawing. If you use WBLOCK to write local blocks to files, the blocks gain global scope because files can be inserted into other drawings as blocks, right? So far so good, but many people are confused about the implications. This is serious stuff; let's figure it out, or you'll never really understand blocks.

To best unravel the problem, a thought experiment is in order. Say you create Block A in Drawing 1. Block A is *local* to Drawing 1. At some point, you decide to WBLOCK Block A out of Drawing 1 into its own drawing file, which is naturally called Block A.dwg. You can say Block A.dwg is a *global* block because it's a drawing file. Are you with us so far?

Then, someone (maybe your CAD manager) revises Block A.dwg. They change it and make it better, faster, stronger than it was before—maybe they make it a dynamic block!

Later, an unsuspecting person uses the DesignCenter or the Tool Palettes to access the global Block A.dwg. They drag and drop Block A into Drawing 1, where it already exists as a local block. What happens?

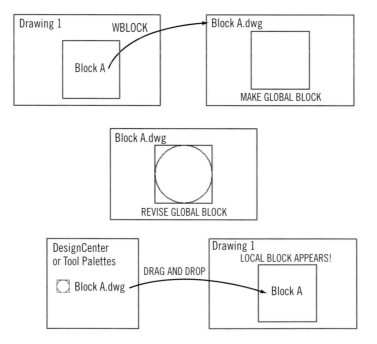

You may expect the local block to be redefined by the global block, but that doesn't happen. Instead, another instance of the original Block A appears. This happens because Block A is already defined in Drawing 1's block table. Ah ha! There's the rub.

If you want a global block to redefine a local block of the same name, you must use the INSERT command. Not only that, you must click the Browse button in the Insert dialog box to access the global block. Choosing blocks from the dialog box's drop-down list inserts local blocks only.

If you browse for a global block and click OK in the Insert dialog box, you see a small dialog box asking you if you really want to update the local definition. Click Yes, and global becomes the new local.

Local blocks   Global blocks

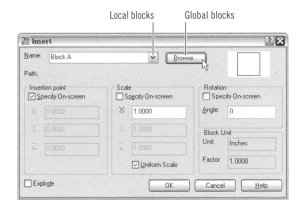

Nest Blocks in the Block Editor

It's easy to create a block and edit it in the block editor, but it may not be clear to you how you go about nesting blocks in the block editor. We have a couple of tricks up our sleeves that will help you quickly define blocks within dynamic blocks.

Before you can nest blocks, you need the block(s) you want to nest defined in the drawing's block table. We're talking block definitions here, not block references. If you want to insert a block definition without any reference, here's how it's done:

1. Use the INSERT command.

2. Click the Browse button in the Insert dialog box, and locate the global block drawing file you're interested in nesting. In this example, insert a Chair block.

3. Click OK in the Insert dialog, and then immediately press Esc. It seems as though you're canceling the command—but believe us when we say the block table has been updated. The global block you selected in the previous step is now a local block definition in the current drawing.

4. Repeat these steps for each block you wish to nest in a dynamic block container.

5. The next task is to draw the geometry that goes in the dynamic block definition. Continuing with this example, draw a simple desk with a set of drawers on one side.

6. Select the geometry you drew in the previous step, type BMAKE, and press Enter. Give this new block the name **Desk** in the Block Definition dialog box. Click the Pick Point button, and select a base point along the upper edge of the desk. Choose the Convert To Block radio button, and check Open In Block Editor.

7. Click OK to close the Block Definition dialog box. The geometry appears in the block editor (with its distinctive yellow background).

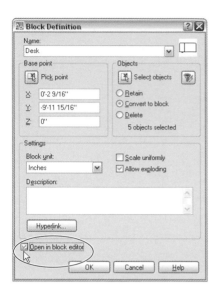

8. Use INSERT, and select the Chair block from the drop-down list in the Insert dialog box. Place the chair next to the desk. Rotate the chair if necessary, and reposition it in relation to the desk. The Chair block is now nested within the dynamic Desk block.

9. Continue adding parameters and actions if you want. Close the block editor, and the nested definitions are complete.

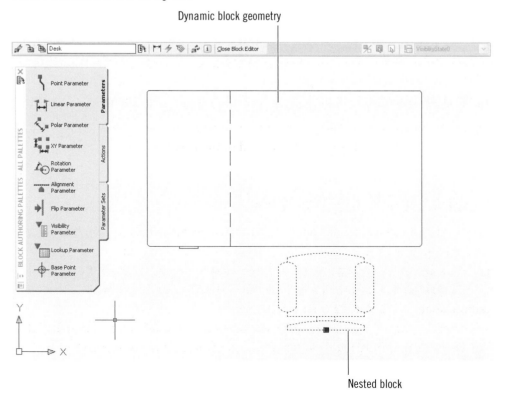

Dynamic block geometry

Nested block

Although you can nest dynamic blocks within other dynamic blocks, only the outer containing block's custom grips will function.

Assign Properties Prior to Insertion

Dynamic blocks usually have custom grips and custom properties—that's what makes them dynamic, after all. Normally, dynamic blocks are manipulated via their custom grips after they've been inserted into a drawing.

Although there is nothing wrong with this method of interaction, it's even more efficient to configure a dynamic block's custom properties before the block reference is inserted into a drawing. That way, you know exactly what you're getting, and you don't have to reposition the block reference after insertion due to geometry changes—it's located perfectly from the beginning. Give it a try:

1. Press Ctrl+1 to open the Properties palette, if it's not already open.

2. Use INSERT, and select a dynamic block. You'll know the dynamic blocks by the lightning bolt symbol that appears in the block preview icon.

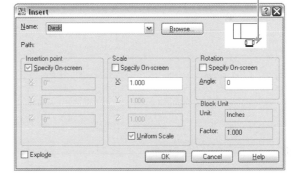

Dynamic block symbol

3. Click OK, but hold off on choosing an insertion point. Unhide the Properties palette if necessary, and edit any of the custom properties. These properties control the dynamic block.

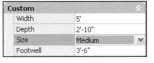

4. Choose an insertion point and/or rotation if the respective Specify On-Screen check boxes were checked in the Insert dialog.

Hey AutoCAD, Don't Scale My Blocks!

Since AutoCAD 2006, a feature has been included that automatically scales blocks when you insert them—and it does so without asking. The nerve! The idea is that AutoCAD matches the scale of the blocks you're inserting to the insertion scale you've set for the drawing. The problem is, if you never set the block scale or the insertion scale—or you don't know what we're talking about—who knows what will happen?

Each drawing not only has units (such as Architectural, Decimal, Fractional, and others), but also has an *insertion scale*, which can be another kind of unit such as Inches,

Centimeters, Angstroms, Hectometers, Light Years (no joke), and many others. You set the insertion scale through the UNITS command from a drop-down in the Drawing Units dialog box.

Blocks also have a kind of unit called the *block unit* that you can set when you create a block. The block unit is set from a drop-down list in the Block Definition dialog box that belongs to BMAKE.

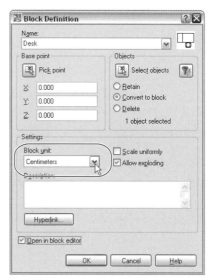

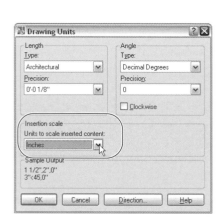

When you insert a block, AutoCAD compares its block unit with the insertion scale of the drawing and comes up with a factor that matches the scale of the block to the drawing. You can see what scaling factor AutoCAD is using in the Insert dialog box—but you can't change it there.

If you don't want big brother controlling your scaling options, set INSUNITS to 0 (alternatively, use UNITS, and set its Insertion Scale drop-down list to Unitless), and AutoCAD won't scale any blocks that you insert into that drawing. It will be entirely up to you to do the scaling (if any) you deem necessary. Power to the people!

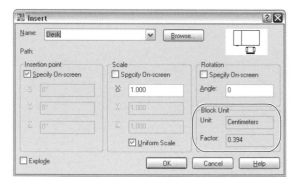

Another feature that affects scale is controlled in the Options dialog box. Use OPTIONS, and choose the User Preferences tab. The Insertion Scale area has two drop-downs that tell AutoCAD what to do when Insertion Scale is set to Unitless (INSUNITS=0).

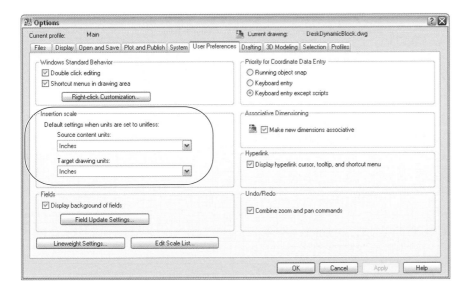

When Source Content Units and Target Drawing Units match, and Insertion Scale is unitless, AutoCAD doesn't scale inserted blocks (default). On the other hand, if you want AutoCAD to scale every block you insert, adjust the two drop-downs in the Options dialog to suit your situation—these settings affect all drawings.

Avoid Nonuniform Scale at All Costs

OK, maybe not at all costs, but nonuniform scale is bad. *Nonuniform scaling* means your block has a different scale in X, Y, or Z. This allows stretching to occur; but in a way, it's cheating.

If you want a block to stretch in some direction, why not build that functionality into a dynamic block? You'll be better off in the long run.

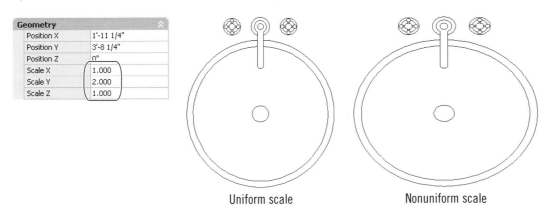

Uniform scale   Nonuniform scale

If you do take the path of least resistance and nonuniformly scale a block to stretch it, be aware that doing so also kills dynamic block functionality in that block. In other words, none of a dynamic block's custom grips appear if it's nonuniformly scaled.

Resetting X, Y, and Z scale factors to equal values restores dynamic block functionality. Even if your block isn't dynamic, why take away that possibility for future generations? It's wiser to leave the door open.

If you really want to be a stickler, you can proactively prevent nonuniform scaling in the blocks you create. Just check Scale Uniformly in the Block Definition dialog box. When these blocks are inserted as references, only their Scale X property is editable—Scale in Y and Z automatically match whatever values are put into the Scale X property.

Try Auxiliary Scale

Auxiliary scale is an optional method for automating block scaling. The idea for auxiliary scale is simple: You insert blocks from a tool palette, and they miraculously appear in the drawing at the correct size, no matter what graphic scale you're working in. Auxiliary scale takes care of it for you by basing its scale factor on either the plot scale or the dimension scale.

Setting up tools to take advantage of auxiliary scale takes some thought. We'll use a real-world example to think through auxiliary scale. Assume you're an architect using Imperial units. You want to place an exit-sign symbol (part of a building's life safety system) in a drawing that will be plotted in $1/8''=1'-0''$ scale. (By the way, this scale shrinks the real world by a factor of 96.) Follow these steps:

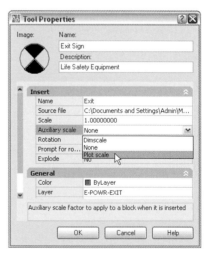

1. Right-click the Exit Sign tool in the Tool Palettes. Choose Properties from the shortcut menu. The Tool Properties dialog box appears.

2. The Auxiliary Scale property has three possible values: None, Dimscale, and Plot Scale. Choose Plot Scale, and click OK.

3. Use PAGESETUP, and modify the current page setup. Choose a plotter driver if one hasn't been selected already, and select $^1/_8˝=1´–0˝$ scale from the drop-down list in the Plot Scale area.

4. Use BEDIT, and select the exit sign symbol to enter the block editor environment. Scale the symbol up so that it measures 96 feet across. You read that right: Make it huge! Close the block editor and save the block.

5. Click the Exit Sign tool, and place the symbol. It appears in the drawing at exactly 1 foot across—go ahead and measure it with DIST. Auxiliary scale multiplied the plot scale of $^1/_{96}$ times the size of the block definition of 96 feet to arrive at one foot.

Auxiliary scale gets its intelligence from either the plot scale or the dimension scale (the dimscale system variable). Plot scale and dimscale are usually reciprocals. So, blocks inserted with an auxiliary scale based on dimscale must be small (just an $^1/_8˝$ in our example). They're scaled up by the dimscale, just as the block in the previous example is scaled down by the plot scale. Pick one (plot scale or dimscale) and go with it, if you plan to design blocks that use auxiliary scale.

Count Those Blocks

Have you ever wanted to tally up how many blocks are in your drawings? The little-known BCOUNT is an Express Tool that acts like a poor man's attribute extractor, but without all the hassle of attributes. True, it's a primitive way of building a bill of materials, but counting blocks will do in a pinch. Now if only your blocks had descriptive names…

This Express Tool can't afford to be in the Express menu; it's only available at the command line. Here's what its output looks like:

```
Command:  BCOUNT

Press Enter to select all or...

Select objects:

Block...................Count

-----------------------------

CHAIR...................38

SPRINKLER...............137

BASEFEED................20

STROBE..................16

EXIT....................16
```

Way Off Base

Every block has a *base point*—the point where a block is attached to your cursor when you insert it into a drawing. You're asked to pick a base point when you create a block, but it's by no means carved in stone.

Have you ever inserted a block and not seen where it appeared on screen? Even if you saw the block, was it attached to your cursor in suboptimal fashion? If so, help is on it way. This section will help you insert blocks right on target.

Set the Entire Drawing's Insertion Base

Every drawing file has a base point. Usually it's 0,0 in the current user coordinate system, but it doesn't have to be. You can adjust the base point location via the aptly named BASE command. BASE is a really old command—maybe it's one that slipped under your radar.

Use BASE (found in the menu under Draw → Block → Base) to select a new insertion base point for the entire drawing. The base point is used as the insertion point when you insert or Xref the entire current drawing into another drawing. A nonorigin base point can potentially be saved in each drawing file.

> BASE is important only when you plan to insert an entire drawing as a block or attach it as an Xref.

Another way of changing the effective base point is to move all the geometry in a drawing relative to its origin point. This approach works—but it can be a recipe for disaster. If we're talking about drawings that are meant to stack one on top of another (like floors in a building, for example), upsetting the relationship between geometry and the origin point can cause alignment problems between drawings further down the line.

Using the BASE command is the better method because with it, you can temporarily alter the base point without upsetting the geometry–origin point relationship. Use BASE again to set the insertion point back to 0,0,0 if you want the original relationship restored.

Insert Blocks with Temporary Base Points

Have you ever wished you could have more than one insertion point for a block? Or, have you taken this one step further and created separate blocks with different insertion points? Yikes! If so, you'll love this new feature that has been sneaked into AutoCAD 2006.

When you go into the INSERT command, you see a new Basepoint option on the command line. That's right: Look at the command line *after* you close the Insert dialog box—there are options available. Here's what the command line looks like:

```
Command: INSERT

Specify insertion point or [Basepoint/Scale/X/Y/Z/Rotate]: b

Specify base point: (click point)
```

The Basepoint option allows you to select a temporary base point while you're in the act of inserting the block. There's less need to redefine a block's base point when you can choose a temporary base point on the fly.

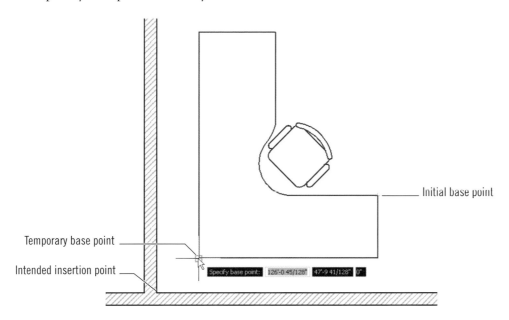

Initial base point

Temporary base point

Intended insertion point

Specify base point: 126'-0 45/128"   47'-9 41/128"   0"

If you use the Basepoint option and still aren't happy, continue to key in **b** until you get it right. The only downside to this technique is you can't use numbers to locate the temporary base point (like "50 cm to the right," for example). However, you can snap the temporary base point to any point on the incoming block or even to other geometry in the drawing, so all isn't lost.

Hide the Insertion Point Grip

Have you ever noticed that dynamic blocks can have any number of custom grips controlling their dynamic behavior, but they also come with one old-fashioned insertion-point grip by default? This blue grip also appears on nondynamic blocks. If you're not one to mix metaphors, you may appreciate this trick, so read on.

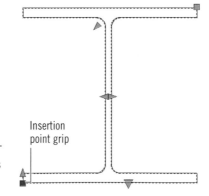

Insertion point grip

Normally, a block's base point is defined when you create the block with BMAKE. The position of the base point is shown in the dynamic block authoring environment by the placement of the UCS icon. (By the way, the UCS command is disabled while you use BEDIT, so you can't move the base point by altering the UCS.)

A dynamic block may have only one Base Point parameter. The optional Base Point parameter can't have actions associated with it. If you add a Base Point parameter, its location determines the base point of the dynamic block, superseding whatever base point was initially defined with the static block. The UCS icon disappears from the authoring environment when you add a Base Point parameter.

Here's the trick: If you want to hide the blue grip in a dynamic block, add a Base Point parameter, and put the Base Point parameter on top of a custom grip. The coincident custom grip hides the blue grip in the block reference—DRAWORDER isn't an issue.

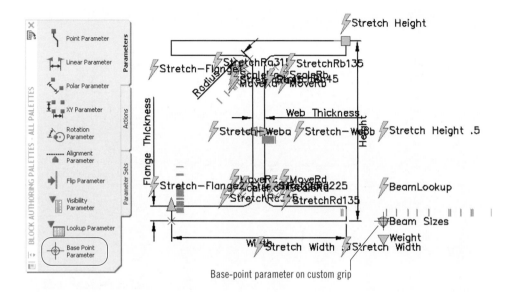

Base-point parameter on custom grip

> If you want the insertion-point grip to stay hidden under a custom grip that moves, you have to include the Base Point parameter in the action selection set responsible for the custom grip's motion.

Cycle Multiple Insertion Points

Wouldn't it be cool if you could build multiple insertion points into a dynamic block? The good news is that you can (thankfully) without having to create multiple blocks. Even though a dynamic block may have only one Base Point parameter, believe it or not, the block can still act as if it had multiple insertion points.

The secret is the fact that every custom grip has the ability to act like an insertion point. Each parameter has a miscellaneous property called Cycling. When Cycling is set to Yes, that grip has the potential to act like an insertion point.

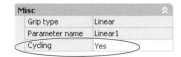

We say "act" because the block has only one true base point; but pressing the Ctrl key while inserting a dynamic block cycles through each custom grip that's preset to cycle, making each one the insertion point in turn.

Don't hold the Ctrl key while inserting a dynamic block. Press and release it repeatedly to cycle through its insertion points.

After you set a few parameters' Cycle property to Yes in the block editor, either select a grip, right-click and choose Insertion Cycling from the shortcut menu, or use BCYCLEORDER to open the Insertion Cycling Order dialog box. This is where you control the order in which grips appear as insertion points.

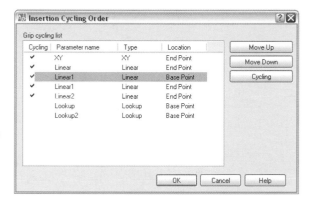

The first item in the list is the insertion point the first time Ctrl is pressed. The next time Ctrl is pressed, the second parameter in the list acts as the block's insertion point, and so on. Use the Move Up and Move Down buttons to alter the cycling order. Click the Cycling button to toggle the Cycling property in the selected parameters. Parameters that are set to cycle are shown with a blue checkmark.

Play with Parameters

Parameters are like interactive dimensions that drive dynamic blocks. They're only part of the overall picture; parameters define custom properties and grips that drive the actions that do the dirty work. We'll play with parameters in this section and see what fabulous tips come of it.

Seven Secrets of Symmetric Stretching

Maybe there aren't seven secrets, but at least alliteration has got your attention! We swear there are at least three secrets of symmetric stretching that we'll now share with you.

Select a parameter grip in the block editor and open the Properties palette. First up: Linear parameters can have 0, 1, or 2 grips. You can't symmetrically stretch without having exactly two grips. Second, linear parameters have two options for Base Location: Startpoint and Midpoint. Choose

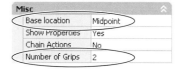

Midpoint: The base point must be in the middle to make stretching equal on both sides.

Finally, both of the linear parameter's grips need a Move or Stretch action associated with them. The linear parameter stretches out equally on both sides when you click either one of its grips, *even though different actions are associated with each of its grips.*

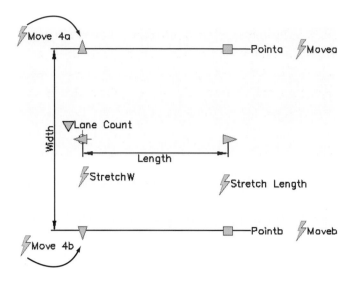

If you have all three ingredients, then your linear parameter stretches out equally on both sides when you click either of its grips. This is the perfect tip for building roadways. Clicking a width grip makes the road wider symmetrically about its midpoint.

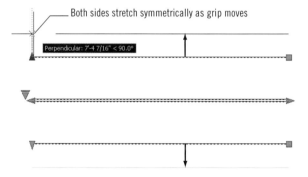

Align Your Blocks

Although it may not occur to you to include one when designing a dynamic block, the Alignment parameter is incredibly useful and deserves your consideration. The Alignment parameter makes it easy to quickly align your blocks with existing geometry (much easier than trying to figure out a rotation angle manually). An Alignment parameter needs no action associated with it—its functionality is contained within the parameter.

When you're in the BEDIT command's authoring environment, add an Alignment parameter to a dynamic block. You can do so either by clicking the Alignment Parameter tool on the Block Authoring Palettes or by using BPARAMETER and choosing its Alignment option.

Either way, you have to specify a base point (usually best along one edge of the geometry) and an alignment direction (following the edge direction). In the example of a water closet—isn't that a nicer way of saying *toilet?*—you may want to place the Alignment parameter a short distance behind the water tank to offset the fixture from the wall. After you specify the Alignment parameter's base point, click a point off to one side using Polar mode so the alignment line is horizontal. The alignment line should line up with the back edge of the water tank.

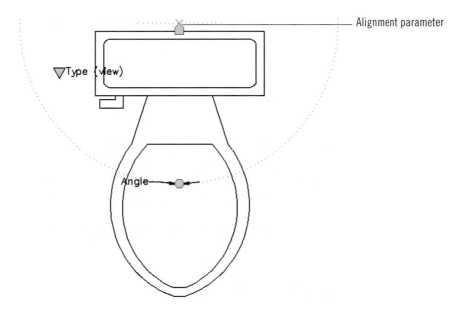

Click the Base Point Parameter tool, and place the Base Point directly on top of the Alignment parameter grip. The Alignment parameter works only if it's coincident with the block's base point—that's a rule. Save and close the dynamic block, and test your new Alignment parameter. Click the alignment grip in the dynamic block reference, and hover the mouse over a wall surface. The water closet moves and rotates automatically to face away from the wall—isn't that fantastic? Move and rotate in one step using the alignment grip.

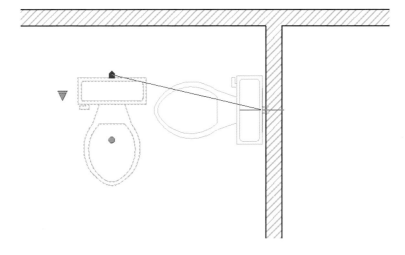

Hide Set Marks for Small Increments

Some types of parameters accept lists or increments that limit their possible values to a set of valid entries. It's smart to use a *value set* in a dynamic block when the values represent a product that is only manufactured in a discrete number of sizes. That way, people aren't able to insert a block that can't be manufactured.

> Value sets are only available for Linear, Polar, XY, and Rotation parameters.

Select a parameter, and look at its Value Set group in the Properties palette. You can change Dist Type to None, Increment, or List.

Set marks can become distracting when there are too many possibilities, something that happens most often with the increment type. If the value set marks become more annoying than they're worth, turn them off.

The BTMARKDISPLAY system variable controls the set-mark display. Set it to 0, and you won't see any more set marks. Unfortunately, this setting affects all dynamic blocks in all drawings. Perhaps in the future we'll have block-specific set-mark display control; that would be better.

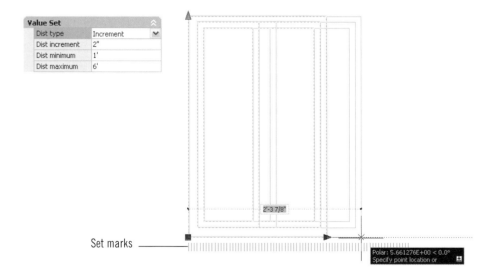

Set marks

Control Object Visibility

The ability to make objects visible and invisible in dynamic blocks is fantastic. This is what allows you to have many blocks in one. To get started with object visibility, add a Visibility parameter in the authoring environment.

Then, you need at least two visibility states. Use BVSTATE to create and manage visibility states.

As you insert blocks into the authoring environment or draw geometry from scratch, the blocks are automatically assigned to the current visibility state—the one that appears in the drop-down list at upper right in the block authoring environment.

Needless to say, you probably won't get all the objects on the correct visibility state from the get go. Select objects, and right-click to access the Object Visibility shortcut submenu. The submenu includes these options:

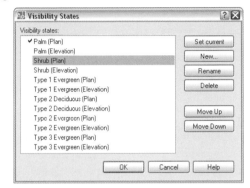

- Hide For Current State

- Show For Current State

- Hide For All States

- Show For All States

Another way to control object visibility is to use BVSHOW. This command shows objects either in the current state or in all states at once. It can be a timesaver especially when you want new geometry (just added to the dynamic block) to be visible in every state. Here's what BVSHOW looks like on the command line:

```
Command: BVSHOW

Select objects to make visible:

Select objects: 88 found

Make visible for current state or

all visibility states [Current/All]<Current>: A
```

Current visibility state

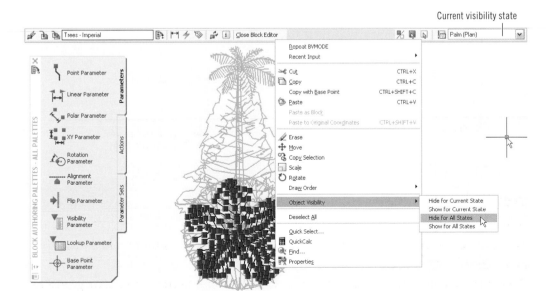

To test your state assignments, set different visibility states current using the drop-down menu at upper right in the authoring environment. If everything looks copasetic, cool— you're nearly done.

You still have to choose which visibility state is the default. This is the state that initially appears when someone inserts the dynamic block. Use BVSTATE to open the Visibility States dialog box; the default state is at the top. Move states up and down if you need to shuffle things around. The order in which states appear in the dialog box is the order they're displayed on the visibility grip in the block reference.

Lose Your Grip

Do you ever feel like you're losing your grip on reality because dynamic blocks are so darn complicated? One way to simplify is to turn off grips that are unused or otherwise unwanted.

Select a parameter with grips you can stand to lose. In the Misc group in the Properties palette, decrement the Number Of Grips if possible. If the wrong grip disappears, it's not your day; you'll have to delete the parameter and create it again. This time, click the startpoint and endpoint in reverse order.

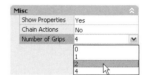

> Command-line aficionados (or those automating the process) may prefer to use BGRIPSET to change the number of grips.

Attributes can have grips that show up in dynamic blocks. These grips allow someone to move the attribute reference in relation to the dynamic block geometry. If you don't think that's a good idea, or if you want attributes to be included in an action-select set, lock them. Locked attributes don't display grips.

> Only locked attributes are affected by dynamic block actions.

You can lock attribute definitions as you create them in the Attribute Definition dialog box, opened with ATTDEF. Check Lock Position In Block at the bottom of the dialog, and the attribute won't get a grip. There is also a Lock Position property that you can edit after an attribute definition has been created.

Associate Actions

Actions make what parameters are asking for actually happen. They're the engineers of dynamic blocks. Actions have to be associated with parameters to get the job done (whether they like it or not). This section leverages lots of action items for dynamic blocks.

Action Selection Tips

When you create an action, you're asked to select which parameter it's associated with and then to select which objects the action will affect. After an action has been created—or if it was created by someone else—you can find out what the action does by selecting the action icon in the authoring environment. Its associated parameter and affected object(s) highlight, telling the story of what the action does. If it's a stretch action, its selection frame also highlights, revealing a crossing window with two blue grips at opposite corners.

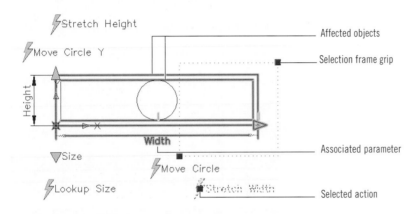

If not everything in the action highlights as you expect, you can easily take corrective action. Here's what to do:

1. Select an action, and carefully observe what highlights.

2. If it's a stretch action, use the blue grips to adjust the selection frame. The action stretches any objects crossed by the selection frame.

3. Double-click the action icon—you know, the one with the lightning bolt.

4. Press Esc to avoid reselecting the selection frame (you already adjusted it with grips). The command line says

   ```
   Select object to add to action set or [Remove]:
   ```

   Click any additional objects that you want the selected action to affect. If you select too many, type **R** and press Enter, and then remove objects from the selection set. Press Enter, and you're done.

Base-Point Independence

The base points of rotate and scale actions are usually dependent on the placement of their parameters' base points. It doesn't have to be this way—you can liberate the action's base point from its parameter's base point. But why would you want to do this?

Occasionally, you'll come across a situation where you want to rotate or scale a dynamic block in an unusual way. To illustrate, we've drawn a Side Table dynamic block that has a round table surface resting on an off-center swiveling post.

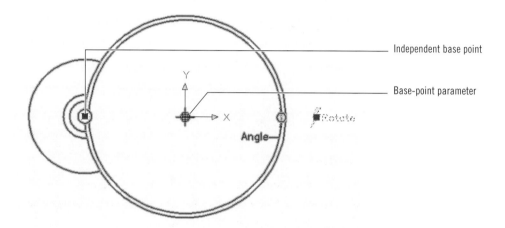

We've created a Rotation parameter whose base point is at the center of the table surface (large circle). Complicating matters is the unrelated Base Point parameter, which is located in this same position; it determines the base point for the entire dynamic block. Here's how you can liberate the action's base point from its parameter:

1. Select the Rotation action.

2. Set the Base Type property to Independent in the Properties palette. A new grip appears at the center of the rotation parameter.

3. Move the new grip to the center of the satellite circle. This is the independent base point about which the dynamic block will rotate.

4. Close and save the dynamic block. Test it: The block rotates around the satellite circle, which is the table's support post in this example.

Adding the Base Point parameter to the rotation action's selection set allows the base point to rotate with the dynamic block.

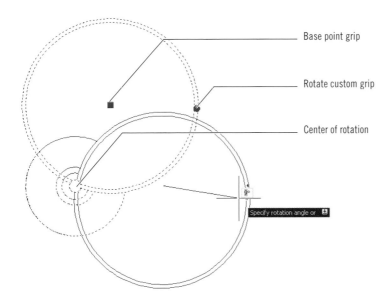

Base point grip

Rotate custom grip

Center of rotation

Specify rotation angle or

One Parameter, Multiple Actions

Kill two birds with one stone by using one parameter to drive two (or more) actions. To illustrate this idea, we've created a simple desk block. It has a set of drawers on one side and a task chair. If you'd like to follow along, draw this yourself. Here we go:

1. Bring the block into the authoring environment (with BEDIT).

2. Add a single Linear parameter called Width. Give it one grip on the side of the desk you want to stretch (away from the drawers).

3. Add a Stretch action, and associate it with the Width parameter. Include the desk rectangle in the Stretch action-selection set. Rename this action StretchDesk.

4. Add a Move action, and associate it with the Width parameter. Select the chair only for this action's selection set. Rename this action MoveChair.

5. Select the MoveChair action, and set its Distance Multiplier property to 0.5. The chair will move half as much as the desk stretches.

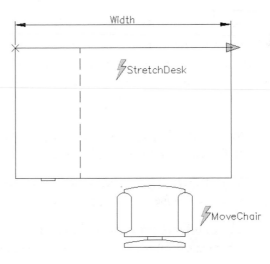

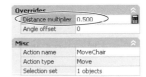

Overrides	
Distance multiplier	0.500
Angle offset	0

Misc	
Action name	MoveChair
Action type	Move
Selection set	1 objects

6. Close and save the dynamic block. Test it by clicking its linear custom grip. The desk stretches, and the chair stays centered in the footwell. Hurray!

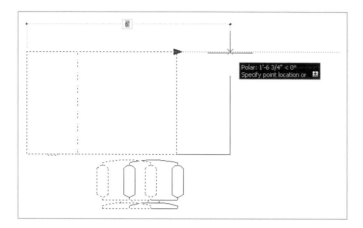

Turn the Tables

Lookup tables are icing on the dynamic block cake. They're the tastiest part of the dessert and can be applied only after the dynamic block has been baked. Don't attempt to take on this recipe until you have a good handle on dynamic blocks. The best way to understand lookup tables is to build one, so let's get cooking:

1. Draw a rectangle, and call it a desk. You can adorn it with accoutrements if you want, such as drawers, a phone, a computer, or whatever. Save it as a block, and enter the authoring environment.

2. Add Width and Depth Linear parameters and corresponding Stretch actions. Test the dynamic block to make sure it's working, and return to the authoring environment.

3. Select the Depth parameter, and change its Dist Type property to List. Click the More button next to the Dist Value List property, and enter a set of values that seem

Value Set	
Dist type	List
Dist value list	2'-8",2'-10",3'

reasonable. The idea is to limit the depth possibilities to a few discrete values given in the list.

4. Repeat the previous step, and make a reasonable value set list for the Width property (we used 4, 5, and 6 feet).

5. Add a Lookup parameter and a Lookup action. Rename the Lookup parameter Size.

6. Double-click the Lookup1 action, and you'll see the Property Lookup Table dialog box. Click the Add Properties button to open the Add Parameter Properties dialog box.

Hold down the Ctrl key, and select both linear parameters. These will be the inputs to your lookup table.

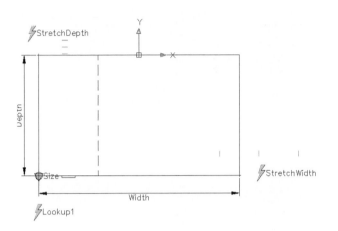

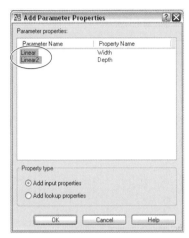

7. Click OK to close the Add Parameter Properties dialog box, and return to the Property Lookup Table dialog box. Select input property values in each cell. Each row in the table corresponds to a lookup property.

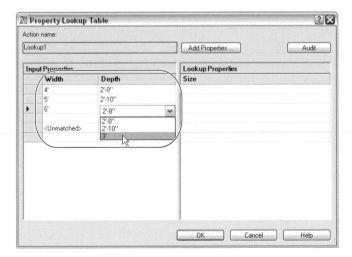

8. Enter the following lookup properties (one in each row): Small, Medium, and Large. Once each row has data, Allow Reverse Lookup is enabled. Reverse lookup means you can select Medium and get a width of 5′ and a depth of 2′-10″. This is what we mean by turning the tables: You can drive multiple input properties with reverse lookup.

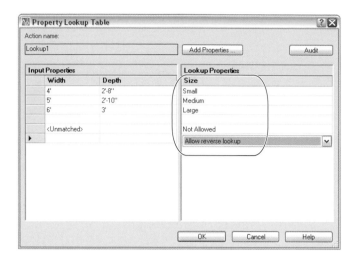

9. Type **Not Allowed** as the lookup property in the <Unmatched> row. Click OK, save, and close the dynamic block.

10. Start playing with Width, Depth, and Size in the Properties palette. Any combinations of input properties that don't correspond to a lookup property (Small, Medium, or Large) yield the message *Not Allowed* in the Properties palette. This is a good warning to users who are manually setting combinations that aren't produced by the manufacturer.

Once you've built a reverse lookup table, you can drive multiple properties by selecting a property from the lookup grip. It's a good thing.

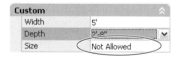

Display Block Properties with Placeholder Fields

Although it isn't technically an action, we couldn't figure out where else to put this important technique. It's certainly dynamic, and it *feels* like an action, so we're morally justified in discussing it here.

BlockPlaceholder is a special field that only works when you put it inside an attribute value in the block editor. As the name suggests, this field is a placeholder for data that appears only when the block is inserted as a reference.

We'll show you how to display Width and Depth property values that were developed in the previous topic. Using BlockPlaceholder fields is a way to see dynamic block property values at a glance—no selection or investigation required. Follow these steps:

1. Open an existing dynamic block in the authoring environment.

2. Add an attribute by using ATTDEF or by clicking the Define Attribute button in the block editor toolbar.

3. Give the attribute definition a tag and a prompt. Click the Insert Field button to assign a field to the attribute definition value.

4. In the Field dialog box, choose BlockPlaceholder from the Field Names list. Select the block reference property you want to display next. In this example, select Width. Set the Format options, and click OK.

5. In the Value text box, append a space, **X**, and another space. This text will appear between field codes in the attribute value.

6. Click the Insert Field button again, and this time select Depth as the block reference property.

7. Check Preset in the Attribute Definition dialog box. Attributes with fields as values should always be preset. Click OK, and place the attribute definition within the dynamic block.

> Put the attribute definition that displays the placeholding fields on a nonplotting layer if you want the information to be for eyes only.

8. Double-click the attribute definition. The default should read *Width × Depth*. The Width and Depth fields' values will be populated once this block is inserted. Click Cancel. Close the block editor, and save changes.

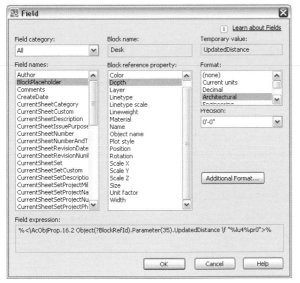

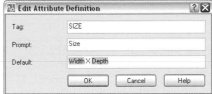

9. Delete the existing dynamic block reference. Reinsert a new reference of the same block. This time, it has the attribute functionality you just defined.

10. Change the Width and Depth property values in the dynamic block, either by manipulating the block's grips or by changing things in the Properties palette. REGEN or use UPDATEFIELD, and the fields will update.

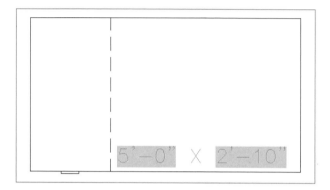

Now the dynamic block tells you its size—how cool is that? We put the attribute on a nonplotting layer, so this is insider information (shhh!). Although it's a bit more work for the block designer, the BlockPlaceholder field makes dynamic blocks more user-friendly and informative.

3D Modeling

ALTHOUGH 3D MODELING has been possible in AutoCAD for a long time, only with the release of AutoCAD 2007 has its 3D feature set really come of age. The last major upgrade of AutoCAD's 3D tools was in Release 13, circa 1994—that's the equivalent of 91 dog years ago! It's interesting to note that dog years (×7) map perfectly to the accelerated pace of software evolution, although we're not sure what this means.

This chapter will throw you a bone, if the last thing you remember about 3D modeling is the 3DFACE command. Obviously, much has changed with 3D modeling, and it's deservedly become one of the hottest topics in AutoCAD 2007.

This chapter's topics include:

- Using Coordinate Systems
- Creating 3D Objects
- Using 3D Editing Tools
- 3D Grab Bag

Using Coordinate Systems

Coordinate systems can be one of the more confusing subjects to those traditionalists who have only used AutoCAD for 2D drafting. You typically still draw objects on the XY plane when you're 3D modeling, so it's conceptually much like 2D drafting. It's just that with 3D modeling, you can reorient the XY plane wherever you want by adjusting the user coordinate system (UCS)—so you can draw anywhere.

In addition, you can access the third dimension without leaving the world coordinate system (WCS). In this section, we'll show you a few techniques that will help you coordinate your modeling.

Access Another Dimension with Coordinate Filters

Multiple universes, hyperspace physics, and a visit from Buckaroo Banzai aren't what we're talking about by accessing another dimension; sorry to disappoint. Instead, we're talking about filtering the input from the mouse while specifying input from a chosen dimension via the keyboard.

Coordinate filters are also known as *point filters*, and that gets to the essence of what they do: They specify points by filtering coordinates. Unless you snap to a 3D object, clicking the mouse on the screen to input coordinates yields only two dimensions. The third dimension can be selected (or keyed in) separately if you know how to ask for it on the command line. Here's how to ask:

1. Switch to an isometric viewpoint so you can perceive three dimensions on your flat 2D screen. One way to do this is to choose View → 3D Views → SW Isometric. This isn't strictly necessary, but it will help you to visualize what's happening in 3D.

2. Switch to the WCS (default) if you aren't already there. Draw a box and an intersecting cylinder for the sake of this tutorial. UNION these two objects together. Switch to the Realistic visual style.

3. Use the LINE command, and click an arbitrary first point to the side of the box.

4. At the Specify next point or [Undo] prompt, type **.xy** and press Enter. This is a point filter (the period puts the *point* in *point filter*). It accepts coordinate input from the selected dimensions (X and Y, here). Any dimensions not in the filter (Z, in this case) are requested on the command line. Notice the word *of* that appears on the following command line—it means the filter is ready to accept a point:

```
Command: LINE

LINE Specify first point: (click arbitrary point)

Specify next point or [Undo]: .xy

of
```

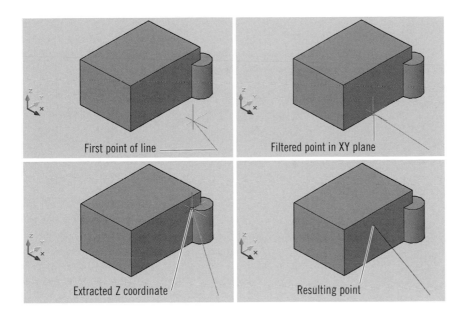

First point of line

Filtered point in XY plane

Extracted Z coordinate

Resulting point

5. Snap to the midpoint of the box along its edge. The point you select will have its X and Y coordinates filtered and input.

6. The command line now says

    (need Z):

    Click a point on the top of the cylinder, and its Z coordinate is extracted. All three coordinate dimensions have now been input and determine the second point of the line. Press Enter again to end the LINE command.

> Instead of clicking a point at a (need) prompt—like you did in step 6—you can enter a numeric value.

You can separate input from any dimension or pair of dimensions with point filters. The following are valid coordinate filters to use at any prompt where you're asked to specify a location:

- .x
- .y
- .z
- .xy
- .xz
- .yz

3D Coordinate Systems

Most people use both Cartesian (x,y) and polar (x<a) coordinate systems in their 2D work. You can expand Cartesian notation from 2D to 3D by adding an additional comma and another coordinate value, making it 3D Cartesian notation (x,y,z). For example, to MOVE an object up 10 units in the Z direction, type the following at the `Specify second point or <use first point as displacement>` prompt:

`@0,0,10`

> ELEV sets the current height of the XY drawing plane in the Z direction.

The polar system can also be extended from 2D to 3D. In fact, two additional 3D coordinate systems blossom from the roots of the polar system: cylindrical and spherical. Few people are aware that AutoCAD has these two additional 3D coordinate systems built in. You might use cylindrical and spherical coordinates if part of the geometry you're designing is roughly cylindrical and/or spherical in form. In any case, it's good to know about these possibilities.

Cylindrical coordinates are like 2D polar coordinates with the addition of a height coordinate; they use both a less than symbol and a comma (x<a,h). Try the following example to understand how cylindrical coordinates work:

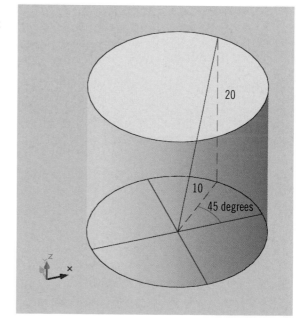

1. Start the LINE command, and click an arbitrary start point.

2. At the `Specify second point or [Undo]` prompt, type the following:

   `@10<45,20`

3. Press Enter to end the LINE command.

> The distance value used in cylindrical and spherical coordinates is measured along the drawing plane—that's the XY plane by default.

Spherical coordinates specify the height above (or below) the drawing plane with an angle instead of a distance. Spherical coordinates use two angle symbols (x<a<b). Here's an example:

1. Start the LINE command, and click an arbitrary start point.

2. At the Specify second point prompt, type the following:

   @10<45<30

3. Press Enter to end the LINE command.

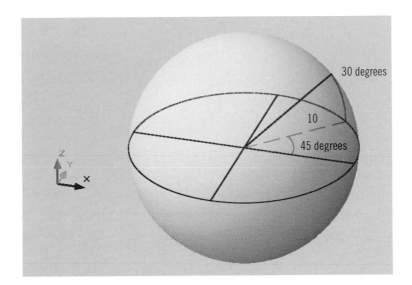

Real-Time UCS

We rely on the UCS to get our 3D work done—but moving from one UCS to another is a tedious process. How often we've wished we could manually grab the UCS and move it around on the screen. Enter the awesome Express Tool Real-time UCS (RTUCS)!

RTUCS lets you grab any axis and rotate it to your liking without fussing with numbers. Easily cycle from one axis to another by pressing the Tab key to cycle through the axes and dragging to rotate the UCS. You can move the origin easily as well, and all this happens dynamically on your screen. What could be better? Here's what it looks like on the command line:

```
Command: RTUCS

Press TAB key to change axis or

[Save/Restore/Delete/Cycle/Angle/Origin/View/World/Undo]

<Drag to rotate>
```

> The current axis and its angle of rotation are shown on the status bar while you're using RTUCS.

Here's a quick summary of the RTUCS options:

Save Stores the current UCS with a name.

Restore Calls back up a saved UCS.

Delete Eliminates a saved UCS.

Cycle Iterates through the six standard orthographic UCS orientations (Top, Front, Right, Back, Left, and Bottom). To cycle, keep pressing the C key—no need to press Enter.

Angle Sets the minimum rotation increment for the current axis.

Origin Moves the UCS origin.

View Rotates the UCS parallel to your current screen view.

World Sets the current UCS back to the WCS.

Unlike regular AutoCAD commands, RTUCS doesn't require you to press Enter after you input an option. This may drive you crazy, but it saves you from extra steps.

Dynamic UCS

The dynamic user coordinate system (DUCS) is new in AutoCAD 2007. If you've ever used Autodesk VIZ or Autodesk 3ds Max, you'll recognize DUCS as being similar to their AutoGrid feature.

DUCS is a mode like OSNAP: When it's on, the UCS is temporarily moved and rotated so the drawing plane (XY) coincides with any surface you hover over. When you're done drawing, the UCS pops back to wherever it was previously.

At first glance, DUCS seems like a godsend—and it is for conceptual modeling. But we recommend you turn off DUCS for precision work where you need to specify coordinates. When you need to be certain you're drawing things where you intend, having the UCS transform without your written consent is unnerving. You have more control with good old UCS and ELEV.

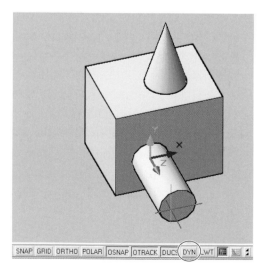

On the plus side, DUCS makes quick work of stacking primitives and drawing objects on the surfaces of other objects—tasks that are practically de rigueur for conceptual modeling.

Ctrl+D toggles DUCS.

You can optionally display the grid and have it follow the DUCS. The grid helps you to visualize where the drawing plane has been dynamically transformed (it's always popping about with DUCS). Use DSETTINGS, and choose the Snap and Grid tab. Check Follow Dynamic UCS in the Grid Behavior area, and click OK.

The next time you draw something using DUCS, the grid pops over to the surface you're drawing on, visually informing you of that fact.

The GRID toggle must be on in order for you to see the grid, and the temporary grid that follows DUCS disappears after the drawing activity is complete. A glimpse of the temporary grid is all you're going to get, but that's all you need.

Set UCSFOLLOW to 0 (off) when you're using DUCS. Otherwise, your view changes to follow the dynamically changing drawing plane, and you can't see what's happening in 3D.

Another issue that comes into play when using DUCS is the fact that the default settings make it impossible to snap to geometry with negative Z values. Don't worry, it's not you—it's the OSOPTIONS system variable. Being prohibited from snapping to things below the XY plane may be good in lots of situations, but if you don't like your options being limited, set OSOPTIONS to 0. This system variable also controls whether object snaps ignore hatch objects. Setting OSOPTIONS to 0 causes AutoCAD to snap to hatch patterns and geometry with negative Z values. If you prefer setting your system variables from friendly dialog boxes, you can find this setting in the Drafting tab of the Options dialog under Object Snap Options (lower-left corner).

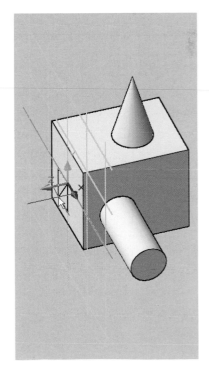

Creating 3D Objects

The intuitive way that you can create 3D objects in AutoCAD 2007 is fantastic. Plus, many new types of 3D objects are available, so you should be able to model just about anything. In the old days, people gave 2D objects thickness to represent the third dimension in a rudimentary fashion. Nowadays, you can create 3D surfaces and solids directly with visually interactive tools. The difference is like night and day.

Primitives Have Evolved

Primitives have become more sophisticated with the passage of time and AutoCAD releases. You've no doubt heard that 3D is super easy now in AutoCAD 2007—visual, intuitive, with no headaches (unlike in previous releases). The new solid primitives work just as your existing commands work—if a primitive is based on a circle (like a cone or cylinder), you see the same prompts you find in the CIRCLE command. A box is created similarly to a rectangle, and so on. Let's look at a few:

Box Comes packaged in a new and friendlier command: BOX. Similar to RECTANG, you dynamically add the height. You can also use a center point to define a cube.

Wedge Created by drawing the base rectangle and the height with the sloped face opposite the first corner. You can also use the Cube option to draw a wedge with equal sides. Just like BOX, you can specify a center point to define the wedge. The 2Point options comes in handy when asked to specify a height.

Pyramid Not surprisingly, draws a solid pyramid (the prompts are similar to those of the familiar POLYGON command). You input the number of sides (3 to 32), inscribed or circumscribed (or use the Edge option), and height.

Cone Offers the same options as the CIRCLE command to define the base (center radius or diameter, 3P, 2P, TTR), followed by the height, which you pick dynamically. You can also specify an elliptical base, believe it or not. The height may be defined by selecting between two points (2P) or an axis endpoint. The Top radius option creates a cone that doesn't meet at a point—cone frustum—OK, how many of you know what a frustum is?

Frustum is a math geek term for a cone or pyramid that's cut off at the top (truncated parallel to base) so it flattens out into a plane rather than coming to a point.

Cylinder Has the same options as the familiar CIRCLE command to define the base, followed by the height, which you pick dynamically. You can also specify an elliptical base—cool, eh? The height of the cylinder can be defined by selecting between two distinct points (2P) or an axis endpoint. It's easy to use the new friendly 3D grips to make changes to the cylinder dynamically at any time.

Sphere Gives you the same options as the CIRCLE command (center point, 3P, 2P, TTR), but you end up generating a sphere.

Helix Allows you to create anything from a flat spiral to a 3D helix to DNA (well, you'd have to make two for a double helix). Specify the center point, base radius or diameter, top radius or diameter, and height. Edit the twist direction and number of turns after the helix has been created in the Properties palette. The helix is a unique wireframe object, not a 3D solid like the other primitives; for example, you can use it as a loft path. If you're using the Dashboard, the 3D Make control panel must be expanded to access the Helix button.

Powerful Polysolids

POLYSOLID is the new polyline, three-dimensionally speaking. Polysolids are made in much the same way as their 2D cousins, with the option to create straight and arc segments within the same object. Unlike polylines, polysolids have a height value, making them 3D solid objects.

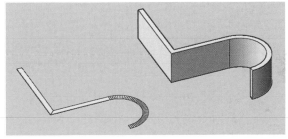

Polyline with width   Polysolid with width and height

```
Command: POLYSOLID

Specify start point or [Object/Height/Width/Justify]

  <Object>: (click first point)

Specify next point or [Arc/Undo]: (notice Arc option)

Specify next point or [Arc/Close/Undo]:

(notice Close option)
```

> You must set height and width options before creating polysolid segments or they will be created with default values. PSOLWIDTH and PSOLHEIGHT are the relevant system variables.

Use grips to manipulate polysolid segments with the simplicity of a polyline. Each straight segment has grips on its endpoints, and arcs have an extra grip that determines arc radius.

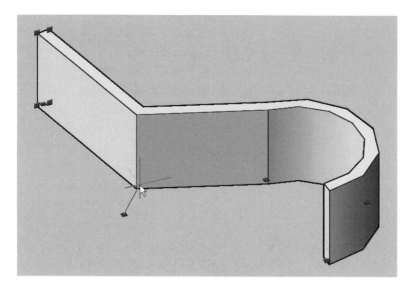

Polysolids have four additional grips at their start point, like any swept object. Use these grips to alter the cross-sectional profile of the resulting 3D solid. Although you can manipulate the cross section, you can't add vertices to it or make the cross section curved.

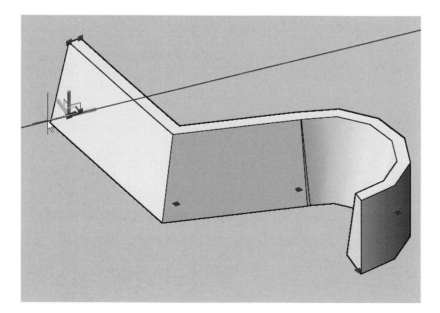

Polysolids are ideal for converting 2D architectural plans to 3D. Set the height and width to match the intended walls, and trace over them with POLYSOLID. Use the command's

Justify option to match the left, center, or right side of the walls you're tracing over. The tracing method creates new 3D solid geometry on top of the 2D linework. Use this method if you want to build a separate 3D model but leave the underlying 2D linework intact.

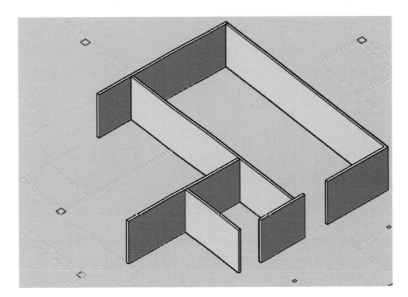

An alternate method for generating a 3D model from 2D plans is to use POLYSOLID's Object option. It converts any line, arc, 2D polyline, or circle into a polysolid. Converting objects in this way doesn't leave the 2D linework intact—it becomes a 3D model instead.

Sweep and Loft Your Way into 3D

SWEEP and LOFT are new 3D modeling commands in AutoCAD 2007. Use them to create objects with complex curvature. Both push profiles along paths to generate geometry. *Profiles* define 2D cross sections of the intended geometry. *Paths* are the journey profiles take on the road to becoming a 3D surface or solid.

Think of *sweeping* as extruding along a curved path, if it helps. Sweeps are good for piping, railings, architectural moldings, screw threads, curbs, cornices—you get the idea.

Normally, SWEEP aligns the swept object (also known as the profile) perpendicular to the path before it's swept. That means you can draw the profile flat on the drawing plane without having to worry about rotating it up into position at the start of the path. If you

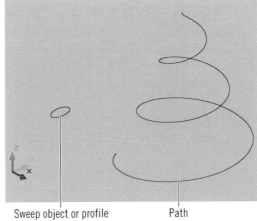

Sweep object or profile   Path

want to align the profile yourself, turn off the Alignment option in SWEEP. Here's what SWEEP looks like on the command line:

```
Command: SWEEP

Current wire frame density:  ISOLINES=4

Select objects to sweep: (select profile)

Select sweep path or [Alignment/Base point/Scale/Twist]:

(select path)
```

The Base Point option is used to choose exactly where the profile rides along its path; if you don't choose, it sweeps along the middle of the profile.

SWEEP, LOFT, EXTRUDE, and REVOLVE all have wireframe geometry that defines their 3D forms, including profile and path objects. AutoCAD tidies up by default, deleting the defining geometry. If you'd like all this defining geometry to stick around after the 3D objects are created, set the DELOBJ system variable to 0. This option can also be found in the OPTIONS command, 3D Modeling tab.

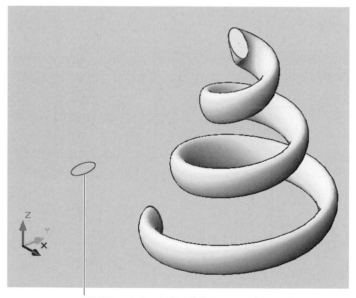

DELOBJ controls whether defining geometry remains.

LOFT allows you to create 3D objects with a series of cross-sectional profiles. You need at least two profiles to generate a loft (path optional). LOFT is great for making boat hulls, mechanical parts, plumbing fixtures, modern furniture, landforms, and whatever other complex surfaces you can dream up. Here we're making a boat hull; the series of cross-sectional profiles is shown in blue, and the path is shown in red.

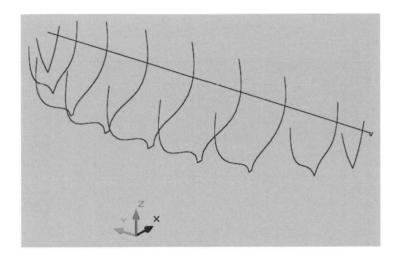

Here's what LOFT looks like on the command line:

```
Command: LOFT

Select cross-sections in lofting order:

(select them in order, one at a time)


Enter an option [Guides/Path/Cross-sections only]

<Cross-sections only>: Path


Select path curve: (click it)
```

Guides are an option and run perpendicular to the cross sections if used. Specify guides if you want finer control of surface curvature; they can prevent wrinkles and twists that may otherwise mess up your beautiful loft.

Using 3D Editing Tools

Although nothing is stopping you from using the tried-and-true 2D editing commands on 3D objects, for best results you may want to reconsider your plan of action. Specialized 3D editing tools can do the job more efficiently—that is, once you learn how to use them. Some 3D editing operations have no equivalent 2D command, so this section is required reading for aspiring 3D modelers.

Transform Objects in 3D

3DMOVE and 3DROTATE are the tools of choice for transforming objects in 3D. Both have grip tools that aid in choosing which direction you want to go. These commands are available most conveniently on the Dashboard, on the 3D Make control panel.

When you click an object's location grip in a 3D viewport with a 3D visual style applied, the Move Grip tool appears. It looks a little like the UCS icon, but without the cone arrowheads and axis labels. You can tell which axis is which by the color mnemonic: RGB=XYZ (see "Crosshairs in 3D" in Chapter 1).

Of course, you don't have to select the objects first in order to move them. Clicking the 3DMOVE tool in the Dashboard and then selecting the objects gives you more flexibility because you get to place the Move Grip tool this way.

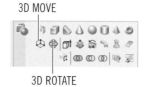

3D MOVE

3D ROTATE

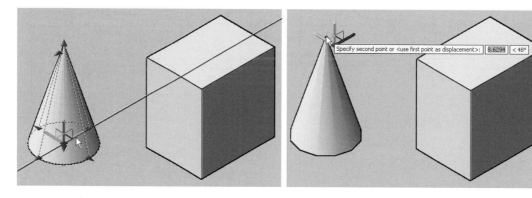

Constrain motion to any of the three axes (X, Y, or Z) with the Move Grip tool by using its axis handles. Did you know that you can also constrain motion to any of the three primary planes (XY, XZ, and YZ) by using the Move Grip tool's center boxes?

3DROTATE's grip tool has axis rings that are likewise color-coded, allowing you to reorient an object about the X, Y, or Z axis. 3DROTATE asks you to select objects and then specify a base point, just like the regular ROTATE command. But then you have to pick the rotation axis by clicking an axis ring on the Rotate Grip tool—a step that's absent in the ROTATE command. Finally, click two points to determine a rotation angle, or type in the number of degrees.

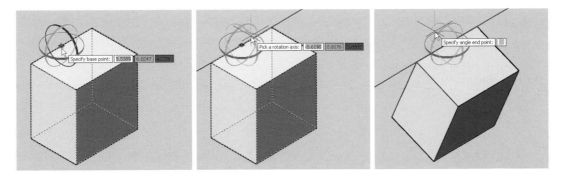

Once you get to know 3DMOVE and 3DROTATE backward and forward, it's time to consider this next tip. If you turn on (set to 1) the GTDEFAULT system variable, it invokes 3DMOVE and 3DROTATE whenever you use MOVE and ROTATE in a 3D viewpoint.

That's right: Then you can forget all about 3DMOVE and 3DROTATE and use your command aliases for MOVE and ROTATE (probably M and RO—if these aren't second nature, then we don't know how to help you).

Leverage the History of Solids

Why use history when you can leverage it? You'll be on your way to robust corporatespeak fluency, at least. Anyhoo, when you get around to learning what history is, and what you can do with it, read on.

Solids have the option to record a construction history. If recorded, history can save you from having to start over if a *composite solid* needs adjusting.

Whenever you use a Boolean operation like UNION, SUBTRACT, or INTERSECT, a composite solid is built. When history is recorded (it is by default), the original forms that make up the composite solid are still there, although they aren't usually visible. This history makes editing solids in AutoCAD 2007 about one million times easier than in previous releases (OK, not a million, but close).

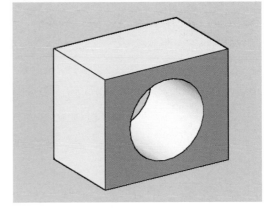

Select what you suspect may be a composite solid, and check out what the Properties palette says. If the History property is set to Record, then the original forms are still there. Change Show History to Yes, and you'll see the ghosted outline of the original forms.

What good would history be if we couldn't learn from it and correct our mistakes? Hold down the Ctrl key, and click a ghosted historical object—now its grips appear, giving you the power to revise history. Wouldn't it be great if the world worked like this?

> FILLET and CHAMFER create composite solids. Access their grips for editing by Ctrl-clicking the filleted or chamfered parts.

On the other hand, it takes some additional memory to store history for solids. You can free up that memory by removing history from selected solids with BREP. This command has no options and makes no exceptions. Once history is wiped, there's no going back—the original parts can't be selected. A new (revisionist) history can be recorded afterward, however.

> Don't use BREP on solid primitives. Doing so strips them of their grips and the ability to edit them as primitives.

SHOWHIST is a system variable that controls how you want to show history on a global scale. When it's set to 1 (default), objects have the ability to show recorded history. A setting of 0 prohibits all solid objects from being able to show history. The opposite occurs when SHOWHIST is 2: All solids show their construction histories on-screen.

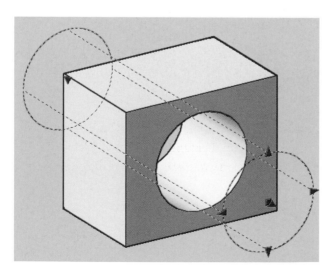

Subobject Modeling Techniques

The Ctrl key is the gateway to subobject modeling. Solids have vertices, edges, and faces that can all be manipulated independently of the object as a whole. Users of Autodesk VIZ and Autodesk 3ds Max will appreciate this modeling modality in AutoCAD, because it offers a familiar and advanced modeling capability.

Even after you start to use subobject grips, a few things may not occur to you at first. For example, did you know that you can rotate subobjects? Make a cylinder, and then select its top face by Ctrl-selecting the center of its top surface. Use 3DROTATE, and place the rotate grip at the center of the top face. As you rotate the face, the rest of the object stays put but remains connected to it—changing its *topology,* or inner structure.

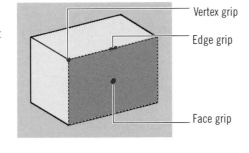

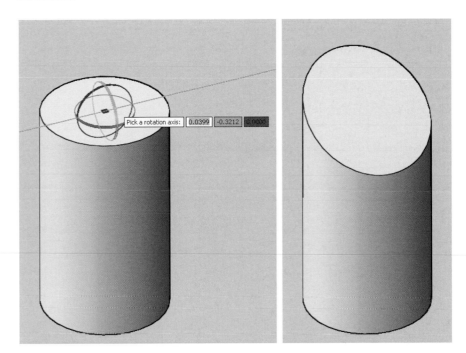

Subobjects move, rotate, and scale according to their topology. You can't create a gabled roof from a box if it doesn't have an edge there to pull up. Fortunately, it's possible to add vertices, edges, and therefore faces by imprinting geometry onto an existing solid. Let's see how this is done in a simple example:

1. Create a box primitive. Its size isn't important.

2. Draw a line across the top edge of the box, spanning between the midpoints of two opposite edges.

3. Use IMPRINT to merge the line into the topology of the box. Select the box first and then the line. The command line says

    ```
    Delete the source object [Yes/No] <N>:
    ```

    Type **Yes**, and press Enter twice. The line becomes an edge.

4. Ctrl-select the two vertices at the ends of the new edge. They're now subobjects of the box.

5. Use 3DMOVE to move the new edge up. Place the Move Grip tool at the midpoint of the top middle edge. Click the blue axis, and move the edge upward to create a gable.

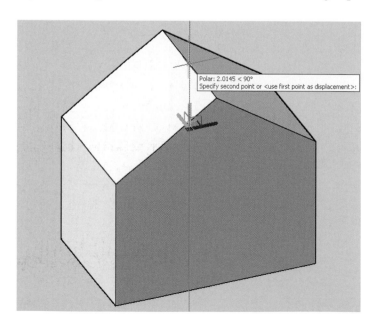

The box is able to fold along its top edge only because it has the topology to support it. You can add as much topology as you want to solids using IMPRINT.

> Transforming multiple subobjects simultaneously gives you additional editing power.

PRESSPULL Makes an Impression

PRESSPULL makes quick work of conceptual modeling. It's an amazingly versatile command that you're going to love—well, as much as one can love an inanimate piece of executing code. PRESSPULL is on the Dashboard's 3D Make control panel, the Modeling toolbar, and the command line, but the fastest way to call up this command is to press Ctrl+Alt.

The most obvious thing PRESSPULL can do is press or pull solid faces. It does this task neatly, without leaving seams behind. It works much like the older SOLIDEDIT command, but PRESSPULL is visually interactive and therefore more intuitive to use.

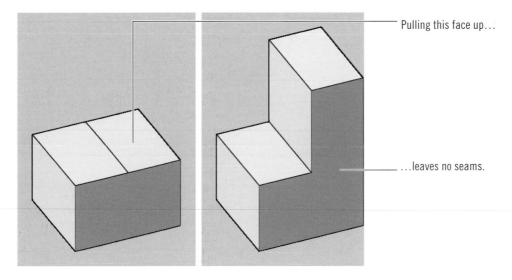

Pulling this face up…

…leaves no seams.

The real power of PRESSPULL comes when you want to press or pull *bounded areas* that are enclosed by coplanar geometry. You don't have to use IMPRINT the way you do during subobject modeling. Instead, PRESSPULL makes an impression of the bounded areas for you and then presses or pulls the new topology as you desire. Give it a try to understand the power of PRESSPULL:

1. Create a box. Orbit to see the box from a 3D viewpoint and display a 3D visual style.

2. Draw a hexagon with the POLYGON command on the surface of one face using DUCS.

3. Press Ctrl+Alt, and click a point inside the edges you drew on the solid face (inside the hexagon). Move the cursor away from the face, and pull the new geometry outward.

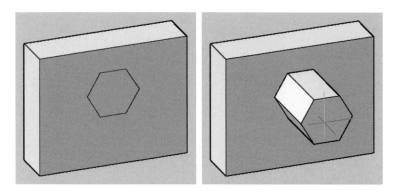

4. PRESSPULL can also press geometry inward, making a depression or even a hole if you press far enough. To see this, draw a circle on the same face where you drew the hexagon using DUCS. Move the circle if necessary so it's not completely on the face.

5. Press Ctrl+Alt, and click a point inside the bounded area within the circle and on the face—the bounded area doesn't have to fit completely within an object. Move the cursor in toward the box volume, and click when you've gone beyond its far edge. A hole appears in the box. PRESSPULL makes a pit or a hole, depending on how far you press.

Click inside bounded area

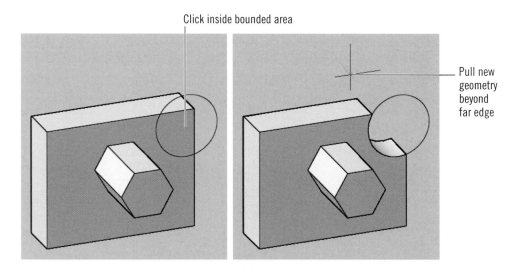

Pull new geometry beyond far edge

Note that the closed area on which you use PRESSPULL needs to be completely displayed on screen; otherwise, Ctrl+Alt won't work (much like the old BHATCH command).

Obviously, PRESSPULL has tons of modeling power. The previous example is food for thought, but you'll have to practice with PRESSPULL to see what an efficient 3D modeler it will make you.

> The system variable IMPLIEDFACE must be set to 1 for PRESSPULL's bounded area magic to work. Otherwise, you have to IMPRINT geometry manually onto solids before their boundaries can be pressed or pulled.

3D Grab Bag

We've swept whatever 3D tidbits were left over on the virtual editing desk into this section for your enjoyment and edification. The grab bag has 3D tips about object snap, thickening surfaces to solids, surface/solid conversion, flattening, accuracy, and accessing content. Reach in, and see what morsels come out.

OSNAPZ

No, this isn't just a cool spelling—OSNAPZ is a system variable that governs what happens when you snap to an object that's not on the drawing plane. ELEVATION sets the height of the drawing plane; that's the height of the XY plane in the current UCS's Z direction.

OSNAPZ gives you two choices: Either it constrains the snapped point's Z value to the drawing plane, or it does nothing and allows true 3D snap to function. The default is 0, so OSNAPZ normally isn't operative. OSNAPZ can be useful in certain situations, so it's good to log it into your memory bank and cash it in when the need arises.

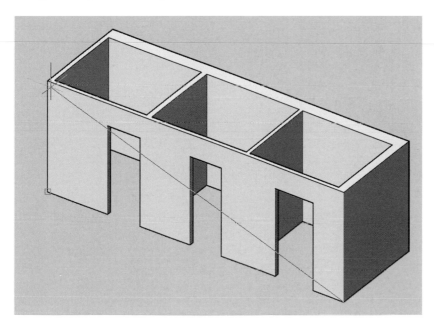

Set OSNAPZ to 1 when you're snapping to 3D objects but want to be sure you're snapping to the XY plane. When it's on, OSNAPZ enforces a kind of 2D snap. For example, if you're drawing lines to calculate an area in a 3D building model, it's helpful know you're snapping on the ground plane. You can then click the top endpoints of walls but actually snap to their endpoints on the ground. You can also set this nifty system variable in the Drafting tab of the Options dialog under Object Snap Options (lower-left corner).

Thicken Surfaces into Solids

Don't fret if you went to a lot of trouble to make a surface but wanted a solid. THICKEN can bulk up an infinitely thin surface into a 3D Solid object. It's dead simple: Say how thick is thick, and voila—instant solid. Here's what it looks like on the command line:

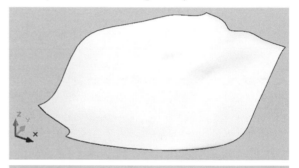

```
Command: THICKEN

Select surfaces to thicken: (select
surface)

Specify thickness <default>: (type
distance)
```

Even though this seems so easy—and it is—don't be fooled into thinking this command isn't important. THICKEN is one of the coolest tools in your 3D toolbox. Check out this lofted terrain that we thickened into a site model. THICKEN can create solids that are well-nigh impossible otherwise.

Converting Surfaces and Solids

A pair of conversion commands is provided to help keep your legacy models up to date: CONVTOSURFACE and CONVTOSOLID. As their names suggest, these commands convert relics from the past to modern surfaces and solids. For example, if you come across a 3D model that is made with wide polylines given 3D thickness, don't freak out. Use CONVTOSOLID, and the polylines will be gone—leaving you with 3D solids, which are much more useful in today's world.

CONVTOSOLID doesn't work on polylines with nonuniform thickness. You'll have to use PEDIT to adjust widths of individual vertices first. Make them all the same width, and then you can convert them to solids.

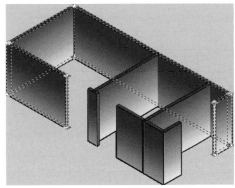

Wide polylines with thickness

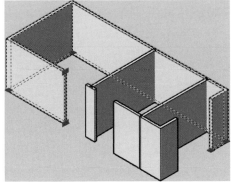

3D solids

DEALING WITH LEGACY 3D MODELS

Polygon meshes can't be converted to modern surfaces and solids. Mesh commands introduced in AutoCAD R10 (circa 1988) included RULESURF, EDGESURF, TABSURF, REVSURF, and 3DMESH; they're still available in AutoCAD 2007. If you encounter these legacy entities, explode them into 3D faces.

Strangely enough, the historically older 3D faces can be converted to modern surfaces. Surfaces can in turn be thickened and made into solids, so all is not lost.

One more tip: Mesh objects usually fragment into tiny pieces when exploded into 3D faces. UNION the fragments together after they've become solids, and you won't be able to tell you're dealing with a legacy model.

EXPLODE is always good for taking objects down a notch. For example, exploding a solid primitive gives you surfaces in the curved areas and regions in planar ones. Exploding planar surfaces yields regions, and exploding regions yields linework such as circles and lines.

Use XEDGES to extract edges from regions, surfaces, or solids. XEDGES doesn't delete its source objects. Rather, it creates new edges on top. You have to hide the source objects—perhaps by putting them on another layer and turning it off—to see the extracted edges. Extracting edges can be just what the doctor ordered when you're building a sweep path along existing edges, for example.

Extract individual edges with XEDGES by Ctrl-selecting them.

Flatten It Out

FLATSHOT takes a snapshot of all the 3D objects on screen and flattens them into a block composed of 2D linework. This is an excellent tool for illustrating complex manufactured parts or for making an old-fashioned 2D isometric drawing of a 3D model. A similar command, SOLPROF, has been around for years, but it only works on objects in a layout viewport and is fussier than FLATSHOT.

Before you use FLATSHOT, change the viewpoint to control how the solids and regions on screen will be flattened; what you see is what you get. When you use FLATSHOT, you immediately see a dialog box in which you can choose whether to show obscured lines. We suggest illustrating obscured lines in another color and with a hidden linetype, differentiating what is hidden from what is plainly visible.

After you click Create, a new block containing the flattened linework is generated. You're asked to choose an X and Y scale factor and an orientation, just like any other block you insert. The new block is placed flat on the XY plane, so you may want to switch to the Top viewpoint to check it out.

> Turn off the layers of objects you don't want captured by FLATSHOT before executing the command.

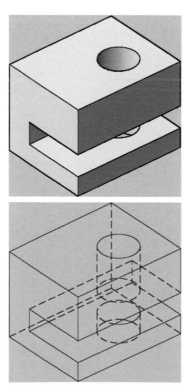

Control Display of Curved Objects

Straight-edged objects are never a problem, but AutoCAD has trouble representing curves on screen with perfect accuracy; programmers call this a nontrivial problem. Perfect 2D curves are often simplified by approximating them with a series of connected straight-line segments. 3D surfaces and solids are approximated by tessellating them into discrete planar facets. You need to know the following system variables to control the appearance of curved objects:

WHIPARC Works only in 2D Wireframe visual style. A setting of 1 completely smooths out circles and arcs, whereas the default setting of 0 approximates curves with straight-line segments. When WHIPARC is 0, VIEWRES controls curve approximation, as it does in all other visual styles.

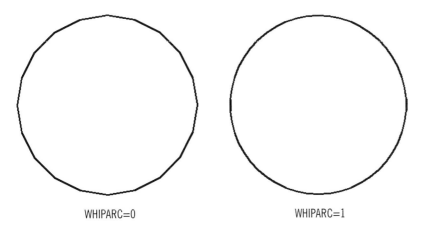

WHIPARC=0   WHIPARC=1

VIEWRES Has a default setting of 1000, which is low enough to produce jaggedness in 2D curves when you zoom in closely in most drawings. VIEWRES officially controls the *circle zoom percent*—meaning it's the percent by which you'd have to zoom in to see approximation artifacts in 2D geometry.

Boosting VIEWRES up to its maximum value of 20000 means you'd have to zoom in an awful lot before jaggedness would become apparent. But beware of boosting the value this high, because VIEWRES also affects 3D objects.

VIEWRES is multiplied by FACETRES to yield the amount of tessellation in 3D objects (are you lost yet?). Increasing VIEWRES adversely impacts regeneration time, so don't go crazy with it. We recommend setting VIEWRES to 10000. Decrease it if your REGENs take too long.

VIEWRES is stored in the drawing, so you have to adjust it in every drawing unless you change it in your template once and for all.

FACETRES (facet resolution) Is multiplied by VIEWRES to yield the amount of 3D tessellation performed. Higher values of FACETRES mean more tessellation and smoother-looking curved 3D objects. FACETRES defaults to 0.5 (pretty low) and can be bumped up as high as 10.

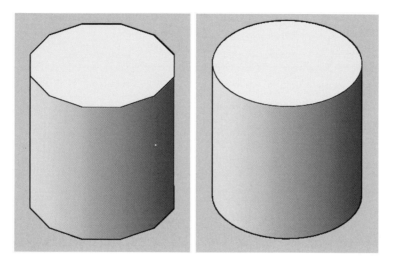

ISOLINES Controls the number of contour lines that appear on NURBS surfaces and solids. NURBS are a kind of fancy math; isolines are contour lines on these perfectly smooth surfaces. Isolines always appear perfectly smooth.

When there are just few isolines (the default is 4), and you're viewing the model in 3D Wireframe display mode, you may not perceive surface curvature. Increasing the number of isolines shows curvature better at no performance cost. We recommend setting ISOLINES to 8.

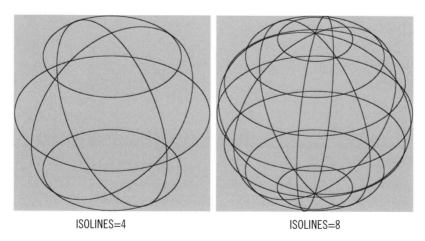

ISOLINES=4   ISOLINES=8

Use the Visual Style Manager to set up the number of ISOLINES you want for each visual style.

Access 3D Content

Did you know a world of already created 3D content is available through the DC Online tab in the DesignCenter? Most of the content is free, and there are advertisements for some pay libraries as well. Drag and drop 3D content from DesignCenter right into your drawings—it doesn't get any easier than that.

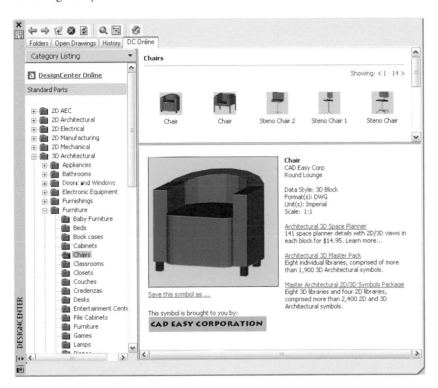

Visualization

WE'VE ALL HEARD that "a picture is worth a thousand words"—but in practice, a picture is often worth incalculably more; it's often the difference between getting a contract and losing one. Visualization is a science of two aspects: interacting with design data in-house and presenting realistic imagery to clients. In the past, these visualization aspects may have been handled with different software packages. Auto-CAD 2007's visualization features have advanced so much that you can handle both facets without leaving AutoCAD.

This chapter will teach you how to navigate virtual space like a pro, whether you're zooming, orbiting, walking, or flying. You'll be styling when you see how to make views, cameras, and visual styles your own. Mastering materials and texturing techniques will raise your 3D models to new heights of realism.

Navigating in Virtual Space

One of the unspoken assumptions in AutoCAD is that the model is static—that is, unless you animate, but that's another subject. Your creations are fixed with respect to the world origin of virtual space. As the all-seeing (but, unfortunately, not all-knowing) navigator, you have the power to change your point of view, to see the model from every angle. Getting around the model is essential, and this section offers a few tricks to make your navigation experience more efficient and intuitive.

Zoom!

You've probably been zooming in and out of drawings for years, so what could you possibly learn that's new, right? Well, you just may be surprised by paying attention to some of the zooming subtleties—they can make you a much more efficient navigator.

Zoom without Interruption

This is an old tip for those die-hards who still prefer using the keyboard. Zoom without interrupting the current command by making the zoom transparent. We don't mean to be opaque, but in this context the term *transparent* isn't to be taken literally. Transparent commands can be executed while you're in the middle of another command.

The secret of accessing transparency is the apostrophe. Let's say you're drawing lines, when it occurs to you that you need to zoom out. Instead of canceling the Line command, zooming out, and then reissuing the Line command to keep drawing, it pays to use zoom transparently to avoid interrupting your flow.

Here's how it works. Draw some line segments, and with the LINE command still running, type **'z**, and press the Spacebar.

AutoCAD includes many transparent commands, and they're all accessed transparently with an

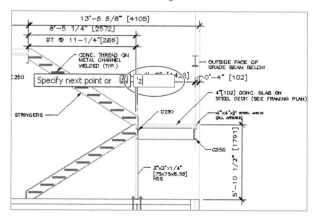

apostrophe. The apostrophe signals a transparent command—in this case, the *z* shortcut for ZOOM. Press the Down Arrow, and observe that the ZOOM command options appear dynamically (if the DYN toggle is off, then look at the command line). Choose Extents, and you're returned immediately to the running LINE command where you left off. Draw a few more segments, and then end the LINE command.

We sometimes take for granted that everyone knows that the Spacebar acts as an Enter (except when you're in text modes). It's a great big key, and it's easy to hit; we suggest you take advantage of it for power productivity!

In case you never noticed, all the places you can issue the ZOOM command other than the keyboard already invoke it transparently. Menus, toolbars, and shortcut menus all use this handy feature. Once you see the utility of command transparency, try it on other commands. It generally works only on commands that neither select nor create objects.

Pay Attention to Cursor Location while Zooming

This is one of those subtleties that, once you see it, will save you tons of time. When you zoom in and out in real time, preferably by turning your mouse wheel, pay attention to where your cursor is on the screen. For example, say you're looking at a lot of geometry on the screen when zoomed out, and you want to zoom in. To observe this effect most strongly, position the cursor far off to one side of the screen.

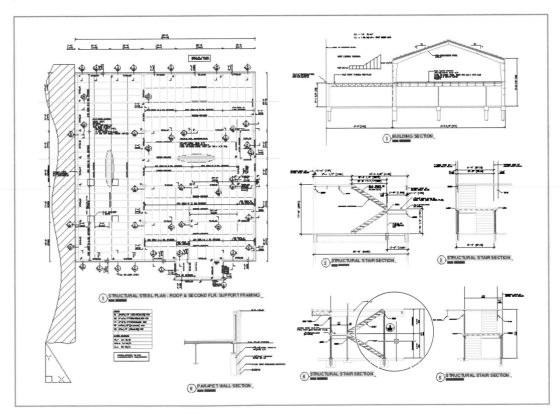

As you start turning the mouse wheel, notice that the enlargement is centered on your cursor location. By strategically positioning the cursor, you can dynamically zoom in to any area of the screen that you want. This form of directed navigation is an alternative to using the more explicit old-school Zoom Window option.

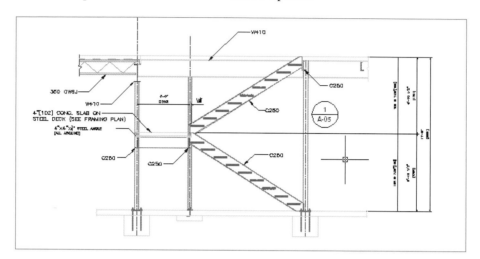

Zoom Extents with the Wheel

A faster way of zooming to the extents of your drawing area is to double-click the mouse wheel. This has been scientifically proven to be faster than typing **Z**, Enter, **E**, Enter (at least, theoretically proven in an armchair). It's even fractionally faster than clicking the Zoom Extents button on the Zoom toolbar (because you have to find the button on screen). Smoke the competition—double-click your mouse wheel!

And you probably thought, the wheel just turned. Now you're privy to the fact that the wheel secretly moonlights as a mouse button. So if the mouse wheel is a button, why aren't the left and right buttons wheels also? That would just be too much!

> See "As the Wheel Turns" in Chapter 1.

Zoom Immediately to Any Object or Selection

In AutoCAD 2007, you can now zoom to the extents of an object or selection of objects rather than the extents of the entire drawing. This turns out to be a useful feature. We wonder whether Autodesk took this good idea from VIZ which has had a similar feature called Zoom Extents Selected for many years. Try it out:

1. Select one or more objects.

2. Type **Z** Enter.

3. Press the Down Arrow key, and choose the Object option. Type **O** Enter if you're using the command line.

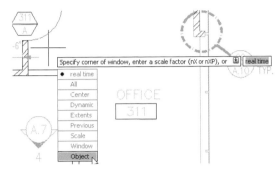

The display immediately zooms to the extents of the selection. Unfortunately, the Object option doesn't work when Perspective is on. This should go on the wish list for the next version of AutoCAD.

Zoom Object is a great macro to assign to a toolbar button for speedy access, (We're so lazy we don't even like to key in options!)

Controlling the Zoom Transition Effect

Do you like to play video games? AutoCAD is now officially trying to keep up with the cool crowd by introducing the *zoom transition effect*. This is probably the first thing you noticed when you installed AutoCAD 2006 or higher—that it smoothly transitions between viewpoints. No more instant transitions like we veterans are used to when zooming. This is definitely news to some longtime users who are unsettled by these disturbing trends. You can turn off this feature or tweak it to your liking using the VTOPTIONS command.

On the plus side, view transitions give a sense of context to navigation by providing visual feedback during transitions. On the downside, view transitions take time. The three check boxes at the top of the View Transitions dialog control where and if this feature is enabled. Uncheck all three, and you successfully turn view transitions off and instant transitions back on (VTENABLE system variable).

On the other hand, maybe delays measured in milliseconds are a small price to pay to gain a sense of context during transition. It's harder to get lost in space with smooth view transitions guiding you along. Set the transition speed in milliseconds by dragging the slider (VTDURATION system variable).

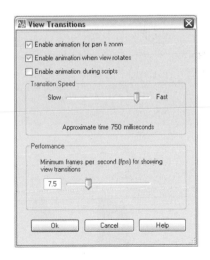

Large drawings tend to overwhelm your graphics card's ability to perform smooth view transitions. Drag the Performance slider to set the minimum frames per second that a smooth view transition is performed (VTFPS system variable). If the transition can't be performed at your set frame rate, an instant transition happens instead.

Orbiting Viewpoints

Working in the third dimension requires the ability to see the model from all angles. 3DORBIT is the right tool for this job. As with ZOOM, paying attention to the subtleties makes all the difference with efficient orbiting.

3DORBIT: Constraint or Freedom?

If given the choice, you'd choose freedom, right? Even though freedom sounds better, orbiting with constraint is the wiser choice. In AutoCAD 2007, the 3DORBIT command has been updated. Where you once had the freedom to orbit in any old way that you wanted, now 3DORBIT has enforced constraint built-in.

The reason for this change is simple. There was (and is) a tendency to become hopelessly disoriented with free orbit. Before you knew it, you'd be upside-down and backward, wondering what happened. Now the tool of choice—3DORBIT—is constrained so that you can't rotate beyond the poles to make more than one complete rotation. That ought to keep you more grounded. The free orbit command is still available (for those with strong stomachs only) under the name 3DFORBIT. Even the name sounds like a bad idea!

In addition, most visual styles (except 2D Wireframe) give you unmistakable visual feedback that makes it hard to become disoriented. When you're looking down on the model, the viewport is medium gray by default. A horizon line appears in the distance as you rotate downward, and the "night sky" gets darker as the viewpoint becomes lower.

By the way, 3DCORBIT is the continuous orbit command, which keeps spinning around and around (possibly good for presentations designed to disorient and for impressive ever-spinning objects).

Intuitive Orbiting and Swiveling

The most intuitive way to pivot around three-dimensional space is to hold a key and drag the mouse wheel. You probably drag the mouse wheel all the time already, to pan. Just hold down the Shift key while you drag the wheel button, and you'll be orbiting—temporary transparent constrained 3D orbiting, to be precise. This is the speedy way to access the new 3DORBIT command.

A further refinement of this technique is to make a selection of one or more objects first. Then, holding down Shift and dragging the wheel button pivots around the selection, rather than around the center of the viewport. In addition, all the unselected objects are hidden while you orbit, so you can focus on orienting the viewpoint in reference to what you're working on.

Think of swiveling as the opposite of orbiting. When you're orbiting, rotation is centered either on the viewport or on the selection. When you're swiveling, the center of rotation is the *camera* you're looking through. Yes, every viewport uses the virtual camera analogy, even if you haven't created a Camera object. The target of the camera is what you're moving by swiveling, while the camera stays put.

Hold down the Ctrl key while dragging the wheel button to swivel. Again, this is a temporary transparent version of the 3DSWIVEL command. In short, hold down the Shift or Ctrl key while dragging the wheel to orbit or swivel intuitively.

One-Button Orbit

Not everyone wants to hold down Shift while dragging the wheel button to orbit—to some people this may seem awkward. Instead, you may prefer to be more explicit in command execution, or maybe you just prefer using the keyboard over the mouse.

For one-button orbit, assign the 3DORBIT command to the F4 function key. If you're an Inventor user, you *must* make this change. Inventor uses F4 to orbit, so this simple alteration will keep you from going crazy as you switch between applications. Even if you never use Inventor, one-button orbit is a great idea.

The F4 key is an excellent choice for reassignment because it currently calibrates a tablet—and let's face it, almost no one in the AutoCAD world uses a tablet any longer (they're so 20th century). To make the easy shortcut reassignment, follow these steps:

1. Use the CUI command. Expand the Keyboard Shortcuts node in the upper-left panel. Expand the Shortcut Keys node as well.

2. Scroll down the command list (in the lower left panel), and locate 3D Orbit. Drag this command up, and drop it anywhere in the Shortcut Keys list. Click the Apply button.

3. Select 3D Orbit from the Shortcut Keys list.

4. Click the Key(s) field under Access in the Properties pane below(in the lower-right panel). Then, click the ellipsis button that appears.

5. Press the F4 function key, and click OK to assign this shortcut key to 3D Orbit. Notice that it claims the F4 key is currently unassigned, even though you know it's already assigned to Tablet. Click OK again to exit the CUI dialog.

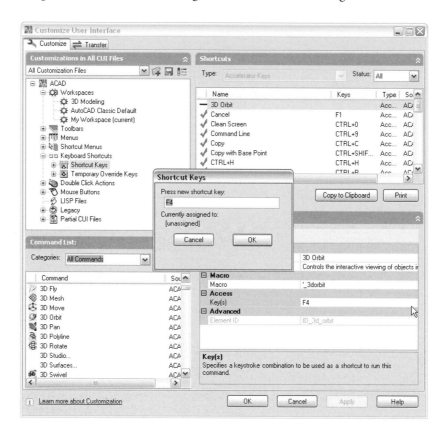

See Chapter 10, "Customization," to learn more about Customization.

Orbit into Elevation and Section

Did you know you can quickly generate elevations of a 3D model by orbiting into a preset view? Interior elevations and sections can also be made by clipping exterior elevations.

Traditional elevations are orthographic projections, meaning they're viewed with parallel projection and usually from a preset view—although you can push elevations beyond the traditional with these tools.

Start by orbiting into a preset view that looks at the side of the model you want to elevate, such as Left, Right, Front, or Back. Quick access to preset views is available from the shortcut menu within the 3DORBIT command. Use this shortcut menu to set parallel projection for a traditional elevation. If your aim is to generate an exterior elevation, then save a named view, and you're done.

If you want to take it a step further and generate an interior elevation, use the 3DCLIP command (it's no longer on the 3DORBIT shortcut menu); the Adjust Clipping Planes dialog appears. It shows a top thumbnail view of the model and has two horizontal lines that represent the front and back clipping planes.

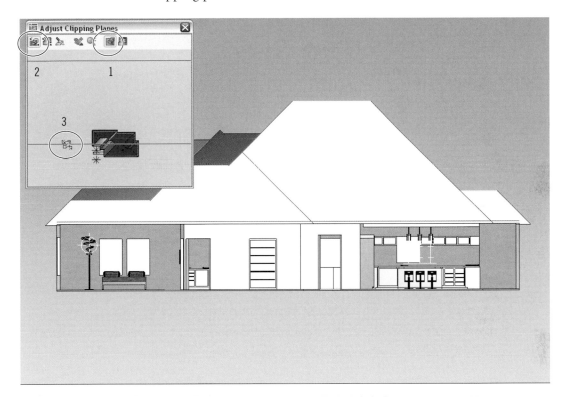

To make an elevation, adjust the front clipping plane to cut away a portion of the model that is obscuring its interior. Here's how it's done:

1. In the Adjust Clipping Planes dialog, toggle on the Front clipping plane by clicking the appropriate button in the toolbar (read the tooltips).

2. Click the Adjust Front Clipping button.

3. Drag the black horizontal line in the thumbnail up until it intersects the model. You see real-time visual feedback in the viewport as part of the model is clipped away. When you're satisfied with the amount of cut away, close the dialog, and save a named view.

You can also try to switch back into Perspective projection while the building is still clipped. Doing so yields a perspective section. Try orbiting slightly for an oblique cut away view of the model, which is a revealing way to visualize a model.

First-Person Navigation

AutoCAD 2007 has fantastic first-person navigation tools (3DWALK and 3DFLY) that put you in the 3D driver's seat. These controls function much like what you'd expect to find in a "first-person shooter" game on Microsoft Xbox or Sony PlayStation.

Before you roll your eyes, give these tools a chance. Orbiting is fine for rotating objects, but first-person navigation is the most effective method for visualizing and getting around interior space. Philosophically, this change in point of view moves you from an all-seeing godlike perspective somewhere up in the sky to a more human one, walking or flying around a defined space.

Would You Prefer to Walk or Fly?

When you walk, your "feet" are constrained to the "ground" of the XY plane, whereas you're free when flying. Expand the 3D Navigate control panel on the Dashboard. Click Perspective Projection (rightmost button) if this mode is not already on. Then click the Walk button (footprints icon), and drag the Step Size and/or Steps Per Second sliders to the right so you can get around more quickly.

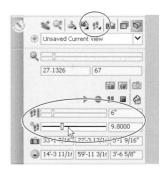

Whether you choose to use 3DWALK or 3DFLY, the navigation controls are the same. There are two identical sets of keyboard controls—one for each hand—so lefties are equally happy. This dual-handed support is welcome because you need one hand on the mouse and one hand on the keyboard to walk or fly in a coordinated fashion.

Press and hold the appropriate keys to walk or fly:

Function	Left Hand	Right Hand
Move forward	W	Up Arrow
Move backward	S	Down Arrow
Move left	A	Left Arrow
Move right	D	Right Arrow

Look and turn by dragging the mouse. Note that you can drag the mouse while holding down keys simultaneously for smoother movement. Pay attention to the target location (green crosshairs) in the center of the screen. This is where you're going, so aim accordingly. If you're walking, you can move up and down relative to the ground plane by dragging (not turning) the wheel button up and down. You can also swivel to the right or left by holding down the first mouse button.

Toggle between walk and fly modes by pressing F while in either mode. The Position Locator palette is another useful aid to navigation. Not only does it always show where you are, but you can also drag the camera or its target to immediately change what you're looking at. Plus, it's helpful in indicating any hiding aliens around the corner (OK…not really).

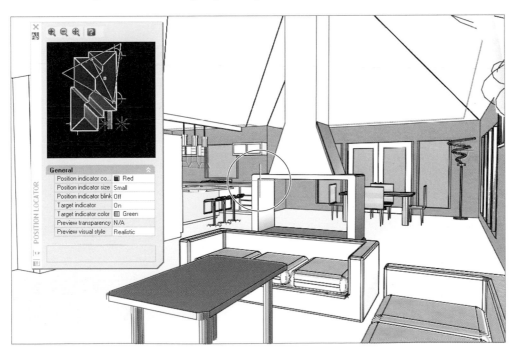

You'll get the best results by practicing first-person navigation in an enclosed space (like the 3D House sample file located in C:\Program Files\AutoCAD 2007\Sample). Better yet, play some console games, and chalk it up to "work research."

Navigation by the Numbers

Effectively getting around in virtual space requires using many different navigation commands. To save time switching between all these commands, a handy shortcut submenu called Other Navigation Modes is accessible from every one of the relevant commands.

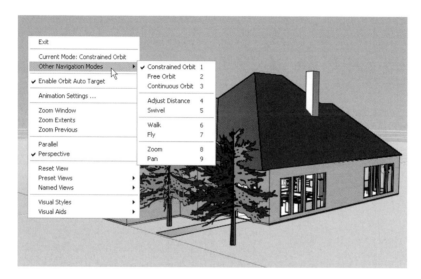

Even better, once you memorize the numerical shortcuts for these commands, just type the number of the command you want to switch to—that's way faster then right-clicking to access the Other Navigation Modes shortcut submenu. Of course, typing numbers only works when you're in any one of the navigation commands; the numbers aren't literally commands themselves.

Navigation Mode	Shortcut
Constrained Orbit	1
Free Orbit	2
Continuous Orbit	3
Adjust Distance	4
Swivel	5
Walk	6
Fly	7
Zoom	8
Pan	9

Work in Perspective

Perspective has been available in AutoCAD for many years, first through the awkward DVIEW command, and later as an option of 3DORBIT. Perhaps it's because we naturally see the world in perspective that this is such a nice feature. Perspective projection in AutoCAD has always been useful for presentation, but for little else—until now.

AutoCAD 2007 finally allows you to snap in perspective. This is a huge development. Now you can work normally in perspective and do what it is we do in CAD: draw precisely with object snap.

This may not sound like much of a tip, but it is. Now that you know, you can make use of this fact and start working in perspective.

There are still a couple of caveats: Perspective isn't available in 2D Wireframe display, and Zoom Object doesn't work in perspective either. But we aren't complaining.

Viewing in Style

AutoCAD 2007 has had a major facelift in the visualization department. Some of the most impressive changes deal with visual styles, cameras, and views. These visual improvements will have you 3D modeling in style.

Develop Your Own Visual Style

AutoCAD has a few visual styles right out of the box, but to really take advantage of this new-found ability, power users will want to develop their own visual styles. Still, let's not reinvent the wheel—it's easiest to get started by copying and pasting an existing visual style. In this example, you'll make a white monochrome faceted visual style that has a nice abstract appeal.

1. Open the Visual Style Manager by clicking the rightmost button on the Visual Style control panel on the Dashboard. You can also get this by choosing Tools → Palettes → Visual Styles.

2. Right-click the Conceptual visual style slot, and choose Copy from the shortcut menu.

3. Right-click in the blank slot, and choose Paste.

4. Right-click the freshly pasted style, and choose Edit Name And Description. Call it White, and describe it as Faceted and Monochrome.

5. Double-click White to make it active. A tiny icon appears on the active user-defined visual style slot.

6. Under Face Settings, change lighting quality to Faceted and Face Color Mode to Monochrome. Click the first icon on the Edge Modifiers title bar to turn on Overhanging Edges, to give this style a sketchy look. Finally, scroll down the palette and turn Fast Silhouette Edges invisible.

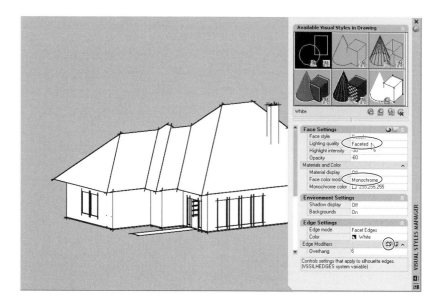

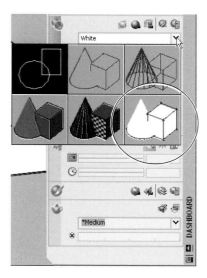

Expand the Dashboard, and open the Visual Style drop-down list. Your new White style appears in this menu, complete with a white thumbnail indicating your assigned settings. That's all it takes to create a custom visual style. With some experimentation, you be stylin'!

Did you know that three more, less obvious visual styles come with AutoCAD? Check out the Visual Styles palette in the Tool Palettes. After you've expanded the Visual Styles control panel on the Dashboard, the Visual Styles palette group should already be active (see "Set Up the Dashboard/Tool Palette Connection" in Chapter 1).

The Visual Styles palette group has one palette called, for lack of a better name, Visual Styles. Click each button to try out the X-Ray, Sketchy, and Shades of Gray visual styles. Drag the White visual style from the Visual Styles Manager onto this palette; it's just that easy. Now you can use White on any drawing you care to open, because its visual style remains on the palette.

That's great if you want to reuse visual styles on your own machine. But what if your colleague saw what a cool visual style you made and wants you to share the wealth? The only way to do this is to export your Visual Styles palette group to a file that your colleague then can import onto their machine.

Use the CUSTOMIZE command to manage tool palette groups. Right-click the Visual Styles palette group on the right, and you'll find its Export and Import options. These deal with files having an .xpg extension, which means eXported Palette Group file.

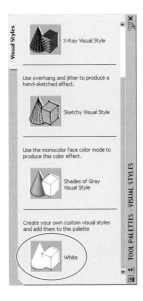

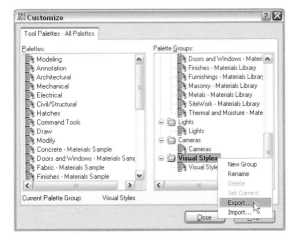

Visual Styles are viewport-specific, whether you use tiled viewports in modelspace or floating viewports in paperspace.

Place Cameras to Gain Perspective

Cameras are more than placeholders—they're a special kind of interactive view. Cameras have a *glyph*, or graphic representation, to interact with and a preview window that helps you to fine-tune the composition. The way you interact with cameras has come a long way since the ancient and awkward DVIEW command. Here's how to get the most out of cameras in AutoCAD 2007:

1. Switch into the Top viewpoint by using the drop-down in the 3D Navigate control panel.

2. Click the Create Camera button in the 3D Navigate control panel, or use the CAMERA command.

3. Click somewhere in the viewport to locate the camera glyph, and then click again to locate its target. Choose Exit from the dynamic prompt, or press Enter to end the command.

4. Select the camera glyph. The Camera Preview window appears. Use the grips on the Camera object to help compose the view you see in the Camera Preview window.

5. Change viewpoints by orbiting, and continue refining the location of the camera, its target, and the field of view using the camera object's grips.

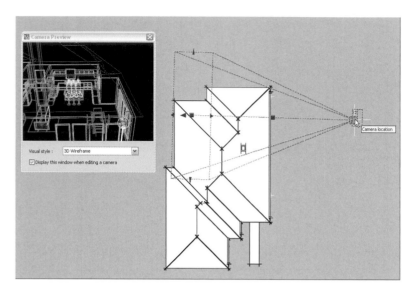
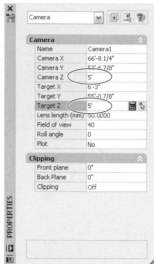

6. If you want numerical accuracy, change the camera properties in the Properties palette. For example, change the Camera Z and Target Z properties to eye level (that's about 5′ in Imperial units).

7. Once you're satisfied with the composition as seen in the Camera Preview, look through the camera lens in the viewport by selecting the camera from the drop-down in the 3D Navigate control panel.

> Set the camera glyph's appearance using the Options command, on the Drafting tab.

If you create lots of cameras and views, their glyphs can be a bit distracting on screen. Hide camera glyphs by clicking the Display Cameras toggle on the expanded 3D Navigate control panel. Otherwise, you can set the system variable CAMERADISPLAY to 0 to turn them off.

Manage Named Views

Named views have been given new life in AutoCAD 2007. Views have been around for many years, but they're finally coming into their own power.

It used to be that views were nothing more than spatial bookmarks; they recorded a place on screen that you could recall easily. Views still do that—but in AutoCAD 2007, views are hopped up on performance-enhancing substances.

At the same time that views record a place in space, they may also save a layer snapshot, named UCS, live section, visual style, and/or background, all at your choosing.

Save Views in Paperspace

There's nothing to saving views in paperspace now. Just use the VIEW command when you're in a layout, and save a new view. It's automatically categorized under the Layout Views node in the Views tree shown in the View Manager dialog box.

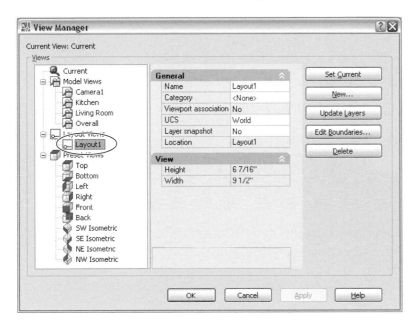

Layout views are most useful when you have many different viewports on a large title block and want quick categorized access to each one.

For example, say you're working away in modelspace and realize something needs your attention on a particular layout—restore the named layout view, and you instantly jump to paperspace, no questions asked! No TILEMODE, no layout tabs, no zooming in, just pure navigational efficiency.

> The fastest way to access named views is with the drop-down on the 3D Navigate control panel on the Dashboard.

Take Layer Snapshots with Views

What's this about layers and views? Never before have these flavors been mixed. It's a delectable combination, as you'll soon appreciate. The New View dialog box that appears when you save a view has a check box (on by default) that allows you to save a layer snapshot with the view.

So, what's a layer snapshot? More precisely, it's a record of the On/Off and Freeze/Thaw status of all layers in the drawing. Think of it as a mini-Layer States Manager that works within views.

Layer snapshots are a friendlier alternative to freezing VP layers, if you know what that means. Sometimes called *viewport layers*, these are freeze/thaw controls that appear in the Layer Manager only when you're in the modelspace of a floating viewport on a layout. Got that?

VP layers have been used for many years by people who like to leave all the layers on in modelspace when they're working but freeze certain layers in viewports to reveal particular plans. It's not right or wrong; it's just one method that has evolved to meet certain needs over time. Consider how much simpler layer snapshots are! Here's a typical workflow:

1. Set up the layer visibility states just as you like them. That means turning on and off certain layers and possibly freezing and thawing others until what you see is what you want.

2. Navigate to the prototypical place where you want to remember this view; it can be either modelspace or paperspace.

3. Create a named view, and leave Save Layer Snapshot With View checked. Choose a UCS, live section, and/or visual style if appropriate. Click OK to save the view.

That's it. Now work some more: Turn layers on and off; freeze and thaw with abandon. Restore the named view whenever you need it.

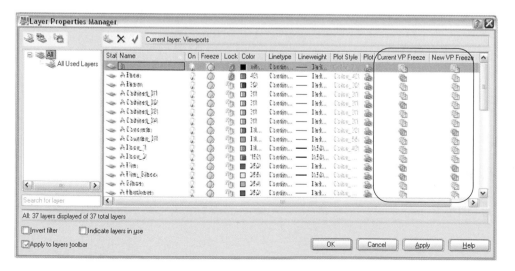

Click the Update Layers button in the View Manager dialog box to save a new layer snapshot with an existing view.

Convert Viewport Layers to Layer Snapshots

Once you realize how nifty layer snapshots are, you may want to convert legacy drawings to use this new feature. If you have some drawings still using VP layers, here is an easy procedure to convert their viewports' visibility status to named views:

1. Open the legacy drawing that uses VP layers. Go to a layout, and double-click the viewport in question. Open the Layer Manager, and click the column heading Current VP Freeze or New VP Freeze to sort the layer list.

2. Notice that all the layers that have been frozen in current and/or new viewports have been sorted so they're adjacent in the layer list. You may need to scroll all the way to the bottom of the layer list to find them. Shift-select all these layers.

3. Click one of the selected layers' lightbulb icons in the On column to turn off the selected layers.

4. Click the snowflake icon in the current or new VP layer column to thaw the selection. Now you have transferred visibility from the viewport to the (global) layers. Click OK.

5. Save a named view centered on the viewport, and make sure Save Layer Snapshot With View is checked.

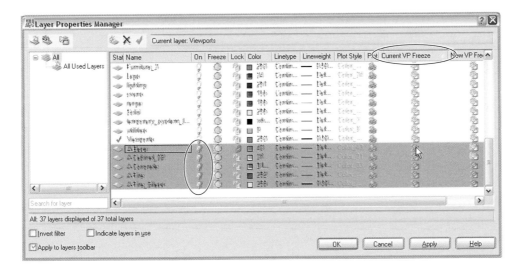

Explore Design Alternatives with Snapshots

You can simulate design alternatives with snapshots. For example, a kitchen designer may have a few different kitchen layouts to present to the client or to think about in-house. Duplicates of the cabinets and appliances can be made and placed on alternate layers, like Alt-A, Alt-B, and so on. Then, the alternate objects can be rearranged according to the design intent. Named views can be saved with snapshots that record one alternate at a time. Here's how it may work:

1. Use the fabulous Express Tool COPYTOLAYER to create duplicates of your chosen objects on new layers. Call the new layers Alt-A, Alt-B, and so on.

2. Turn off all the layer alternates except Alt-A, and save a view with a layer snapshot. Call the view Alternate-A, for lack of a more interesting title.

3. Turn off the Alt-A layer, and turn on Alt-B.

4. Save another view called Alternate-B with a layer snapshot.

5. Repeat steps 3–4 for as many alternate layers as you have.

6. Recall named views at will to reveal the design alternatives during a presentation or brainstorming session.

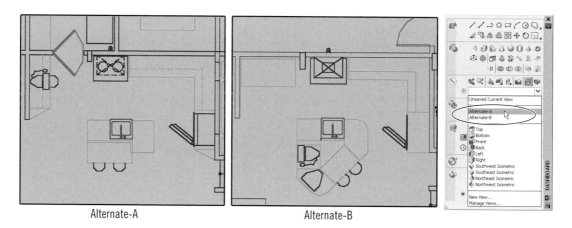

Alternate-A   Alternate-B

See the Background behind Views

A nice way to spice up on-screen presentations is to show a background image behind views. Every named view has the ability to display a background color, gradient, or image. Of these, images are probably the spiciest choice. You like spicy?

1. Save a named view or edit an existing one by opening the View Manager.

2. Open the Background override drop-down, and choose Image.

3. Browse for a suitable background image file on your hard drive. Skies, cityscapes, even real photos of the project site will do.

4. Click the Adjust Image button in the Background dialog if you want to play with the offset and/or scale of the image. Click OK.

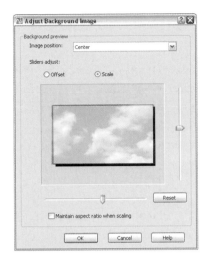

5. Apply and save the named view, and then call it up again from the 3D Navigate control panel in the Dashboard. You may have to restore the view if the background doesn't show up immediately on screen. What a difference a background makes—now we're cooking!

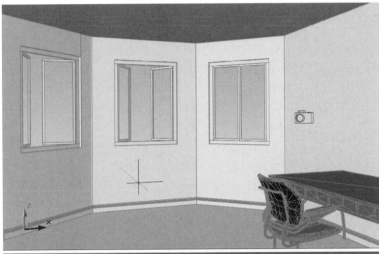

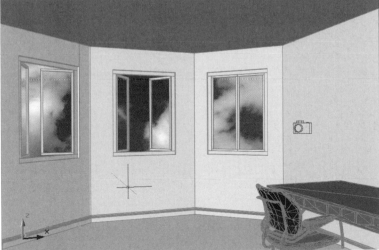

Presenting Realistic Imagery

Never before has it been so easy to present your designs in a realistic light with AutoCAD. AutoCAD 2007 has new materials and lights, mental image's mental ray rendering engine, and amazingly, the ability to save animations. This section will teach you the ins and outs of making your 3D models look absolutely fabulous.

Materials

Materials are all about surface—defining how light is reflected, absorbed, and/or refracted and transmitted all the way through. Is the surface smooth or bumpy, matte or shiny, reflective or translucent? You'll be able to dial in exactly the look you're looking for with materials.

Install the Material Library

The number one thing you should do if you're at all concerned about making your life easy is to install the optional materials library. Although we're not too sure why it's an option (maybe to save hard-drive space), the materials library offers you multiple palettes of 300 professionally built real-world materials.

In the AutoCAD installer, a page in the wizard asks if you want to install the Express tools and/or the materials library. If you clicked Next a little too hastily, there is a way to add these features later, after you've installed AutoCAD:

1. Go to the Start menu → Settings → Control Panel → Add, and Remove Programs.

2. Locate AutoCAD 2007 in the list of programs, and click its Change button. Be very, very careful not to click Remove.

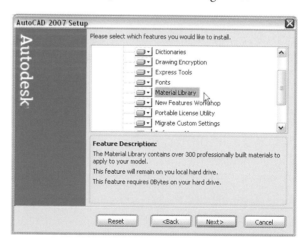

3. Choose Add Or Remove Features in the wizard, and then locate Material Library in the list. Choose "Will be installed on local hard drive."

4. While you're at it, also make sure to install the ultra-useful Express Tools. Complete the install wizard, and you're back in business.

After you've installed the materials library, you're probably wondering why your life doesn't seem any easier yet. To reap the true rewards, you also have to know how to access the materials library.

Open the Tool palettes, and click its Properties button (at the bottom) to access additional palette groups. Notice that both Materials and Materials Library appear—Materials is standard, and you just installed the Materials Library palette group. Select Materials Library, and examine the plethora of pre-made materials on the following palettes:

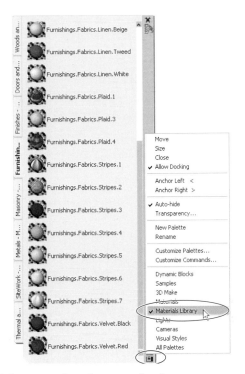

- Woods And Plastics

- Doors And Windows

- Finishes

- Furnishings

- Masonry

- Metals

- Sitework

- Thermal And Moisture

Many of these palettes are repeated in the Materials group, but there are far fewer materials on the standard palettes as compared to those in the library. The Materials palette group also includes these palettes, in case you were looking for them:

- Concrete

- Fabric

- Flooring

If your palette groups are empty, use the CUSTOMIZE command, and drag the appropriate palettes (ending with Materials Sample) under the Materials group. Drag palettes that end in Materials Library into the Materials Library palette group, and you'll be all set up.

Optimize 3D Performance

Displaying materials and textures in the viewport is a great way to visualize surface qualities, but doing so can also greatly impact 3D performance—which is especially troublesome in large models.

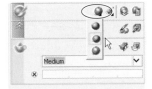

You can toggle the display of materials, textures, or both by using the first flyout button on the Materials control panel. Use the first button to turn off both materials and textures, the second button to turn off textures, and the third button to leave both on.

Materials determine surface qualities like color, shininess, and translucency, whereas textures are images mapped onto surfaces that add much more realism. Unfortunately, your graphics system has to calculate all these interesting qualities in real time, so leaving both materials and textures on while you're navigating and working can bog you down.

Turning off textures and materials speeds things up; that makes sense. But now using AutoCAD isn't much fun because you can't see all the pretty surfaces you've spent time beautifying. You're in luck: There is an alternative that may keep you smiling.

Another way to optimize your 3D performance that isn't as black and white as turning off the interesting bits is to prioritize the adaptive degradation for materials and textures. What's that, you say?

The 3D performance can be *degraded* in real time, meaning turned down a notch or two when necessary. This can happen adaptively, so only as much of the good stuff is taken away as is needed to maintain your chosen frame rate—and that ensures smooth navigation. We suggest moving textures and materials up in the adaptive degra-

Top: Materials and textures off
Middle: Materials on and textures off
Bottom: Materials and textures on

dation priority list, so they get degraded first. That way, you can leave the display of materials and textures on, and you'll see them only when it's not hurting your 3D performance. To see how this is done, follow these steps:

1. Use the 3DCONFIG command.

2. Scroll down the list that determines the priority for what gets degraded first. Select Materials, and leave it checked.

3. Click the Move Up button repeatedly until Materials is at the top of the degradation order.

4. Select Textures, lower in the list, and move it all the way up to the top of the list. You want Textures to get degraded first because they hurt performance the most. Click OK.

5. Turn on materials and textures by clicking the third option on the first flyout button on the Materials control panel. Now you have the best of both worlds.

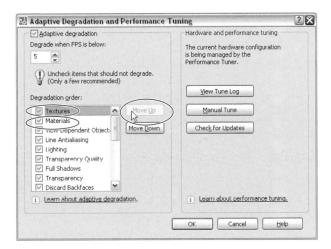

Customize Materials to Get the Look You Want

You probably don't have a lot of time to play with materials—you have a job to do, and you want to prepare your drawing quickly for rendering. Customizing existing materials is the fast track to getting what you want. It beats creating materials from scratch. Fortunately, there are lots of preset materials to choose from, especially if you install the Materials Library (see the first topic in this section).

Maybe you can find a material in the library that represents the surface of your model just as you imagined. If so, attach it and move on. If it's a close match, but not perfect, then learn to customize. Here's how it works:

1. Open the Tool palettes, and browse either the Materials and/or Materials Library palette groups.

2. Use the MAT command to open the Materials palette.

3. When you find a potentially interesting material, drag it from the Tool palette, and drop it into one of the slots in the Materials palette.

4. Customize any of the parameters that define the material to suit it to fit your needs.

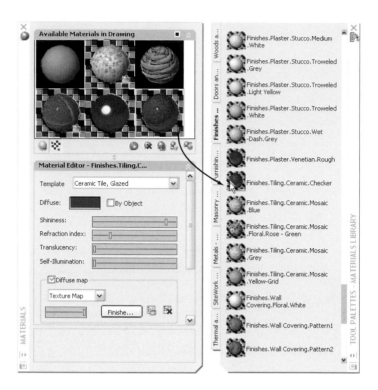

5. If you make extensive changes, right-click the swatch in the Materials palette, and choose Edit Name And Description. It pays to be descriptive. Changes you make in the Materials palette affect the current drawing only.

6. Attach the material to objects or object faces (see the next topic).

Drag materials you have customized and want to reuse in other drawings to a tool palette.

Clever Ways to Attach Materials

Do you want to attach a material to a single object or selection of objects and/or faces, or hand-attach it by layer? Each method has its plusses and minuses. Choose the method that suits you:

Attach By Layer The method chosen most often by neat, tidy, organized folks. Attaching materials to layers is the most powerful method, but it requires *planning*. You need to have thought ahead when you were modeling to end up with all the parts that require separate materials on different layers. If this is you, congratulations. Most people use a hybrid approach.

Use the MATERIALATTACH command, which can be found as the Attach By Layer button on the Materials control panel. Drag material icons from the left pane to icons in the right pane of the Material Attachment Options dialog.

You'll need to load the materials you want to attach prior to using this command—see what we mean about planning?

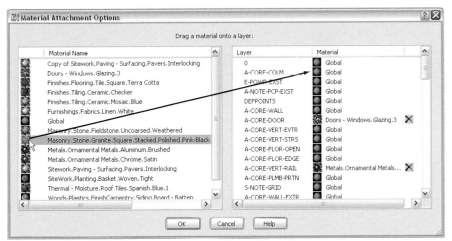

Attach By Object The most obvious method, right? Drag a material from the Tool palettes, and drop it on an object to attach intuitively. This is both easy and dangerous. It's easy to attach a material to the wrong object when dragging and indiscriminately dropping.

To avoid these dangers, click a material tool in the Tool palettes, and then make a selection of objects and press Enter. This method has the added advantage of being able to attach a material to multiple objects in a selection.

On the other hand, if you've been customizing materials, then the natural next step is to click the Apply Material To Objects button in the Materials palette toolbar.

This method can be tedious and slow if you find yourself attaching materials individually to hundreds of objects. A little time spent planning to attach materials by layer may really be worth it.

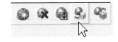

Attach By Face Often used in exceptional circumstances. You want a different material on one surface of an object that already has a good material applied. Instead of slicing the object into two parts and possibly putting the parts onto two different layers, attach the material to the face in question. Attaching material per face is a much more direct approach.

To attach per face, all you need is a subobject selection. Hold down Ctrl, and select a face or two. Then, right-click the material's slot in the Materials palette, and choose Apply Material To Selection.

Convert Materials from/for Other Programs

If you open an old drawing from a previous version of AutoCAD that has materials defined, use the CONVERTOLDMATERIALS command to bring it up to snuff in AutoCAD 2007. Also do this if you've imported a 3ds file using the 3DSIN command, to ensure everything is hunky dory.

If you're opening an old drawing that has materials defined, chances are it also has maps, as in bitmaps or textures. In all probability, you're now missing those maps because they're separate files after all, not part of the drawing file you opened. In order for the materials to render correctly, they need to know where their dependent maps are located. Here's how you fix it:

1. Use the Options command, and select the Files tab.

2. Scroll down, and expand the Texture Maps Search Path. Click Add and then Browse.

3. Locate the maps folder where the texture image files are located, and add it to the texture search path. Click OK.

If you plan on using Autodesk VIZ and/or 3ds Max instead of AutoCAD for your visualization needs, there is no need to export your drawings to any other file format. Although most (if not all) Autodesk products can read the DWG format, only contemporaries can understand each other. In other words, you need 3ds Max 8 or VIZ 2007 if you want to open native DWG files written by AutoCAD 2007.

> See Chapter 8, " Sharing Data," to learn how you can use the freely available DWG TrueConvert to convert files to different versions.

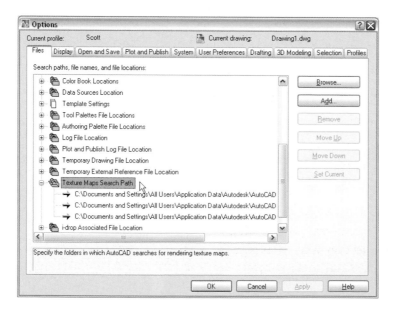

If you're planning to use VIZ and/or 3ds Max with AutoCAD you'll be happy to hear that materials are preserved in translation. 3ds Max 8 users have to download the free RealDWG 2007 extension to read DWG 2007 files, though.

Other tidbits: AutoCAD's materials that use the Realistic shader get converted to Architectural materials. Materials that use the Advanced shader get converted to Standard materials. All objects coming from AutoCAD have real-world mapping coordinates applied.

Textures

Textures are also known as maps, or *bitmaps* to be precise. *Bitmaps* is the $2 word for images—although with the devaluation of the dollar, maybe that should now be a $20 word. Being images, bitmaps are naturally made of pixels that need to be told how to stretch across geometry in AutoCAD. This stretching, and possibly repeating process (known as *tiling*) of getting pixels arranged on geometry is called *mapping*.

Mapping Coordinates Scaled to Fit

Objects get *mapping coordinates* assigned automatically in AutoCAD. Mapping needs a coordinate system to know how much to scale and/or tile images in relation to geometry.

The letters X, Y, and Z were already taken by the philosopher Descartes in his namesake Cartesian coordinate system to represent the primary axes of 3D space; the mapping coordinate system gods had to look for other letters.

Not being able to think of anything better, they chose U, V, and W to represent mapping coordinate space for the obvious reason that these precede the other letters—as in U, V, W, X, Y, Z. Incidentally, this is a good way to remember that UVW is a different sort of space than, well, XYZ space. UVW space is on the surface of objects that exist in XYZ space. Get that?

Generally in AutoCAD you only worry about mapping when you're not happy with the way UVW coordinates were assigned by default. There are two possible culprits: the material and the object itself. Of these, the material is the more likely suspect. Let's bring it in:

1. Use the MAT command to open the Materials palette.

2. Select the material in question—the one that is disturbing your happiness because its mapping doesn't look right.

3. Click the "Adjust scale/tiling, offset, rotation values of bitmap" button in the Materials palette. That was a mouthful.

4. By default, textures are set to scale, and even though no units are set, the texture repeats. In many cases, this isn't what you want. For example, let's say you're making a picture frame with a piece of artwork on it that you want to see without repetition (it's not pop art).

5. Click the Fit To Object radio button in the Adjust Bitmap dialog.

Use MaterialMap to manually set and adjust planar, box, spherical, and/or cylindrical mapping coordinates.

When a bitmap is scaled to fit an object, it's displayed exactly once in U and V (it doesn't repeat). Use this technique whenever you have a bitmap that you want to see without tiling—signs, logos, photos, paintings, and other forms of *entourage* (see "Add to Your Entourage") are likely candidates.

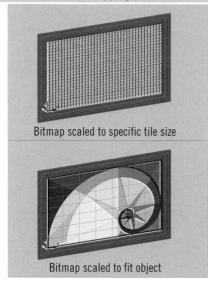

Bitmap scaled to specific tile size

Bitmap scaled to fit object

Scale Bitmaps for the Real World

If you have samples of the materials used in your project, and a digital camera, you can make accurate AutoCAD materials based on your real-world materials. We've seen it in action at the office, and it's pretty cool. It's simple: Take photos of the samples, and clean them up and crop them in Adobe Photoshop if you're able. Once you have a digital image file, follow these steps:

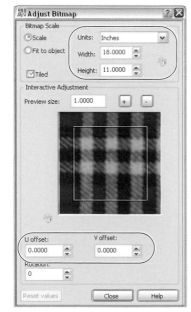

1. Create a new material in AutoCAD on the Materials palette.

2. Select Texture Map in the drop-down list in the Diffuse Map area. Click the Select button, and locate the bitmap on your hard drive.

3. Click the Adjust Bitmap button next to your new texture map.

4. In the Adjust Bitmap dialog, select the Scale radio button.

5. Select a unit of measurement in the drop-down list. What you choose here determines the units of the values in the Width and Height parameters.

6. Estimate the real-world width and height of the photo, and enter those values.

7. Optionally, adjust the U and V offsets to center the bitmap in the frame. Whatever is inside the frame gets tiled in real-world scale.

Real-world scale is turned off if you select None in the Units drop-down of the Adjust Bitmap dialog.

Quickly Tint Textures

Have you ever found the perfect texture—except for the fact that it's the wrong color? The texture is fine, but it needs to have a specific hue. Don't despair: There is quick fix that doesn't require advanced knowledge of Photoshop.

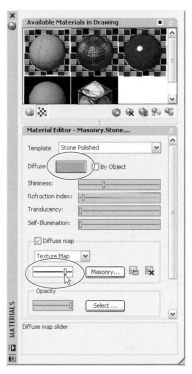

For example, let's assume you're looking for a square stacked polished granite material—but in green. There's a material like this in the library, in gray. Here's what to do:

1. Load the material in question into the Materials palette.

2. Click the Diffuse color swatch to open the Select Color dialog box, and select an exaggerated hue similar to what you're looking for. If you want a medium green, choose a very bright saturated green instead.

3. Drag the diffuse slider to the left slightly, maybe just to 85 percent. This decreases the amount the texture map is used and mixes it with the diffuse color you chose previously. Be careful not to drag the slider too low, or you'll lose detail in the texture as the color takes over. This technique works best with neutral or gray bitmaps.

> Take grayscale photos of real-world textures, and mix in color in the material to cover all possible hues.

Add to Your Entourage

It's easy to identify beginners to computer visualization, because their images are almost always devoid of life and lack real-world context. Bring an otherwise boring rendering to life by adding people, plants, cars, furniture, and anything else you can think of to make your designed environment or object more believable. These added elements that dress up your visualization are called *entourage*, technically speaking.

An incredibly difficult and time-consuming way to do this would be to make 3D models of all your desired entourage. Don't go there unless you need absolute realism! An easier way is to make opacity-mapped materials and map them onto flat surfaces. This photographic technique is enough to fool the camera—and, you hope, your audience as well.

To do it right, you need Adobe Photoshop to produce opacity-mapped entourage from photographs. Extracting images from their backgrounds is an involved process that requires more space to describe than is available here.

> See *Enhancing CAD Drawings with Photoshop* (Sybex, 2005) by Scott Onstott to produce entourage from photos.

We'll explain how to use ready-made entourage in AutoCAD. In addition to making entourage yourself, there are a few places on the Internet where you can purchase entourage. Check out the following sites:

- realworldimagery.com

- marlinstudios.com

- archvision.com

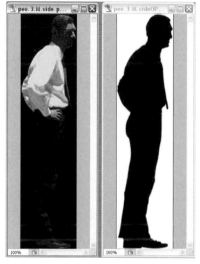

Entourage always has two parts: a color photograph and a corresponding grayscale opacity map (called an *alpha channel* in Photoshop). In AutoCAD, these need to be separate image files.

The opacity map tells AutoCAD where the material is opaque (black) and where it's completely transparent (white). The edge often has shades of gray that are partially transparent. Let's use this entourage in AutoCAD 2007:

1. Use the PLANESURF command to create a flat surface. Rotate it up, and position it in your model where you want the entourage to appear.

2. Edit the plane object, and roughly match its aspect ratio with the entourage.

3. Create a new material on the Materials palette and choose the Advanced template.

4. Assign the color photo as the material's diffuse map.

5. Assign the corresponding grayscale image as the material's opacity map.

6. Drag the Shininess slider to 0.

The diffuse map appears in the viewport, so you still see the black fill surrounding the cut out. The entourage appears correctly only when rendered.

Sharing Data

THERE ARE ZILLIONS of ways to share design data with AutoCAD. Not only is it essential to share data with outside consultants, but sharing is equally important within your in-house team. How you share depends on the relationship you want to have with the design data, and the applications you use.

This chapter examines the ins and outs of exchanging data via the clipboard, DesignCenter, and i-drop. You'll also be able to increase Xref performance, underlay DWF files, and learn top-secret techniques that will save you loads of time. This chapter gives you tips on how to share and play nicely AutoCAD-style.

This chapter's techniques are organized into the following topics:

- Moving Data between Drawings
- Making External References
- Working with Other Applications

Moving Data between Drawings

There are several ways to get the stuff you've drawn from one drawing into another. Cut, copy, paste is the most intuitive way to move data between two drawings, whereas the DesignCenter is better used for multiple drawings and symbol libraries. If you're accessing drawing content on the Internet, then i-drop is the technology for you.

Cut, Copy, and Paste

The Clipboard sure beats the old fashioned way of moving drawing data with the WBLOCK and INSERT commands. When you cut, copy, and paste drawing entities with the Windows Clipboard, folders, files and filenames don't even enter into the picture.

There is more to using the Clipboard than meets the eye, at least as far as AutoCAD is concerned. Cut (Ctrl+X), Copy (Ctrl+C), and Paste (Ctrl+V) will do the job, but you'll lose the objects' place in space if you use the Clipboard with these defaults.

We suggest using alternative commands to preserve the spatial context of objects transferred between drawings via the Clipboard. Right-click in the drawing window, and you'll see a shortcut menu grouping the Clipboard commands together.

One possibility is to copy source objects to the Clipboard using the default copy—either Ctrl+C or COPYCLIP. Then, switch to the target drawing, and choose Paste To Original Coordinates from the shortcut menu, or use PASTEORIG. This form of pasting from the Clipboard preserves the spatial context of the source objects, meaning they appear in the target drawing exactly where they were in the space of the source drawing.

Another way to go is to capture the all-important spatial context by preselecting a base point when you copy the objects to the Clipboard. This is accomplished with Ctrl+Shift+C or COPYBASE, which asks you to specify a base point in the source drawing. Follow this up with the default paste—either Ctrl+V or PASTECLIP. The pasted objects appear relative to the base point you preselected.

Paste As Block (Ctrl+Shift+V) is another choice on the shortcut menu. Use this if you ever want to paste the contents of the Clipboard as an anonymous block into a target drawing. Be warned that anonymous blocks have names like A$C1BD953EC that aren't exactly descriptive. Therefore, it's probably better to avoid using Paste As Block unless you come up with a good reason to do so—such as sheer laziness, for example. You can always use the RENAME command to change the name to something recognizable if you want.

Change the shortcut key for Ctrl+Shift+V from PASTEBLOCK to PASTEORIG if you do more pasting to original coordinates than pasting as block. See Chapter 10, "Customization," for more information on customizing the user interface.

DesignCenter

If you're still accessing blocks from your symbol library via the INSERT command, please stop already. DesignCenter is much better—it allows you to access everything in a symbol library at a glance. DesignCenter lets you store related blocks that might have previously been written to separate files, all in one file. This means you can do away with arcane file-naming conventions and concentrate more on accessing design content.

Just type **DC** or press Ctrl+2 to open DesignCenter—the formal command name is ADCENTER. Expand the tree until you get to the level of individual drawings. It's then possible to expand the drawings to access their symbol tables, which include blocks, dimension styles, layers, layouts, linetypes, table styles, text styles, and Xrefs.

So you see, DesignCenter is much more powerful than the INSERT command—you can access all kinds of blocks and styles stored within drawing files in this one-stop shop. You may want to aggregate all related content in an existing symbol library into a few well-named files such as Electrical, Mechanical, Fasteners, and so on. Then, you'll be able to quickly browse through numerous blocks contained within these few files in DesignCenter.

Maybe you've noticed that the folder tree doesn't have a path text box. If you already have a path open in the Windows Explorer that you want to access with DesignCenter, copy the path in the Explorer to the Clipboard. Use the ADCNAVIGATE command in AutoCAD. Then, right-click the command line, and choose Paste from the shortcut menu. Press Enter, and the path you've pasted appears in DesignCenter.

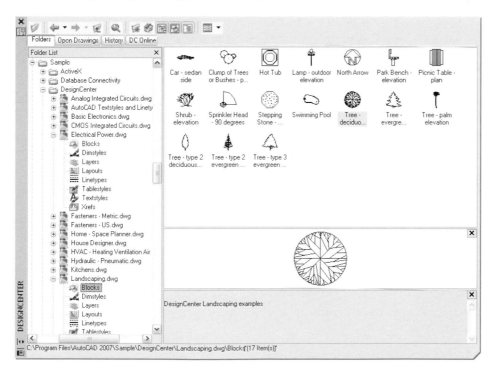

i-drop

I drop, you drop, we'd all like to drag and drop data from the Web right into AutoCAD. The technology behind i-drop is XML based, so it's easy for anyone who's ever done any web design to understand and code.

To use i-drop, you need to install a browser plug-in (available for Internet Explorer only). Then, when you access an i-drop–enabled web page, you'll see the i-drop indicator cursor, which (not surprisingly) looks like an eyedropper.

To use this remarkably seamless technology, drag the i-drop indicator from the web page right into AutoCAD. Whatever you're dragging is downloaded and inserted into your current drawing. It couldn't be any easier.

Not to be confused with the noneditable drawing web format (DWF), i-drop is better suited to transferring DWG files over the Web—you can put any type of file in an i-drop package. No security is built into i-drop, so have your network administrator set up a password-protected folder on your web server if you want to keep your DWG files a secret.

You'll need some basic web design skills to create i-drop–enabled web pages. Autodesk has an i-drop developer center on its site that has all the samples and documentation you need to get going with this technology. Just search for *i-drop* on the Autodesk website: http://www.autodesk.com/

An i-drop enhancer extension is available to subscription customers only. It adds right-click mouse functionality, automatic URL attachment, and activity logging for those who want to get the most out of this exciting technology.

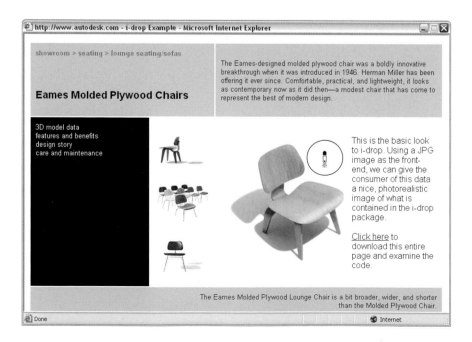

Making External References

External references (Xrefs) allow people to work simultaneously on different parts of a design. This section offers you a few tips and tricks for dealing with the ubiquitous Xref.

Who Has My File?

Ever try to open a drawing file, only to find out someone else is already in it? Maybe you absolutely need to get into this drawing and consequently need to go find that person right away! What to do? Send an e-mail? Stand up and shout? No, no, no—use the WHOHAS command.

At the command prompt, enter **WHOHAS**, and you'll be asked to select the drawing file in question from the Select Drawing To Query dialog. After selecting the drawing file, the AutoCAD detective returns you its findings, as seen here.

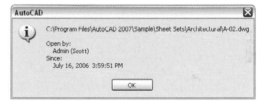

Now you can go have a chat with the offender who wasn't psychic enough to realize you were going to need to use this drawing!

Xtreme Xrefs

Xrefs have gone extreme in AutoCAD 2007—they support DWG, DWF, and tons of image formats all in one palette. The new updated External References palette is the place to find and control everything that's attached to your drawing. But don't type the lengthy new EXTERNALREFERENCES command—use the shortcut XR instead, or choose the command from the Insert pull-down menu.

For all the power of the new External References palette, it's more efficient to be able to reload Xrefs without opening it. If any of your externally referenced drawings change while you're working, a balloon will appear notifying you of this important fact only if XREF-NOTIFY is set to 2.

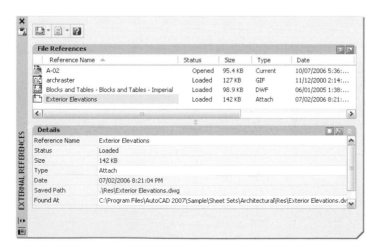

Normally, we don't go for balloon help, but this one is a winner. Just click the hyperlink inside the notification balloon to instantly reload the Xref—no questions asked. In a similar vein, to instantly reload all Xrefs, right-click the Xref icon in the status bar tray, and select Reload Xrefs from the shortcut menu.

If your system bogs down when opening files with large Xrefs, there are several things you can do to speed it up. First, unload any Xrefs that you don't need. Right-click the

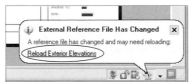

unwanted node in the External References palette, and choose Unload from the shortcut menu. Unloading isn't as serious as detaching—you can always reload without having to search for the right file to reattach later.

The next tip to increase performance is to load only those parts of an Xref that you need. If you're only viewing part of an Xref, there's no need to load the entire file. Open all referenced drawings, and see if there are any layers that you can freeze. Set the system variable INDEXCTL to 3 to save layer and spatial indexes in the files to

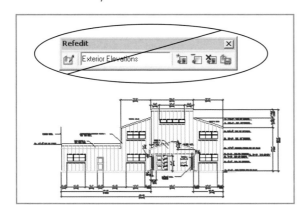

be referenced. Saving indexes takes extra time and increases file size but accelerates Xref loading.

Go back to the parent file, and set the system variable XLOADCTL to 2—this will demand-load a copy of each reference, just the parts you need, thus speeding up load time. Finally, use XCLIP if you can clip away any portions of the Xrefs that you don't need to see referenced into in the parent file.

Have you ever wished that you could turn off in-place Xref editing? You know how easy it is to edit an Xref (within the referenced drawing) using the Refedit toolbar. The problem comes when other "professionals" in your office mess up your Xrefs! If you want to make it harder for others to edit Xrefs, set XEDIT to 0 in drawings where you want to disallow in-place editing. At least they'll have to know this system variable to get around the system.

Top Secret: Reference Manager

All Autodesk had to do to make the Reference Manager virtually top secret was to make it a stand-alone application. It's been there in your Start menu since AutoCAD 2004, but almost nobody knows about it because it's not part of AutoCAD. Now you know where to find it, and knowledge is power!

The Reference Manager will save you loads of time, should you decide to move drawing files to other folders or disk drives—it's the re-pathing tool extraordinaire. It can change paths to externally referenced files, images, fonts, plot configurations, and plot styles in multiple drawings all in one place and all at one time. If you've ever had a coworker rename an Xref directory or move Xrefs from one directory to another, you can appreciate the hours this tool can save you.

Using the Reference Manager is simple. Just add drawings, select the parts you want to re-path, and click the Edit Selected Paths button. Browse for the new path, and that's it. You can even export a .csv file of the paths you've changed, for your records.

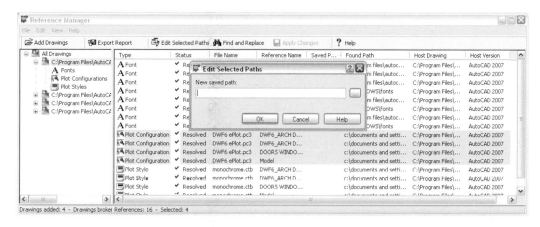

Edited paths for TrueType fonts aren't saved in the Reference Manager. This is good because AutoCAD always searches for TrueType fonts in the Windows Fonts folder anyway.

Wouldn't it be nice if you could launch the Reference Manager from within AutoCAD, rather than from the awkward Windows Start menu? Good news—you can! Use the Express Tool ALIASEDIT to alter the acad.pgp text file via its nice Graphical User Interface (GUI). Here's how to do it:

1. Click the Shell Commands tab in the AutoCAD Alias Editor dialog box, and click the Add button.

2. In the Edit Shell Command dialog box, type **REFMAN** as the alias. This is the command you'll issue in AutoCAD to launch the Reference Manager application.

3. Type the following in the Command text box in the Edit Shell Command dialog box:

```
START AdRefMan.exe
```

4. Choose 1 from the Flag drop-down menu. This flag means AutoCAD won't wait for the Reference Manager to do anything—REFMAN launches AdRefMan.exe.

5. Click OK in every open dialog box, and you're done. Use REFMAN now and forever more to launch the Reference Manager within AutoCAD.

Framing Images

In order to edit an image (move it, erase it, and so on), you need to have the frame on (IMAGEFRAME set to 1). Often, however, we prefer to have the frame turned off for printing (IMAGEFRAME set to 0). You want folks to focus on the image, after all, not its rectangular frame.

Consequently, we find ourselves flipping this system variable back and forth from 0 for editing to 1 for printing. How tedious (yawn).

Fortunately, you can now have the best of both worlds. Setting IMAGEFRAME to 2 means the frame displays for editing purposes, but it doesn't print—awesome!

Underlay Those DWFs

The Drawing Web Format (DWF) is fantastic for publishing on the Web because

- It's a vector format that allows infinite zooming.

- It has layers (which you can make inaccessible if you choose to).

- You can plot DWF files accurately without AutoCAD.

- It's not editable.

- The format is highly compressed and has a small file size.

Until AutoCAD 2007, all you could do was export DWF files from AutoCAD. You were stuck if you wanted to get someone else's DWFs into AutoCAD. No longer—use the External References palette or DWFATTACH to directly underlay those dwifs.

DWF files are handled much like images in the way they're linked but not embedded in a drawing file. All the layers within the DWF are flattened into a single layer—that's why it's called an *underlay*.

DWFs are better than images because they have vector resolution, which means you can zoom in indefinitely—plus you can snap to DWF geometry. Use DWFOSNAP to control whether object snap works on DWF files—1 means it does, and 0 means no snapping is allowed.

> Check out Project Freewheel from Autodesk labs at http://dwfit.com. This technology preview offers DWF viewing on the Web without installing any client software. With Freewheel, you can see DWF files on a Mac, on Linux, on a PDA, on a cell phone, on your toaster (if so equipped), or in Firefox—very cool.

Working with Other Applications

AutoCAD doesn't do everything, and chances are you regularly use lots of other applications in your work. We often have to move data from one application into another, and the trick is getting applications to play nicely together. This section offers you a few techniques that make working with other applications (and AutoCAD) go more smoothly.

¡Olé!

Object Linking and Embedding (OLE) is an ages-old technology that is built into Windows—it transfers data between applications via the Clipboard.

You can drag just about anything into AutoCAD (spreadsheets, databases, text documents, images, and more), and if the originating application supports ActiveX technology, you can link or embed what you're dragging into AutoCAD.

Linking versus Embedding

Linking is like having an Xref to a document created in an external application within Auto-CAD. You need both the originally linked file and the application that created it installed on your machine. For these reasons, linking is extremely dangerous—it's far too easy to break OLE links. An OLE link that works fine on your machine—say, to an Excel spreadsheet—won't work on another person's computer if they don't have Excel installed.

Therefore, we recommend embedding over linking in most situations. The only downside is that the embedded version is a copy, and it won't get updated should the source data change. But at least embedded OLE objects don't have links that can be broken.

If you drag and drop an object from another application into AutoCAD, you're embedding—likewise if you copy and paste.

> Hold down the Ctrl key while dragging between applications to leave a copy of the original behind. Without Ctrl, it's a cut 'n paste job.

Changing Embedded Font Scale

Fonts in embedded documents seemingly appear at any ole size. If you want the fonts to appear at a specific scale—say, to match the rest of your drawing—here's a tip for you.

Select an embedded object, and then type the **OLESCALE** command—it doesn't work the other way around. The font and point size from the originating application show up in the OLE Text Size dialog box. It's up to you to select how many drawing units you want the text height to be. The result is a much friendlier object that matches the size of the other text in your drawing.

Paste as AutoCAD Entities

If you're embedding an object made in another application that contains geometry, there is a good chance that it can be interpreted as native AutoCAD entities such as arcs, lines, text, and circles. These entities are infinitely more usable in AutoCAD than an embedded picture that can't be edited.

For example, if you want to embed a chart made in Excel in AutoCAD, don't just copy and paste it. Instead, use the PASTESPEC command in AutoCAD, or choose Edit → Paste Special. Choose AutoCAD Entities in the Paste Special dialog box, and you'll be better off.

Link or Embed Audio

Have you ever wanted to be able to leave audio commentary in a drawing file? Recording audio is a lot easier and surely is less formal than leaving written comments to your colleagues in a drawing. Give it a whirl:

1. Record an audio file using a microphone and your favorite recording software.

> Windows has an audio program built in under Start menu → Programs → Accessories → Entertainment → Sound Recorder.

2. Highlight the sound file you recorded in the Windows Explorer, and copy it to the Clipboard by pressing Ctrl+C.

3. Switch to AutoCAD, and use PASTESPEC or choose Edit → Paste Special.

4. Select Paste Link in the Paste Special dialog box. Linked audio files can be embedded in multiple drawings and can be updated centrally. Embedded audio is unique to the drawing where it's embedded.

5. Check Display As Icon, and click the Change Icon button. Change the Label

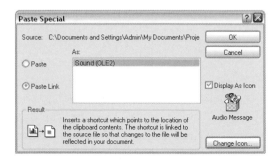

text and/or the icon in the Change Icon dialog if you want. Click OK and OK again, and place the link icon in your drawing.

6. Double-click the link icon in your drawing to launch the audio—or right-click and choose OLE → Open. Your listeners will see a Packager dialog that warns them about only opening trusted files. Clicking Open plays the audio in the default audio player.

Architectural Desktop to AutoCAD

You can already open Architectural Desktop (ADT) drawings in AutoCAD because AutoCAD has the ADT object enabler built in. Although the enabler shows the ADT objects, it's not empowered enough to edit them.

You can explode all the ADT proxy objects into basic AutoCAD entities with AECTO-ACAD. This command creates a new drawing file and allows you to also bind or insert-and-explode Xrefs at the same time. AECTOACAD's command-line interface looks like this:

```
Export options [Format/Bind/bind Type/Maintain/Prefix/Suffix/?]

<Enter for filename>:
```

The Bind option controls whether you want to bind. Bind Type can be set to Bind or Insert, just as you'd expect for any Xref. Prefix and Suffix allow you to append a different prefix or suffix compared to the current filename. In any case, the output of this command will be a new file.

> AECTOACAD is the same command as -EXPORTTOAUTOCAD (note the preceding dash to indicate command-line use only).

The new drawing loses the intelligence of the Architecture Engineering and Construction (AEC) objects, but at least the objects can be dumbed down to linework so that older versions of AutoCAD can understand them—all the way back to R14. ADT users can choose File → Export to AutoCAD (within ADT) to export files all the way back to Release 14.

AutoCAD to Photoshop

For best results, you want to set up a new printer driver to get AutoCAD linework into Photoshop where it can be greatly enhanced for presentation. Scott has written an entire book on this subject called *Enhancing CAD Drawings with Photoshop* (Sybex, 2005) that is definitely worth checking out. Follow these steps to set up a driver for exporting drawings from Auto-CAD to images in Photoshop:

1. Use the PLOTTERMANAGER command to open the Plotters support folder.

2. Double click the Add-A-Plotter Wizard icon.

3. Advance to the next page of the wizard, and select My Computer. Click Next.

4. Select Raster File Formats from the Manufacturers list and Portable Network Graphics PNG (LZH Compression) from the Models list.

> The PNG image file format is an excellent choice for image output because it has lossless compression and very small file size.

5. Click Next four more times, and then click the Edit Plotter Configuration button. Expand the Graphics node in the Plotter Configuration Editor dialog box, and select Vector Graphics.

6. Select Monochrome and 2 Shades Of Gray as the resolution and color depth. This will capture linework in the most efficient manner possible and keep file sizes small. Click OK and then Finish to close both dialog boxes.

7. Plot using your new driver, and you'll output linework in image files that you can open with Photoshop.

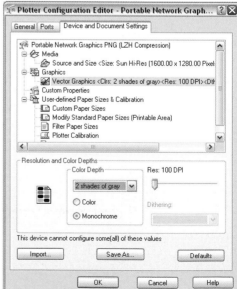

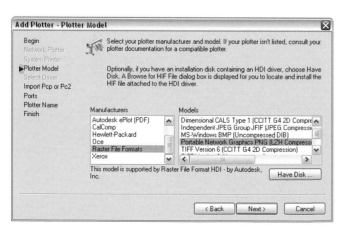

AutoCAD to Office

Do you ever need to get AutoCAD drawings into Microsoft Office applications such as Word, Excel, and PowerPoint? The Windows Metafile is the ideal vehicle for this kind of transfer—the .wmf format is both vector and raster, and it's supported on all versions of Windows. Here's how to do it:

1. Open the drawing you want to transfer in AutoCAD, and zoom extents in modelspace.

2. Use the WMFOUT command. Save a .wmf file on your hard disk, giving it a file name. Select the objects you want to transfer, and press Enter.

3. Switch to the Office application you want to use—PowerPoint, for example.

4. In PowerPoint, choose Insert → Picture → From File (this menu option is the same in all Office applications). Select the file you saved in step 2. It appears as a PowerPoint slide.

5. Use the tools on the Picture toolbar to adjust the image if necessary. That's it!

If you'd like to have an interactive drawing file (in DWF format) embedded into your PowerPoint presentation—one in which you can zoom and pan, control layers, move from layout to layout, and so on—you can do so via DWF. You need to make sure you have the DWF viewer installed on your system first. (You can get it at: www.autodesk.com; do a

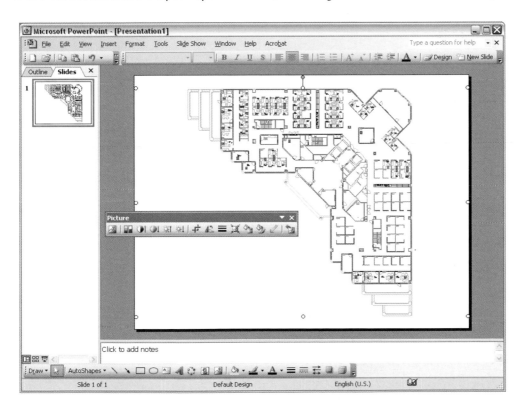

search for *dwfviewer*). Select Insert → Object → Autodesk DWF Viewer Control from the menu. An image displays in the center of the slide. Right-click the image, select Autodesk DWF Viewer Control Object → Properties from the menu, and select the DWF file you want to display on your PowerPoint slide. The DWF only displays when the slide show is playing (so don't be alarmed when you don't see it). But you'll be able to interactively zoom in, pan, control layers, and so on during the PowerPoint presentation—very impressive!

Truly Free DWG Conversion

Autodesk has finally given up on forcing people to upgrade (or at least embarrassing them) with file formats. Have you ever had to call a consultant or even a client to ask them to "save down" their .dwg files for you? How humiliating not to be as up-to-the-second technology-wise as your peers.

Have you been on the other end of the stick and had to save different versions of your drawings in older file formats for those Luddites who haven't upgraded to the latest version of AutoCAD? What a hassle!

Autodesk has a free program on its site called DWG TrueConvert that translates any AutoCAD drawing file between any of the following file formats:

- AutoCAD 2007/LT2007

- AutoCAD 2004/LT2004

- AutoCAD 2000/LT2000

- AutoCAD R14/LT97/LT98

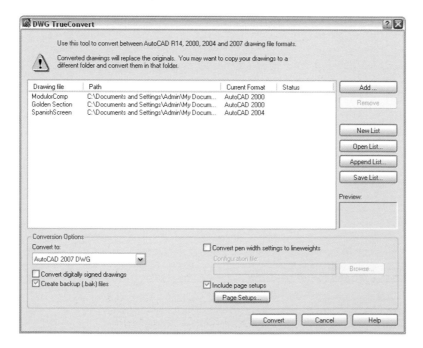

AutoCAD has clearly been updated more frequently than its file formats. TrueConvert doesn't work with DXF or DWF files—only DWG files can be converted. AutoCAD doesn't need to be installed on your computer to convert drawing files with TrueConvert—download it from www.autodesk.com (33 MB).

You can even convert pen widths to lineweights and add page setups to drawing files. Best of all, TrueConvert can batch process multiple .dwg files so you don't have to sit there and tediously convert each one manually. Hurray!

Did we mention that TrueConvert is free?

View and Plot DWG without AutoCAD

Are there folks in your office who need to review and/or plot drawing files, but who would be a danger to themselves and others with a full version of AutoCAD?

Save some bucks, and get these individuals DWG TrueView. With it they can open, zoom, pan, and print drawing files. Again, this is a free download at www.autodesk.com (119 MB). Now if only you could get a bonus for saving your firm the cost of one AutoCAD seat…

TrueView also lets you view, plot, and publish DWF files.

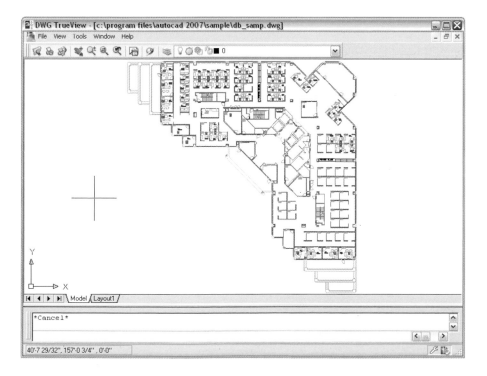

If you've already downloaded the free viewer, we have a little tip for you. On occasion, if you've zoomed in close, you may get the message *Already zoomed in as far as possible*. No worries; switch between the model and layout tabs once to force a regeneration, and you'll be good to go (hey—you get what you pay for).

Round-Trip Design Review

Electronic markups are the way to go if you want to realize a colossal jump in efficiency for your team. Why not eliminate traditional design reviews marked up with red pencil on paper, save tons of plotting time (not to mention ink cost), and save the trees while you're at it?

Autodesk has a low-priced product ($199 at the time of this book's publication) called Design Review—formerly known as DWF Composer. Design Review is used by a *reviewer* to mark up drawings made by a *designer*.

The electronic markups are brought back into AutoCAD as DWF underlays where the designer integrates the changes shown in the markup set into the design drawings. The data goes full circle and is kept digital throughout the entire design-review process. The changes shown in a DWF markup set can be viewed through AutoCAD's Markup Set Manager palette. The designer selects each markup, and AutoCAD automatically loads that drawing file and zooms in on the task at hand. Comments can also be stored with each markup. After correcting the drawing, the user checks this markup off the list. After completing all the markups, the touch of a button makes it easy to send the modifications back to the reviewer. Everything is kept nice and organized, shaving time off the entire design-review phase of a project.

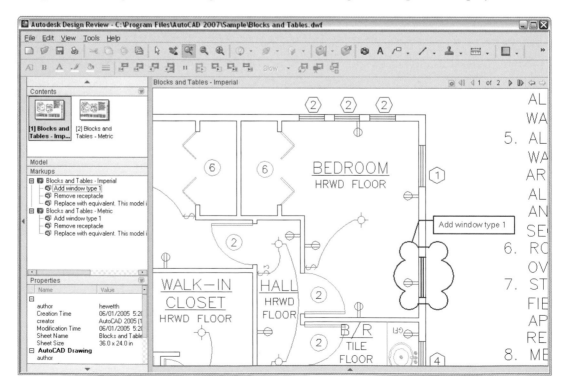

One of the coolest features in Autodesk Design Review is the ability to combine numerous project documents into a multipage DWF file. Drag project-related documents made in Microsoft Office (and other applications) into Design Review for inclusion in the DWF file. You can purchase Design Review and download it immediately (or have a CD shipped to you) from the following URL: http://www.autodesk.com/designreview

If you just want to print out DWF files without marking them up, Autodesk offers the lightweight (2 MB) DWF Viewer for free at http://www.autodesk.com/dwfviewer.

Plotting and Publishing

PLOTTING AND PUBLISHING are flip sides of the same coin. You *plot* when printing a single layout or model space view and *publish* when printing information from more than one drawing—it's output by any other name.

Bear in mind that the commonplace act of printing has become an abstraction in AutoCAD. No trees are felled when you plot and publish in intangible electronic forms such as DWF, PDF, ZIP, or even HTML—and great efficiencies are realized for those who go 100 percent digital. But for the traditional majority who isn't quite there yet, plotting and publishing still have the connotation of printing on paper.

However you and your organization go about creating output, this chapter offers you tips and techniques for communicating your design ideas to the rest of the world.

It's organized into two topics:

- Plotting
- Publishing

◼ Plotting

In all other applications it's called printing, but AutoCAD is so special that making output deserves its own verb. You *plot* in AutoCAD. We feel (and some people remember) that the origin of this term hearkens back to the days of vector pen plotters: When the paper moved back and forth in the X direction, the pen carousel moved in Y, and lines were plotted within this physical coordinate space.

Today, almost all output devices are *raster*, meaning they translate the vector math from AutoCAD into pixels just prior to printing. We're not really plotting anymore—technically speaking, that is. But don't think that's ever going to stop us from plotting!

Plot in the Background

If you have big drawings with lots of Xrefs, you're probably tired of waiting for plots to finish so you can get back to work. Are you forced to go on a coffee break when you plot these big boys?

The good news—or maybe it's not so good, depending on how you see it—is that you can set AutoCAD to plot in the background so you can keep working without interruption. You'll have to think of other ways to justify your next coffee break.

Background processing is enabled for publishing by default, but not plotting—go figure. Use OPTIONS, and choose the Plot And Publish tab. Check Plotting in the Background Processing Options area.

If you opt for background plotting, you won't see the Plot Job Progress dialog box, informing you of plot status with an animated progress bar. More important, you won't be able to use that dialog box to cancel the plot at the last second when you realize you've omitted something important.

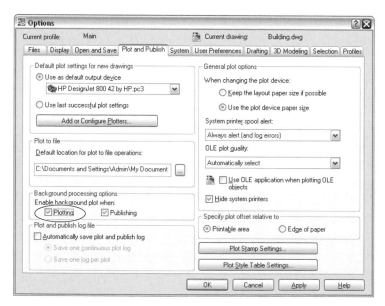

Don't worry—you're not left out in the cold. When you plot in the background, an icon appears in the status bar tray. Right-click this icon, and you can choose Cancel Sheet or Cancel Entire Job. Incidentally, you can also view plot and publish details on this shortcut menu, or use VIEWPLOTDETAILS.

Only one job at a time can be processed in the background.

Hide Unused Printers and Paper Sizes

Reduce clutter in the Plot dialog by hiding unused printers and paper sizes. Doing so saves you time and gives you peace of mind when plotting—you don't have to wade through long lists of plotters or paper sizes that you don't have or use.

When you purchase a printer, it comes with a driver that interfaces between the device and the operating system; this driver is called a *system printer*. AutoCAD in turn has a driver that interfaces between the system printer and AutoCAD; this is called a *plotter* or plotter driver. AutoCAD's default is to show you both the system printers and the plotter drivers in the Plot dialog box. We highly recommend that you hide the system printers.

Why, you ask? In a nutshell, you'll get the best results by plotting with an AutoCAD plotter driver, not to the system printer directly. AutoCAD's plotter drivers do a much better job of sending nicely formatted drawing information to the device than the system printers do by themselves. It's better to hide the system printers in AutoCAD (although they're still available to other applications) to avoid the temptation of using them. Here's how it's done:

1. Use OPTIONS, and select the Plot And Publish tab.

2. If you haven't already done so, create AutoCAD plotter drivers to match any system printers you have. If this is the case, click the Add Or Configure Plotters button. If you already have AutoCAD plotter drivers set up, skip the next step.

3. Go through the Add-A-Plotter Wizard, and create an AutoCAD plotter to match each system printer. Normally, this is a CAD manager's job; talk to this person if they exist in your firm.

4. Check Hide System Printers in the General Plot Options area of the Options dialog box. That's all there is to it.

The next order of business is to evaluate each plotter and think about what paper sizes are used in your firm. This doesn't mean all the paper sizes the plotter driver supports—list only the sizes you actually use. Chances are, you use only a handful, so it should be easy

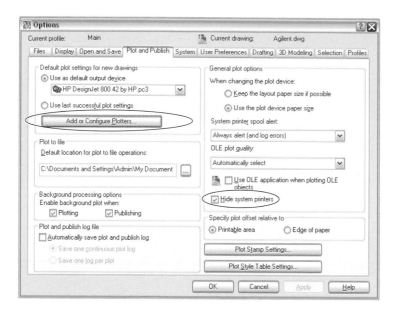

to come up with a short list. For example, you may have an HP Designjet 800 plotter and use only the Arch C, Arch D, and Arch E paper sizes. Now you can filter the plotter driver's paper sizes to reflect what you use in the real world:

1. Press Ctrl+P or use PLOT to open the Plot dialog box.

2. Select a specific AutoCAD plotter driver from the Printer/Plotter Name drop-down list.

3. Click the adjacent Properties button to open the driver-specific dialog box called the Plotter Configuration Editor.

4. In the Plotter Configuration Editor, expand User-Defined Paper Sizes & Calibration if necessary, and click the Filter Paper Sizes node.

5. Click the Uncheck All button to deselect all of the hundreds of paper sizes. This is an exhaustive list that includes all the paper sizes used worldwide in every discipline.

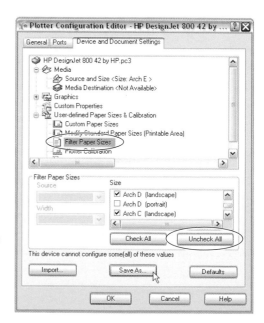

6. Scroll through the Size list, and check only the paper sizes you actually use.

7. Click the Save As button at the bottom of the Plotter Configuration Editor dialog box. You're prompted to save a PC3 file with the same name as your plotter driver; do so by clicking Save. This opens a Save As dialog noting that the filename already exists.

8. Click OK to close the Plotter Configuration Editor.

9. A small dialog box appears, giving you options for how to save the changes to the PC3 file. Choose the Save Changes To The Following File radio button, and click OK.

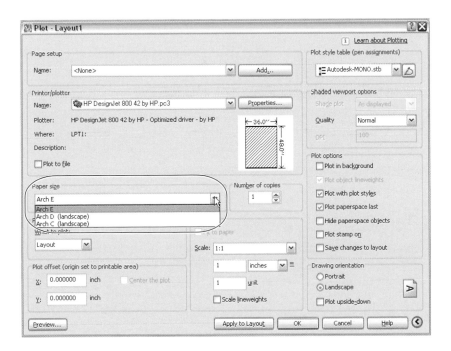

10. For the big payoff, press Ctrl+P, and select the plotter driver you've been working on. Click the Paper Size drop-down list, and verify that only the sizes you filtered appear in the list. Yippee—no more clutter! That was a lot of work, but it will be totally worth it in the long run.

Liberate Color from Plot Style

Why do so many AutoCAD users still plot using color-dependent plot styles—you know, so all green objects plot the same way? It made a lot of sense to plot by color when about a dozen colors mapped to pens in a pen plotter, but those days are long gone.

When you liberate color from plot style, your color options open up tremendously. The AutoCAD Color Index (ACI) has exactly 255 colors to assign to layers and objects, and most of the ACI colors are too dark to use effectively. True Color has over 16 million color choices, so why not have salmon, bisque, coral, tomato, or honeydew layers? At least you'll be able to match your outfit.

Named plot styles can be assigned to layers, to layouts, and even directly to objects—and best of all, color has nothing to do with it. Color is then free to do what it does best in AutoCAD: identify and differentiate layers and objects on screen. Color can do more work for you in True Color mode.

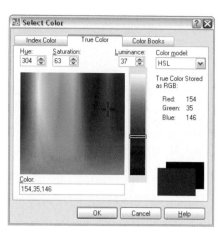

Drawings can either have color-dependent plot styles or named plot styles, but not both. To see which type of plot style your drawing has, use PSTYLEMODE. It's 0 for a named plot style or 1 for a color-dependent plot style. PSTYLEMODE is read-only, so it's just FYI.

If you want to convert an existing drawing from a color-dependent plot style to a named one, use CONVERTCTB. First you're prompted to select the drawing's current CTB color table file. Then, you're prompted to create an STB style table file that's based on the CTB file.

Finally, you see a warning dialog informing you that there's more work to do.

Use STYLESMANAGER to open the Windows Explorer to the Plot Styles folder. Although you can use the STB file you just converted, we recommend customizing one of the out-of-the-box STB files to suit your needs. `Autodesk-MONO.stb` already has lots of screened styles that you may find useful. Double click it to open the Plot Style Table Editor. Review the style table and make any changes you deem necessary (maybe none). Click Save & Close when done.

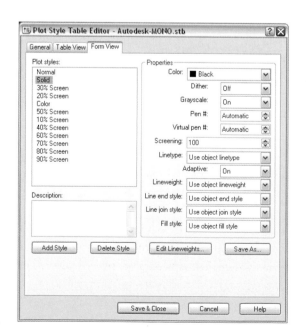

Back in AutoCAD, use CONVERTP-STYLES to toggle the current drawing from one plot style table mode to the other. You're prompted to select the STB file that you converted earlier using CONVERTCTB. Once your drawing is set to use named plot styles, use PAGE-SETUP to open the Page Setup Manager. Click Modify and assign the STB file you customized (we suggested `Autodesk-MONO.stb`) to your current page setup.

Finally, assign plot styles to each layer. You're also free to pick more interesting True Colors for each layer.

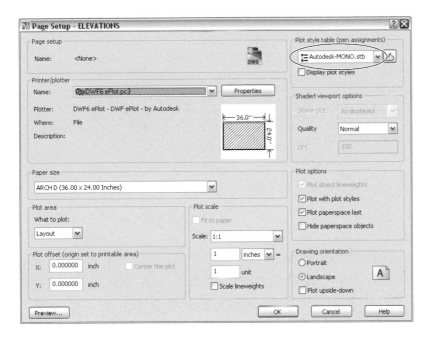

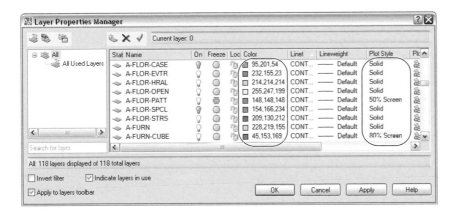

Use PLOTSTYLE to set the current (named) plot style. All new objects are created with the current plot style. It's a good policy to leave ByLayer as the current plot style and assign plot styles to layers.

Whew! That was a lot of work converting an existing drawing to use named plot styles. If you plan to stick with named plot styles, set PSTYLEPOLICY to 0. Then, all new drawings you create will utilize named plot styles. The only thing that can mess this up is if your drawing template still uses color-dependent plot styles (the template overrides PSTYLEPOLICY). Convert your templates to named plot styles, and never look back.

Output Images from AutoCAD

Aside from the technique of creating a raster printer driver, which we showed you in Chapter 8 ("AutoCAD to Photoshop"), there are several quicker ways to get pixels out of AutoCAD.

The most basic technique uses the Print Screen key to capture whatever is on your screen at the moment. But this captures your whole screen, Windows toolbar and all. Press Alt+Print Screen to capture just the current application. The captured pixels are copied to the Clipboard. You need image-editing software into which to paste the pixels (like Photoshop), but that's another story.

Other ways to output images from AutoCAD include JPGOUT, PNGOUT, BMPOUT, and TIFOUT. Each outputs an image file based on the objects you select to its corresponding file format. Super easy, no worries—peace out.

> Using a raster printer is the only way of outputting more pixels than are visible on screen.

Publishing

The term *publishing* sounds formal, but it just means you're plotting more than one drawing or sheet. AutoCAD makes this an efficient experience with its publishing feature. You can publish an entire sheet set from the Sheet Set Manager (SSM) or output all the open drawings by using PUBLISH. It sure beats plotting drawings one at a time.

Go Digital with DWF

The drawing web format (DWF) has been around for years, but not everyone has embraced this important technology. DWF files have the potential to remove the inefficiency of publishing on paper from the design process, not to mention its cost. Your entire drawing set can be published as a multipage DWF file that encapsulates all your hard work on a project. And because the DWF Viewer is a free download on www.autodesk.com, anyone can view a DWF file. We realize that many of you use PDF as your preferred output file when going digital; but we highly recommend DWF due to its much smaller, vector-based output, which packs more intelligence than a PDF file.

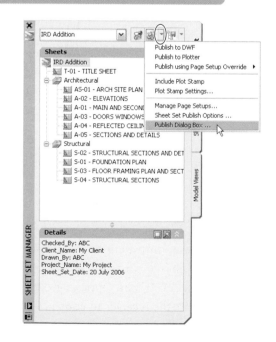

Old habits die hard, but perhaps now is the time to go 100 percent digital. Stop printing on physical media, and start publishing DWF files. Here's how it's done:

1. If you're using the Sheet Set Manager, click the Publish button's drop-down arrow to open its shortcut menu, and select Publish Dialog Box. If you're not using the SSM, use PUBLISH to create a sheet list from all open drawings.

2. Choose the Publish To DWF File radio button. If you want to publish to physical media, select the Publish To Plotter Named In Page Setup radio button, instead, and then select a page setup that references a plotter for each sheet in the list.

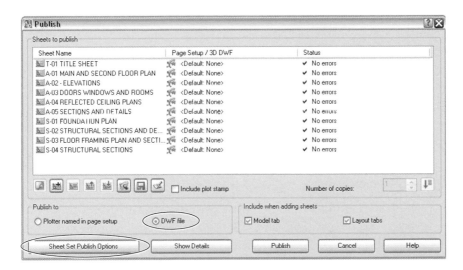

Drag sheets around in the Publish dialog box to reorder the list. Sheets are processed in the order in which they appear in the sheet list.

3. Click the Sheet Set Publish Options button in the Publish dialog box.

4. Review the Sheet Set Publish Options dialog box. If you're concerned about security, set Password Protection to Specify Password, and then type a password immediately below. But be warned: If you forget your password, don't call us—there's no way to get it back!

5. Layer information isn't included in a DWF file by default. Choose Include next to Layer Information in the DWF Data Options group, if you prefer. This permits the receiver to control the layer visibility in the DWF file.

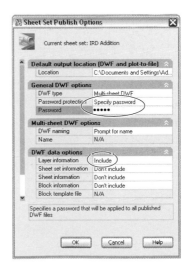

6. Click OK to close the Sheet Set Publish Options dialog box. Click the Publish button in the Publish dialog box. Specify a filename and location, and you're done.

Save all drawings you plan to publish. Then click the Save Sheet List button in the Publish dialog box to save a drawing set description (DSD) file. The same sheet list can be published again at a later date by using +PUBLISH. The plus symbol requests a DSD file before opening the Publish dialog box.

DWF files can accelerate your in-house design review process. Reviewers can use Autodesk Design Review to mark up DWF files. Then, the DWF files take a round trip back into AutoCAD as underlays, where designers integrate the markups into the source DWG files. See Chapter 8 ("Round Trip Design Review") for more information.

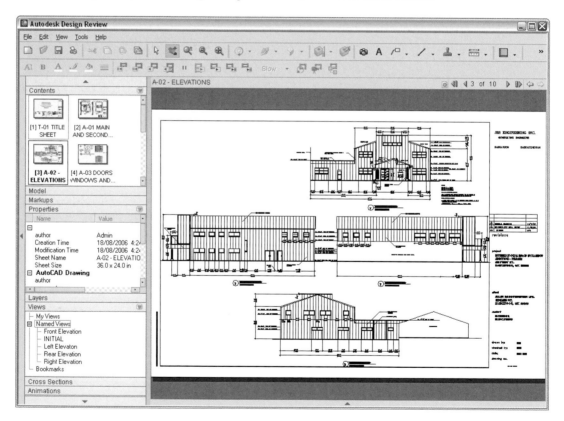

Don't Ship It, eTransmit!

If you're printing drawings on paper and shipping them to consultants by courier or FedEx, you're doing it the hard way. Why not specify in your contract that your deliverables will be digital, and pass along reprographics costs to consultants who are stuck in the dark ages?

ETRANSMIT puts drawings and their dependents into a nice neat package for electronic transmission. The drawings and their Xrefs, font map, plot style table, plotter configuration file, sheet set data file, and sheet template files are examples of dependents that can be included.

> Consider sending DWF files instead of eTransmitting DWG source files. DWF files are smaller and can't be altered. If your recipient needs the ability to alter your design data, then eTransmit is the way to go.

Have you ever gotten a call requesting missing Xrefs that delayed a project? It's far too easy to forget some of the dependents when you package files manually; let ETRANSMIT remember to include them for you. Here we go:

1. If you want to electronically transmit a single drawing file, save it and use ETRANS-MIT. If you want to send multiple drawing files, select them in the SSM, right-click, and choose eTransmit. Either way, the drawings and their dependents will be packaged in the transmittal.

2. The three tabs in the Create Transmittal dialog box show the same information in different ways. You can view the included sheets for an overview, the file tree for a categorized look, or the files table for the nitty-gritty details.

3. Uncheck any sheets or files that you don't want to include. Before sending the package, it behooves you to check the transmittal setup first. Click the Transmittal Setups button.

4. Create saved setups for easy reuse in the Transmittal Setups dialog box, or click Modify to alter the Standard setup.

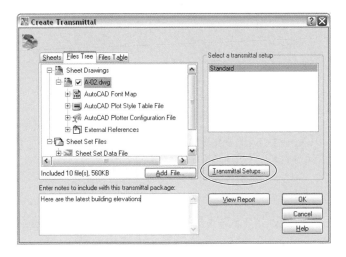

5. The Modify Transmittal Setup dialog box has all the options. Choose Self-Extracting Executable (*.exe) as the Transmittal Package Type to avoid hearing complaints from uneducated consultants who don't know what to do with a ZIP file. Choose ZIP (*.zip) if you're concerned about EXE files not making it through a corporate firewall.

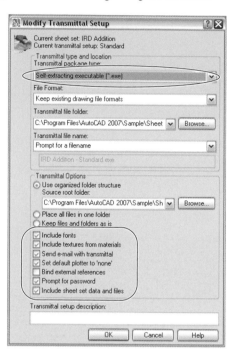

6. Pay attention to the check boxes at the bottom of the Modify Transmittal Setup dialog box. If you include fonts, be aware that you'll be violating intellectual copyright laws if the recipient doesn't own the commercial TrueType fonts you're sending. Check Send E-mail With Transmittal if you're planning to send the package as an attachment.

7. Click OK or Close in each of the three dialog boxes to send the transmittal. Send it as an e-mail attachment if it's small enough; FTP is the wiser choice if your attachment is over 5 MB.

ARCHIVE is similar to ETRANSMIT, but you specify a folder for the package for yourself rather than sending it to another party. Right-click the top node in the SSM, and choose Archive to package the entire sheet set for storage. Burn the archive onto a DVD for cold storage, or record it onto a backup hard drive for peace of mind. This is especially useful should you need to send your drawing set to a client before the drawings are completed. You eTransmit the files to the client and archive the files for yourself. If the client calls with a question, you can open the archive to see what they're referring to.

Let AutoCAD Be Your Web Designer

AutoCAD can create basic web pages for you that showcase your drawings. The web pages can even have i-drop functionality so those who've installed the DWF Viewer or Autodesk Design Review can interact with the drawings on screen. On the other hand, you can post images of drawings instead of i-drop to prohibit detailed examination and quality printing. PUBLISHTOWEB is a wizard that takes you through a 12-step program to produce web pages. The wizard tells the story.

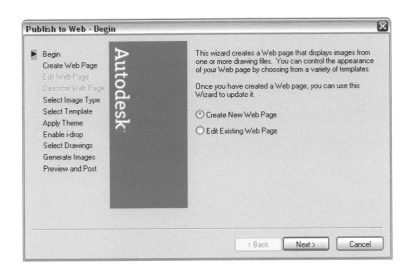

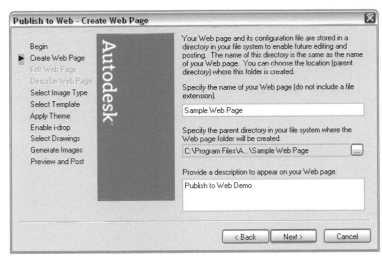

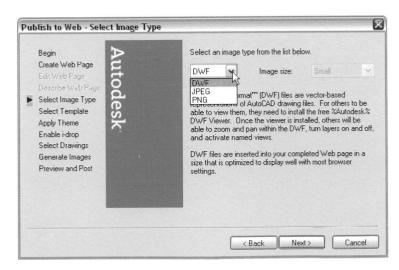

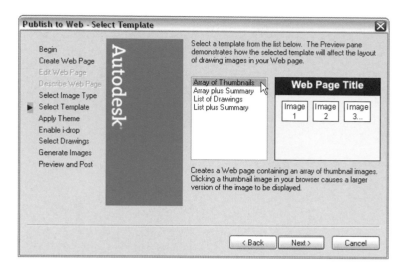

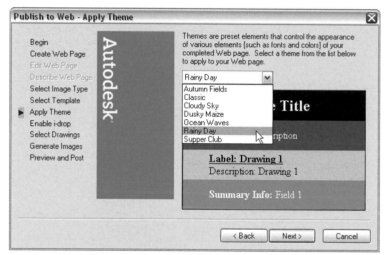

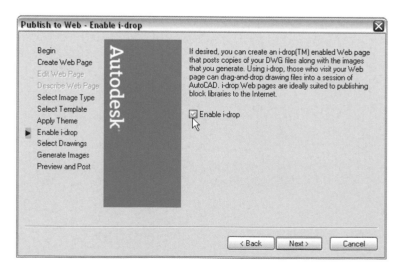

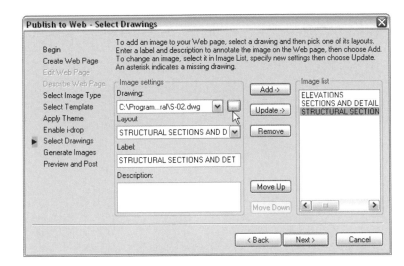

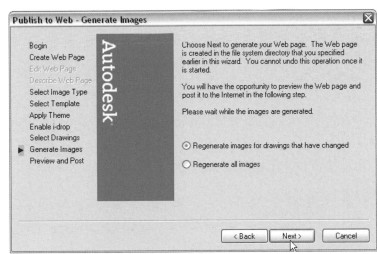

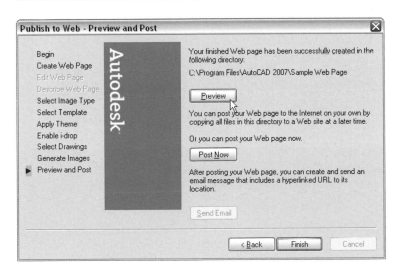

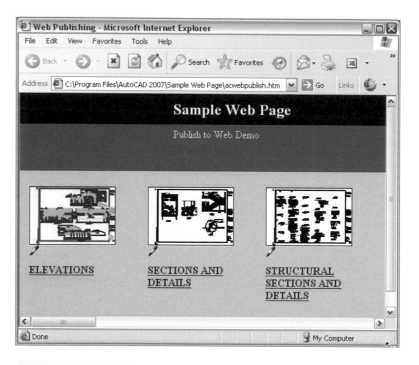

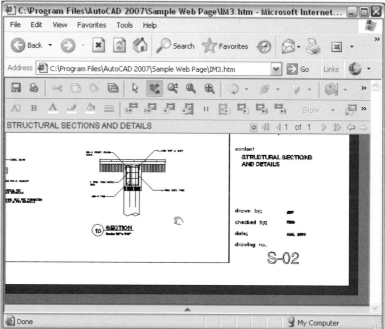

Customize publish-to-web templates for more control over the appearance of pages generated by PUB-LISHTOWEB. The templates are located here: `C:\Program Files\AutoCAD 2007\UserDataCache\Template\PTWTemplates`.

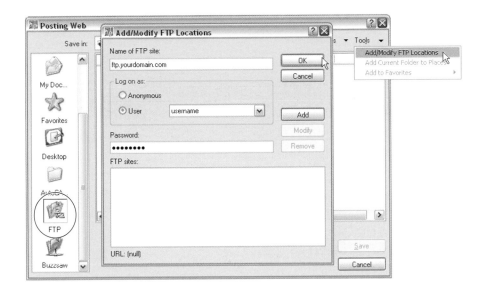

Publish and View 3D DWF Files

If a picture is worth a thousand words, then consider how much an interactive 3D DWF model is worth—practically a novel! 3D DWF files are one of the most effective means of communicating spatial design ideas.

Use 3DDWFPREC to control the precision of your exported 3D DWF files prior to export. Its values vary from 1–6, with 2 being the default. Larger values like 5 or 6 make big DWF files. Bump 3DDWFPREC up to 3 or 4 to capture more detail and have your 3D models appear smoother.

Export a 3D DWF file from the Model tab of the current drawing with 3DDWF, or export several with PUBLISH. If you go the PUBLISH route, you have to choose the 3D DWF page setup for each drawing you wish to export.

Once the drawing's been exported to a DWF file, locate it using the Windows Explorer in the folder you published it to. Double-click the DWF file, and the Autodesk DWF Viewer launches (it's installed with AutoCAD)—or Autodesk Design Review launches preferentially, if you have it installed too.

Click the arrow next to the Orbit button, and choose Turntable. Turntable is the preferred tool for examining architectural models; it keeps the vertical axis fixed. Use Orbit if you're looking at a mechanical part or manufactured object. Explore the navigator pane with its rollout palettes to see what you can do with the 3D DWF.

If you have any web design experience, you can embed 3D DWF files in web pages for a more elegant user experience. Here's a typical code snippet that embeds the file 3D.dwf into a web page:

```
<object id = "viewer"

 classid=

  "clsid:A662DA7E-CCB7-4743-B71A-D817F6D575DF"
```

```
CODEBASE=

  "http://www.autodesk.com/global/dwfviewer/

  installer/DwfViewerSetup.cab"

border = "1"

width = "640"

height = "480">

<param name = "Src" value="3D.dwf">

</object>
```

The viewer of your page will be prompted to install the free DWF Viewer if they don't have it. They aren't prompted if they already have it or Autodesk Design Review installed; then the DWF file appears embedded in the web page.

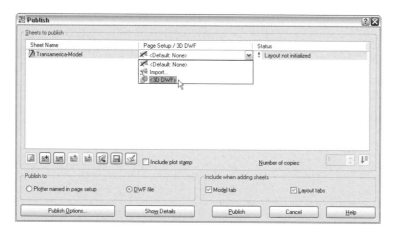

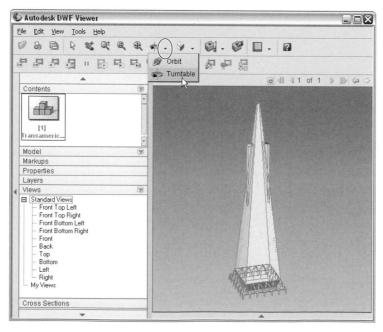

Customization

CUSTOMIZATION HAS ALWAYS been a subject near and dear to the hearts of CAD managers, AutoCAD power users, and those who want to be. This chapter offers such folk tips and techniques in the art of customizing AutoCAD.

From tool palettes, to menus, to the UI, you'll be able to customize AutoCAD just the way you want it to be from the tips in this chapter. In addition, we offer you some workspace power tips and important techniques for customizing AutoCAD at the enterprise level.

The following topics cover many of the disparate customization options available in AutoCAD:

- Customizing Tool Palettes
- The Menu Legacy
- Customizing the User Interface
- Customizing Workspaces
- CUI for the Enterprise

Customizing Tool Palettes

Tool Palettes were designed to be customized—in fact, they're begging for it. Although you probably know that you can drag just about anything onto a tool palette and have it automatically appear as a tool, this topic covers some of the Tool Palette's finer points—so you can create the right tool for every job.

Organize Palettes with Palette Groups

The primary means for organizing tool palettes is often overlooked. Palettes should be logically grouped into collections for ease of use. So many palettes and palette groups ship with AutoCAD that it's hard enough to find what you're looking for as it is.

Access palette groups by right-clicking the Tool Palettes menu at the extreme bottom edge of its title bar. All the existing palette groups appear below the bottom separator bar. Choose Customize Palettes from this menu, or use the CUSTOMIZE command to open the dialog box of the same name.

Two lists appear in the Customize dialog box: Palettes on the left, and Palette Groups on the right. Create a new palette by right-clicking in the Palettes list; that's easy enough. The trouble comes when you want to create a new palette group by right-clicking in the Palette Groups list. If you right-click anywhere *within* the list, you'll get a subgroup that's nested within an existing group—undoubtedly not what you want.

To get a top-level palette group, you have to right-click just below the last palette group in the tiny whitespace that's available. You may have to minimize the groups list to create some white space to click in. Then, choose New Group from the shortcut menu, and the result is the palette group you were looking for.

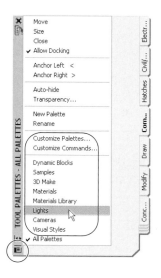
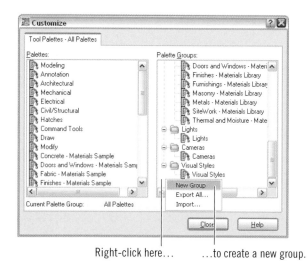

Right-click here...   ...to create a new group.

Once you've created at least one new palette and a new palette group, drag the palette(s) into the group, across the dialog box from one list to another—easy as pie. Click OK to close the dialog box.

Now the new palette group is accessible from the Tool Palettes menu, and the group contains just as many palettes as you dragged in while you were in the Customize dialog box.

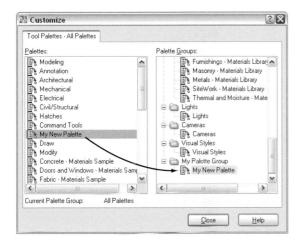

Customize Commands on Palettes

AutoCAD 2007 has a new feature that greatly simplifies the former confusing workflow for customizing commands on palettes. This "feature" is so intuitive that you'll wonder how it could have been any different in the past. Who cares? Now you can drag commands directly from the Customize User Interface dialog box into the Tool Palettes. Give it a shot:

1. Set your chosen palette group current by choosing it from the Tool Palettes menu.

2. Right-click the Tool Palettes menu, and choose Customize Commands. This is the nice way of opening the Customize User Interface dialog box when you want to work with commands, because it maximizes the Command List (and minimizes the Customizations In list).

3. Filter the lengthy Command List by choosing a category from the drop-down list if you want. Scroll through the Command List, and locate the command you're interested in palettizing.

4. Drag the command you located in the previous step directly to the Tool Palettes. Your chosen tool appears on the palette—end of story.

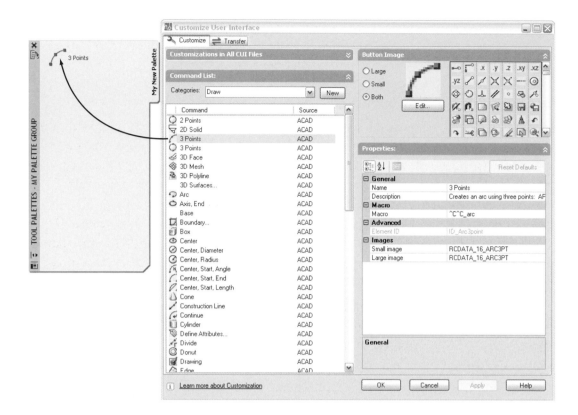

Organize Palettes

All you neat and tidy folks will appreciate this one. You can organize (compulsively or not) individual palettes by adding separator bars to visually group related tools and/or add descriptive text that explains things in plain English, or whatever it is you're speaking.

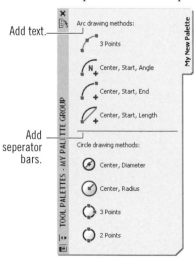

Add text.

Add seperator bars.

Right-click anywhere in the body of a palette, and choose Add Text and/or Add Separator as you see fit. If you don't like the position of the text or separators you've added, drag them elsewhere in the palette, and they will oblige by automatically relocating as you wish.

If you like this tip, you'll appreciate knowing how to access the (almost hidden) view options. Right-click the actual palette tab, not its body or title bar, which open different shortcut menus.

The View Options dialog box allows you to control the tool icon size with a slider. This is great if you want to fit more tools per palette: Drag the slider to the left. Plus, you can opt to display the icon only, icon plus text, or text only in list view. The drop-down lets your chosen view options affect the current palette only or propagate to all palettes on your machine.

Drag Blocks to Palettes

One of the best things about Tool Palettes is the fact that you can drag blocks to palettes for easy reuse in other drawings. The only aspect that spoils this sweet functionality is the reality of hard-coded paths. Tools created by dragging blocks to palettes reference their actual source files. If you ever move, rename, archive, or otherwise alter the path of the source drawing where the blocks initially came from, then your tools won't work.

The secret to eternal palette happiness is: Be mindful of where your blocks' source files are. The easiest way to do this is to first transfer interesting blocks that you'd like to palettize into one or more files for safekeeping. We recommend that you place these files in a special folder on your file server, so that others in your organization can access them. Make the block transfer with copy and paste, or WBLOCK and INSERT if you prefer; it doesn't matter.

Once the blocks have been collected into a file or files in the designated folder, here's what you do:

1. Open DesignCenter by pressing Ctrl+2.

2. In the DesignCenter palette, navigate to the folder you designated as the repository of blocks, forever accessible to Tool Palettes.

3. Expand said drawing, and select its Blocks Symbol Table node.

4. Drag the blocks you want to convert to tools directly from DesignCenter onto the Tool Palettes. The tools you create are automatically hard-coded to the source files in the repository. As long as you never upset the absolute location of the block folder on the file server—or its contents—all your block tools are guaranteed to work.

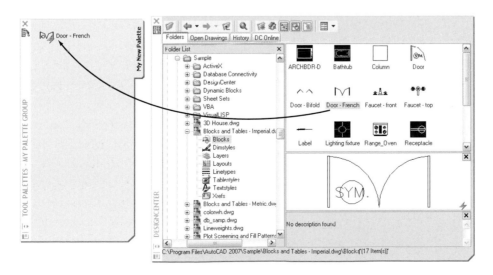

But what about block scale? Do you work in different scales and need your blocks to come in scaled accordingly? There is absolutely no need to make duplicate blocks in different scales, or even to add a scale action to a dynamic block to solve this problem.

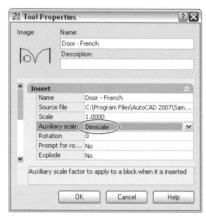

Right-click a block tool on the Tool Palettes, and choose Properties from the shortcut menu. Each block has a unique set of tool properties that control how it's inserted. Change the Auxiliary Scale property to either Dimscale or Plot Scale to have the block automatically sized according to these well-known scales. Auxiliary Scale is None by default, so you have to manually change the tool properties if you want automatic scaling to occur when the tool is used.

Drag Dimension Styles to Palettes

Most people know that you can drag objects and even blocks to Tool Palettes, but fewer realize that there are benefits to dragging dimension styles to palettes. The savvy know this isn't literally true, because you can't drag styles directly to palettes—you must drag a representative object instead—but the effect is much the same.

You don't need to worry about hard-coded paths as you do with blocks, because the dimension styles don't reference external files when they're turned into tools. What is most attractive about this method is the flyout menu that appears next to dimension style tools: It lets you access many dimension commands right from the palette in an efficient manner. Here's how it works:

1. Create a dimension style worthy of becoming a tool. This is a style you plan to use in multiple drawings in the future.

2. Create a single dimension object in a drawing. Make sure this object has the style you created in step 1.

3. Drag the dimension object onto a tool palette. Right-click the new tool, and rename it with its style name.

4. Access the tool properties, and click the more button (…) for the Flyout Options property. Uncheck any dimension types you never use with this style in the Flyout Options dialog box. Doing so simplifies what you see in the next step. Click OK in both open dialog boxes.

5. The new tool that appears on the palette does more than just insert the object you dragged over to create it. Notice the flyout arrow next to the dimension tool: Click it, and you see a flyout menu. Use this flyout menu to create any dimension object type in the tool's style—no need to hunt for the right dimension tool on a toolbar or in menus when they're all right here on the Tool Palettes.

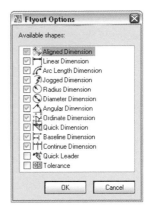 

The same concept can be used to place your most popular hatch patterns on the palette. Select a hatch pattern object on your drawing with a pattern you use all the time, and drag it over to your palette. Doing so saves the pattern, angle, spacing, layer, color, and so on for future use. When you need to hatch, select the hatch pattern from the palette, and drag it to the proper location in your drawing—it works like magic! Taking the time to set up your palettes properly saves loads of time in the long run.

Edit Tool Properties

Before we tell you about maximizing your results with tools, we feel compelled to give you a friendly overview of the menu codes we'll mention in this section:

- ^C means Cancel (some commands require two cancels to get out so we always use ^C^C).

- ; means Enter.

- \ means Pause for user input.

Now that that's settled, to get the most out of tools, it behooves you to edit their properties—that's where you have access to the macro that's executed when the tool is clicked. In some situations, dragging an object to the Tool Palettes isn't enough, and you need to do more customization to get the tool to behave the way you want.

For example, let's say you want to create a tool that draws a polyline of a given width. Dragging a polyline to the Tool Palettes only generates a generic drawing tool. You have to edit the tool properties to add more specific customization. Give it a try:

1. Draw a polyline. Drag the polyline to the Tool Palettes, and a new tool appears.

2. Right-click the new tool, and choose Properties from its shortcut menu.

3. Type the following into the Name text box: **Polyline 1″ Width**.

4. In AutoCAD 2007, change the Use Flyout property to No. This enables the Command String property. When the flyout is enabled, the tool remains generic, and no custom command string is possible.

   The Command string says `^C^C_pline` by default. This macro reads like this in English: Cancel twice (to ensure you're at the command prompt) before localizing the PLINE command into the current language, and then execute it. If you never plan to use your palettes in any other language, you can remove the underscore, and the command will work fine. Because AutoCAD comes in so many different languages, all the commands are prefaced with an underscore. The `^C` should look familiar to many of you who've used AutoCAD for ages—back when we used Ctrl+C to cancel commands.

   When using the PLINE command, you first have to click a start point on screen before you get to select options. The macro equivalent of this is the backslash: It means pause for user input. Now you know just enough to code the command string.

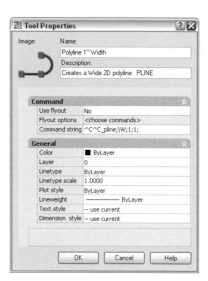

5. Type the following into the Command String property:

   `^C^C_pline;\W;1;1;`

   This means cancel twice, localize and execute PLINE, Enter, pause for user input, Width option, Enter, 1 (inch), Enter, 1 (inch), Enter. Got that?

6. Click OK to close the Tool Properties dialog box, and try your new command. It lets you draw wide polylines without any further ado.

> The Ctrl key lets you select multiple tools simultaneously. Right-click when you have several tools selected, and you can edit properties that the selected tools have in common.

The Menu Legacy

If you've been using AutoCAD for more than a year or two, you've probably edited menus the hard way. In versions prior to AutoCAD 2006, the AutoCAD menus were stored in massive text files with .MNU, .MNS, and .MNC extensions. Editing these beasts was tricky because if you had one typo—poof!—the whole menu wouldn't work.

Fortunately, menus are handled in a more robust way in recent versions of AutoCAD: through a nifty graphical user interface. This means you no longer have to edit text files to customize the menu, so broken menus are a thing of the past. This section has a few tips for readers migrating away from legacy menus.

> Command aliases aren't part of the seemingly all-encompassing CUI dialog box. See "Board the Command Alias Express" in Chapter 1 to learn how to codify abbreviations such as C for Circle.

Menu Migration

Before migrating from legacy MNU, MNS, and MNC menu files, it's important to know something about the way it was done in the old days. See? You can't avoid learning this stuff, even if it's a bit late.

The ACAD.MNU text file was the menu template, and it had comments as well as menu code. Often the comments were helpful as you learned how to customize menus. The ACAD .MNS file had all the comments stripped out but was still a text file (and AutoCAD preferred this file to the .MNU file . Finally, the ACAD.MNC file was a compiled version of ACAD.MNS, so it wasn't editable. By the way, the MNS file diverged from the menu source as customizations were made through the user interface. So, the most up-to-date menu was the MNS file. Confused yet? Not surprising.

> The MNL file type still exists and is used to load Lisp code. It's loaded automatically with its corresponding CUI file. Never rename this file, because it only knows to load when the CUI file with the same name is loaded.

If you want to migrate from an old menu into AutoCAD 2006 or 2007, choose the MNS file as the means of transfer. Use the MENU-LOAD command, and select the legacy MNS file. AutoCAD automatically converts this legacy file into a CUI file. Then, use the CUI command to open the Customize User Interface dialog box. The legacy menu appears as a partial menu. We suggest renaming it to something other than ACAD (which is the main customization group name). Each CUI file must have a unique top-node name.

Transfer Legacy Menu Items

Once you've loaded a legacy menu as a partial CUI file, it's harvest time! Switch to the Transfer tab of the Customize User Interface dialog box to reap your rewards.

The Transfer tab's purpose is to move customizations from one CUI file to another. You don't strictly have to move customizations items—you can have multiple partial menus loaded at any given moment, but it may simplify things for you to put all your apples in one basket (or CUI file).

To transfer legacy menu items, expand the appropriate nodes in the tree in the right pane, and drag them to their respective locations in the left pane—it's that easy. No cutting and pasting text is necessary, just a little drag and drop. You can transfer toolbars in this way, too.

> If your toolbar icons display with a question mark after you transfer them, AutoCAD can't find your custom icon bitmaps. Use the OPTIONS command, and choose the Files tab. Expand Customization Files, and browse for a new Custom Icon Location.

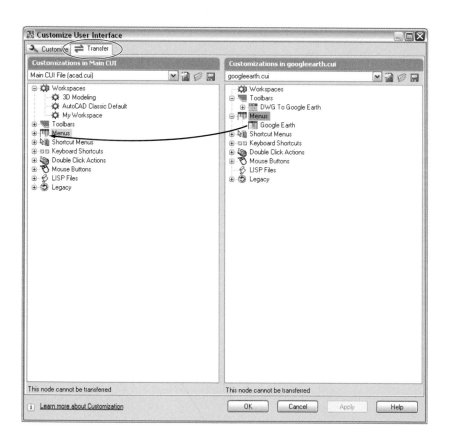

Customizing the User Interface

Ever since AutoCAD 2006, everything having to do with customizing the user interface has been stored in CUI files, which are based on the Extensible Markup Language (XML). All you power users with XML experience will be tempted to edit the CUI files manually in a text editor, just like you did with legacy menu files—but don't do it!

To edit CUI files by hand is to miss the point, plus you'll risk making them nonfunctional. CUI files are made and edited automatically through the Customize User Interface dialog box, accessed by the CUI command. Leave well enough alone, and be happy that your days of hand-coding customizations are over. This section has a few tips and tricks for getting the most out of the Customize User Interface dialog box.

Reassign F1 to Cancel

How many times have you accidentally hit the F1 key when you meant to press the adjacent Esc key? We recommend reassigning the F1 key from its default of asking for help to something you probably do a lot more of: canceling commands. If you're a bad shot (perhaps too much caffeine?), you won't have to wait around for the Help command to load anymore. Here's how to do it:

1. Use the CUI command to open the Customize User Interface dialog box.

2. Scroll down the command list until you find Cancel; press C to quickly jump to the commands that start with this letter.

3. Expand Keyboard Shortcuts in the Customizations In list. Drag the Cancel command up, and drop it on the Shortcut Keys node. You need to do this because Cancel isn't normally assigned to a shortcut key (Escape is handled separately by Windows, for reasons unknown).

4. Select Cancel in the Customizations In list. This command's properties appear in the lower-right pane of the Customize User Interface dialog box.

5. Click the blank Key(s) field, and click its more button (…). A tiny Shortcut Keys dialog box appears; press the F1 key, and click OK. It will probably tell you that the F1 key isn't assigned (even though you know it is).

6. Click OK in the Customize User Interface dialog box, and you're done. Remember to ask for help (not that you'll ever need it) through the Help menu from now on, or key in **?** or **Help**.

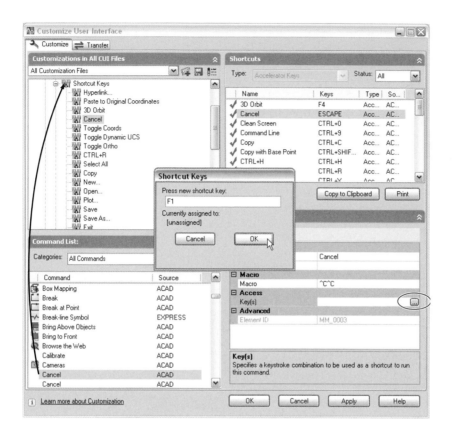

Assign Double-Click Actions

We love the double-click capability in AutoCAD. Double-click an object, and you can quickly edit that object—no questions asked. In AutoCAD 2007, you can assign specific double-click actions for each object type.

Are you tired of seeing the Properties palette open every time you double-click a line? Wouldn't it be cool if you could copy a line just by double-clicking it? Or would you prefer to use the EATTEDIT command over DDEDIT when you double-click an attribute block? These are just two scrumptious possibilities. The good news is you can have your cake and eat it too—bon appétit:

1. Use the CUI command to open the Customize User Interface dialog box.

2. Expand Double-Click Actions in the Customizations In list. Select the object type you're interested in; for this example, expand Attribute Block. Select its indented action node.

3. The Properties pane of the right half of the Customize User Interface dialog box is where you enter the macro that executes when this type of object is double-clicked. Type the following macro for Attribute Block (if it's not already there):

```
^C^C_eattedit
```

4. Click Apply and OK, and test your newfound powers by double-clicking an attribute block. The Enhanced Attribute Editor appears—hurray!

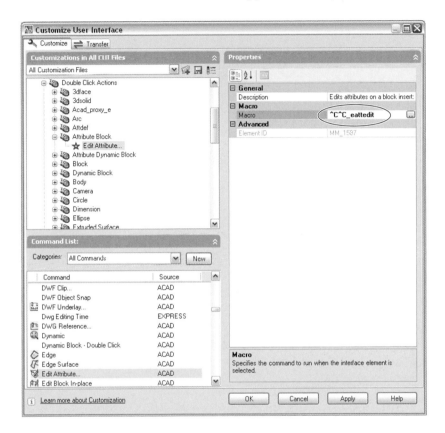

Create Custom Commands and Icons

It's great to be able to create custom commands and icons and quickly get them integrated into the AutoCAD user interface. In case you've always wanted to do this but have been afraid to ask, we'll hold your hand through the process. It's not that scary and can be very satisfying.

The LAYON command is useful but sadly underrepresented in the user interface. LAYON turns on all layers; it can be helpful to instantly turn all those light bulbs back on if you're one to progressively turn off layers as you work. LAYON was formerly an Express Tool, but it's now part of the AutoCAD core; so, you don't have to code this command from scratch, although you can do so with custom commands.

You'll first add LAYON as a command in the command list—it's necessary to add it to the user interface even though you know this code is loaded in memory already. Then, you'll add the command to a toolbar and customize its button icon. Here we go:

1. Use the CUI command to open the Customize User Interface dialog box.

2. Click the New button in the Command List pane. A new node called Command1 appears in the list.

3. In the Properties pane on the right side of the Customize User Interface dialog box, type **All Layers On** in the Name property. Make the Description say **Turns on all layers**. Put the following code in the Macro property:

   `^C^Clayon`

   Click Apply at the bottom of the dialog box. You've successfully added this command to the user interface.

4. Expand the Toolbars and Layers II nodes in the Customizations In pane.

5. Drag the All Layers On command from the Command List, and drop it just below Layer Off on the Layers II toolbar.

6. With the All Layers On command still selected in the Command List, scroll through the list of icons in the upper-right pane. Locate the icon that looks like a stack of layers—it's the one used for Layer Isolate. Select this icon. It's a good place to start, but you'll customize the icon for your new command.

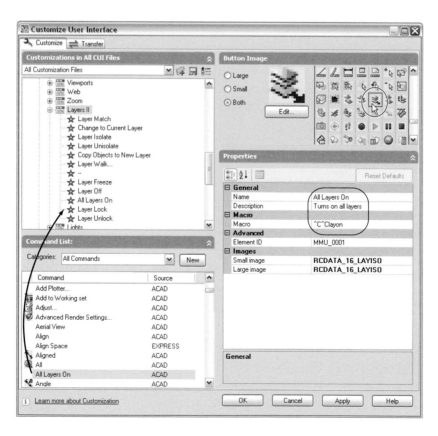

7. Verify that the Both radio button is selected in the Button Image pane, and click the Edit button. You'll be editing both large and small icons.

8. The Button Editor dialog box is like a primitive paint program. Click the yellow color swatch, and use the pencil tool to color in the three layers in the image with yellow pixels. If you find yourself struggling with the Button Editor, any small child can help you!

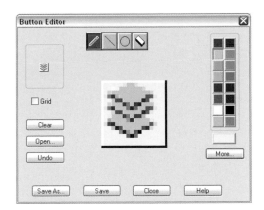

9. When you've finished your masterpiece, click the Save As button in the Button Editor, and give the image file the name **LAYON.BMP** (it's saved in the custom icon folder as defined in Options). Click Close to dismiss the Button Editor dialog box.

10. Scroll to the bottom of the icon list, and select your masterpiece. Click Apply, and OK to close the Customize User Interface dialog box.

11. Open the Layers II toolbar, if it's not already, and check out your new custom command and icon. Restart Auto-CAD if you don't see it.

> If you need to create many icons, you won't be happy using the wimpy AutoCAD icon editor. There's nothing to keep you from using another friendlier program like Paint or Photoshop. You need to create icons that are 16 pixels by 16 pixels for the small icons, 32 by 32 for the large ones (be sure to do both!).

Customizing Workspaces

Workspaces are collections of menus, toolbars, and dockable windows; they provide a quick way to call up different arrangements of user interface elements for each set of tasks you want to perform. This section offers you a few workspace power tips.

Customize a Workspace in the CUI Dialog Box

You've probably already experimented with workspaces through the Workspaces toolbar (see "Using Workspaces" in Chapter 1). If you've saved workspaces via its toolbar, you were taking the bottom-up approach of customizing a workspace from within.

The more powerful top-down approach is to customize workspaces via the Customize User Interface dialog box. There, you can choose which menus, toolbars, and dockable windows belong to each workspace, all in a one-stop-shop. Here's how it's done:

1. Use the CUI command to open the Customize User Interface dialog box.

2. Select a workspace you want to edit in the Customizations In pane on the left.

3. Click the Customize Workspace button in the Workspace Contents pane on the right. Everything turns blue to indicate that it's now editable—only not from this pane.

4. Expand the Toolbars and Menus nodes in the Customizations In pane on the left. Notice that each menu and toolbar has a check box next to it. Any partial CUI files you've loaded also have these check boxes.

5. Check any menus or toolbars that you want to add to this workspace, and uncheck any you want to remove.

6. Expand Menus in the Workspace Contents pane on the right. Drag menus around to change their display order to the way you like it.

7. Click the Done button to finish editing the workspace.

8. Repeat this entire procedure for each workspace you want to customize. Click OK to close the Customize User Interface dialog box, and you're finished.

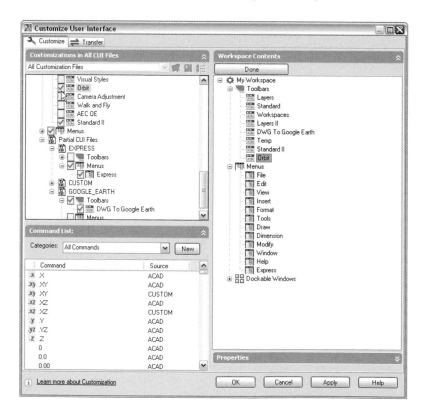

Restore a Workspace with a Command-Line Switch

If you're using partial and/or enterprise CUI files, your toolbars may not stay put when you close and restart AutoCAD. You can fix this easily by making one of your workspaces current. However, wouldn't it be better not to have to think about this every time you start up AutoCAD? If you agree, launch AutoCAD with the /w command-line switch, and you'll have your chosen workspace up and running. Here's how to make the switch:

1. Use the Windows Explorer to locate `C:\Program Files\AutoCAD 2007\acad.exe`, right-click, and choose Send To → Desktop (create shortcut).

2. Minimize everything by pressing Windows key+M. Right-click the shortcut to acad.exe on the desktop, and choose Properties.

3. Place the cursor at the end of the text in the Target text box, and type **/w** **"MyWorkspace"**. You must enter a space before the forward slash to separate the switch from the executable. All startup switches are options that immediately follow a forward slash. The /w switch takes one argument: the name of the workspace, in quotes. This option is passed to the executable when it starts up. Click Apply, and rename the shortcut **AutoCAD 2007**.

4. Launch AutoCAD with the shortcut, and observe that your toolbars are right where you left them last time.

See "Prepare for AutoCAD Launch" in Chapter 1.

Create Workspaces for the Enterprise

When editing a workspace in the Customize User Interface dialog box, you may have noticed the Dockable Windows node in the Workspace Contents pane. There are no check boxes for dockable windows in the Customizations In pane on the left (like there are for toolbars and menus), so maybe you wonder why dockable windows are part of workspaces. What can you do with them?

Dockable windows' appearance and size are stored by the workspace—but did you know that you can lock down the dockable windows' appearance by taking the top-down approach? It's perfect for CAD managers who are designing an enterprise CUI file for everyone to share. The enterprise workspace allows you to enforce consistency.

The point of an enterprise CUI file is that it's read-only, so no one (except someone as knowledgeable as yourself) can edit it. Here's the rub: To edit an enterprise CUI file, you must swap it with the main CUI file. Make alterations to the enterprise CUI while it's masquerading as the editable main CUI file, and then swap them back when you're done. Here's what to do:

1. Use the OPTIONS command, and select the Files tab of the Options dialog box.

2. Expand the Customization Files node. Notice there are two flavors: Main and Enterprise.

3. Swap the main and enterprise customization files. It helps to copy and paste each path to Notepad to make the switcharoo without typing or browsing.

4. Click Apply and OK to close the Options dialog box.

5. Arrange the dockable windows on the screen just as you want them to be for the enterprise.

6. Use the CUI command, and edit the enterprise workspace.

7. Select the dockable windows you want to lock down in the Workspace Contents pane on the right.

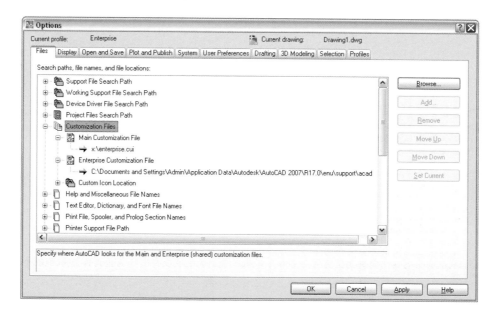

Select multiple dockable windows in the Workspace Contents pane of the Customize User Interface dialog box by holding down the Ctrl key.

8. In the Properties pane, set any of the following appearance properties to Do Not Change: Show, Orientation, Allow Docking, Auto Hide, and/or Use Transparency.

9. Apply the changes, and close the Customize User Interface dialog box. Go back into the Options dialog box, and swap the Main and Enterprise CUI files (repeat steps 1–4).

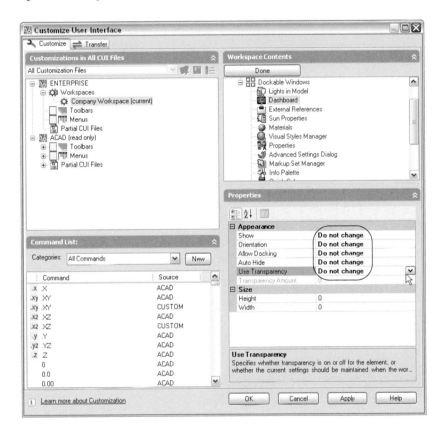

CUI for the Enterprise

Before you dive into designing an enterprise CUI customization file, it's important to understand a little background. AutoCAD uses three kinds of customization files: main, partial, and enterprise. Each CUI file has a unique *customization group name* (formerly called a *menu group name*) that identifies it. The main CUI is typically named ACAD—it's the top node you see in the Customize User Interface dialog box.

The main CUI is editable by each user, so there's an ACAD.CUI residing locally on each machine in an enterprise. The main CUI is meant to record each user's personal preferences; it gives people the freedom to arrange things the way they like.

Partial CUI files can be loaded with the CUILOAD command and are best used for third-party tools. You can load or unload partial CUI files whenever you want without affecting the main CUI. Partial CUI files are editable and are loaded on top of the main CUI, superseding it.

Enterprise CUI files are best used to hold company standards. The enterprise CUI file is up to the CAD manager to create and isn't meant to be editable by the typical user. The ENTERPRISE. CUI file should be stored on the network, because it will be shared among all the AutoCAD users in the enterprise. This section will focus on this last type of customization file.

CAD Managers: **Create an Enterprise Profile**

In the "Create Workspaces for the Enterprise" topic, we showed you how you have to swap the main and enterprise CUI files in the Options dialog box in order to edit the ENTERPRISE. CUI file.

It's a hassle to have to copy and paste paths into the Options dialog box, and we don't expect CAD managers are satisfied with this clunky workaround.

A more elegant approach is to create an Enterprise profile on the CAD manager's machine that references the swapped customization files, so that ENTERPRISE.CUI is considered the main customization file for editing purposes.

Then, all you have to do to work on the enterprise customization file is set the Enterprise profile current—no more awkward copying and pasting path information on the Files tab.

Consider using the /p command-line switch in a shortcut that you, the CAD manager, use to launch AutoCAD with the Enterprise profile. That's the ultimate in enterprise customization file editing convenience.

See "Prepare for AutoCAD Launch" in Chapter 1.

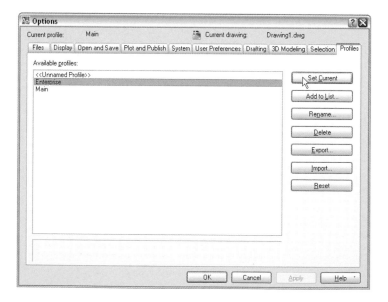

Enterprise CUI Deployment

Once you're happy with the state of your enterprise CUI file, it's time to get it out to all the AutoCAD users on your network. The ENTERPRISE.CUI file must be referenced in each user's profile, which is stored in each system registry.

If you work in a two-person office, no big deal. But if you're supporting dozens or even hundreds of CADsters, this is no laughing matter. Here's a tip that will save you a lot of running around: Use the Deployment Wizard to install AutoCAD across the network.

First, you have to create a network share location where you want to store the enterprise CUI file. This is a folder that everyone in the enterprise can access.

Then, consider that no security is built into the whole enterprise customization file business. If you want to protect your precious read-only enterprise CUI file from power users who a) are very knowledgeable or b) have read this book, you or your network administrator must take extra steps.

A network administrator can restrict write access to the folder where the enterprise customization file is stored on the file server. Only those individuals authorized to edit the ENTERPRISE.CUI file should be granted write access in this location.

Install the Deployment Wizard from the AutoCAD installation disc. It's available when you click either Multi-Seat Stand-Alone Deployment or Network Deployment. Read the Network Administrator's Guide in the AutoCAD Help system to bone up on the Deployment Wizard. You can tell the Deployment Wizard where the enterprise customization file is on the network, and it pushes it out to all the users automatically.

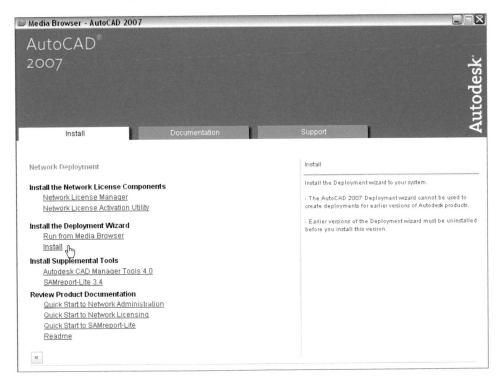

Index

Note to the Reader: Throughout this index **boldfaced** page numbers indicate primary discussions of a topic. *Italicized* page numbers indicate illustrations.